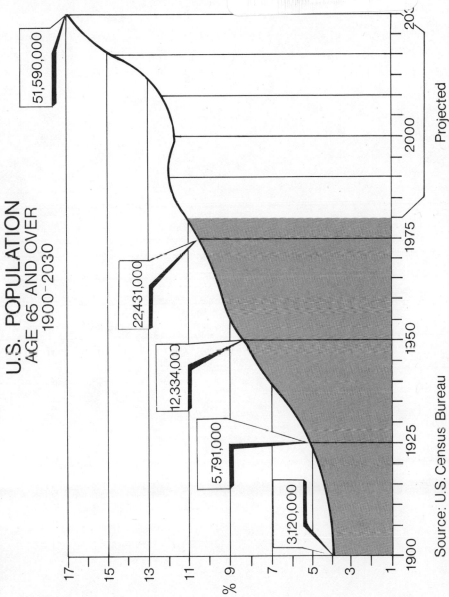

U.S. POPULATION
AGE 65 AND OVER
1900–2030

Source: U.S.Census Bureau

AGE GAUGE – Chart shows the percentage of the American population 65 and older from 1900 to 1975, with predictions for 1980 to 2030.

LATER LIFE

LEWIS AIKEN

University of the Pacific
Stockton, California

1978
W. B. SAUNDERS COMPANY
Philadelphia   London   Toronto

W. B. Saunders Company: West Washington Square
Philadelphia, PA 19105

1 St. Anne's Road
Eastbourne, East Sussex BN21 3UN, England

1 Goldthorne Avenue
Toronto, Ontario M8Z 5T9, Canada

Library of Congress Cataloging in Publication Data

Aiken, Lewis R., 1931–

Later life.

Bibliography: p.
Includes indexes.
1. Aging.   2. Aged.   3. Gerontology.   I. Title.

QP86.A38   362.6   77-11326

ISBN 0-7216-1070-6

Later Life   ISBN 0-7216-1070-6

Last digit is the print number: 9   8   7   6   5   4   3   2   1

The sounds of the city,
Sifting through the trees,
Settle like dust
On the shoulders
Of the old friends.

Can you imagine us
Years from today,
Sharing a park bench quietly?*

Preface

There are many reasons why a particular subgroup of the population becomes singled out for special study. The seriousness of the problems posed or the benefits offered by the subgroup to society as a whole and an increase in the power of the subgroup by virtue of its size and leadership are two related reasons why gerontology has become a more popular field during recent years. In terms of problems posed, old age is costly to society. The costs of health care, retirement payments, housing, and social services are all increasing rapidly. People who are 65 years of age or older compose 10 per cent of the American population, but they account for 40 per cent of physicians' office visits and occupy 33 per cent of the hospital beds in the United States. Because of the growing power of the elderly and their spokespersons, Medicare and Medicaid may eventually give way to some form of national health insurance, which may well cost society even more money. With respect to retirement income, the Social Security system is fast becoming overburdened, being supported by a ratio of 3.2 workers for every beneficiary today, compared to a projected ratio of 2.2 to 1 in the year 2020. In spite of these costs and recent improvements in services to the elderly, many continue to be treated as second-class citizens who are waiting on the shelf for death to overtake them. Furthermore, costs are assessed not only in monetary units. It is costly to the young and middle-aged as human beings, both now and in the years ahead when they will be the aged, to treat older people as anything other than respected, valuable members of society.

Older people can offer skills, wisdom, and psychological support to younger age groups. The anticipated labor shortages of the 1980s and 1990s in many countries, produced by low population growth during the 1960s and 1970s, will make it necessary to retain people in the work force for a longer period of time. This circumstance could also help to relieve the financial stress on the retirement system. The findings of several surveys and many other research investigations have shown that most elderly people desire to be and are capable of being productive members of society.

If for no other reason, the sheer numbers of elderly people will force society to take greater notice of them in the future. Today, there are approximately 23 million Americans over 65 years of age, a figure that will most likely rise to over 30 million by the end of the century. Not only are the elderly increasing in numbers, but the proportion of the over-65 group in the total population is increasing even faster. These numbers mean political power for the elderly, power that will undoubtedly result in better medical care, increased housing subsidies, larger retirement incomes, and expanded social services for this age group.

Thus far, research and other efforts directed toward understanding the aged have not been very systematic or ambitious. A few centers have concentrated on topics such as personality development and sexual behavior of the elderly and attitudes of younger people toward the elderly, but few comprehensive longitudinal interdisciplinary investigations have been conducted. Encouraged by federal and private foundation support and stimulated by the growing social, economic, and political significance of the aged, professional interest and hence the body of information on later life has expanded greatly in recent years.

One purpose of this book is to identify and review what is known about later life and the methods by which this information was obtained. The author has attempted to accomplish this purpose in a fairly nontechnical manner, but a certain amount of specialized language has proved necessary. The Glossary, which appears at the back of the book, contains definitions of most of the technical terms used in the book. The Index of Terms and Organizations should also prove helpful.

Another, perhaps even more important, purpose in writing the book was to motivate and point to some directions for further study and research on this most interesting and increasingly influential stage of human existence. Gerontology and geriatrics are still not especially popular as fields of specialization in the social sciences and medicine. The situation appears to be changing, however, and the author would like to help accelerate the pace.

The emphasis of the book is on the psychology of later life. But psychology is actually a multidisciplinary field, and later life is merely the final stage in the developmental progression of a biosocial organism. Consequently, the reader will encounter many facts and concepts from biology, sociology, economics, philosophy, and even a few literary quotations in this book. Some information about the earlier stages of life and how they help prepare a person for old age has also been included. All of this material can contribute to our understanding of the total human being—a biological, social, economic, philosophical, and sometimes poetic creature. The many-sided character of human nature becomes especially clear when looking at old age, the final developmental period of life and a time for summing up.

LEWIS R. AIKEN

Contents

Chapter 1

Introduction

Growth and aging are complementary biological processes, with aging being a leveling-off or decline in the size and/or efficiency of an organism. However, human development does not stop with the cessation of physical growth and lessened efficiency in some areas.[1] The final period of development is old age, a period which may be the best or the worst time of life. The definition of this final developmental period changes with time and place. It depends not only on the characteristics of the individual but also on the attitudes and needs of the culture. The meaning of "old" also varies with the stage of development of the observer. To a child, a person of 40 may appear old, whereas a middle-aged adult may consider old age as 75 years and above.

Affected to a great degree by retirement legislation, society as a whole has come to view the period of 60 to 65 years as the beginning of old age. But people age at different rates, both physically and psychologically. In fact, age can be judged medically in terms of a person's *functional capacity*—the ability to engage in purposeful activity—rather than by chronological age. Physicians also distinguish between primary aging, or senescence, and secondary aging, or senility. *Senescence* refers to genetically determined changes in body structure and function, while *senility* refers to disabilities produced by illness or injury as a person ages. Thus, a person can be old at 40 as well as 80, depending on overall health, attitude, and other circumstances.

LONGEVITY AND LIFE EXPECTANCY

There is great variety in the developmental patterns of organisms, and the life span of an organism is related to the rate and

1

pattern of its growth. The length of an animal's life—its *longevity*—varies from a few hours in adult mayflies and a few days in fruit flies and houseflies[2] to over a hundred years in some humans, large birds, and Galapagos turtles. Even greater longevity is found in the plant kingdom, where giant redwoods and bristlecone pines live for thousands of years.

Human Longevity

On the human level, the longevity record is held by Methuselah, who is reputed to have lived for 969 years. The *Guinness Book of World Records* lists Delina Filkins of New York, who died in 1928 at the age of 113, as having the longest known life span in modern times. Other famous, perhaps exaggerated, accounts of very old people are the cases of Thomas Parr, who was presented to Charles I of England as a 152 year old curiosity, and Javier Pereira, a Colombian Indian who visited the United States in 1956 claiming to be 167 years old. Physicians who examined Pereira concluded that he was indeed "very old," but they could not determine his exact age. More recently, a Russian, Shirali Mislimov, is said to have been 167 when he died in 1972 ("Soviets Say," 1977). Another Russian, Rustam Mamedov, who clearly recalls the Crimean War of 1854 and the Turkish War of 1878, maintains that he is 142.

Human life expectancy and the proportion of old people in the population vary with such factors as historical period, sex, ethnic group, heredity, technology, and life style. The number of people in the United States who are 65 years of age and older has increased from approximately three million (4 per cent of the population) in 1900 to 16.6 million in 1960, 20.1 million (9.9 per cent of the population) in 1970, and 23 million in 1977. Every day there are approximately 1600 more Americans over 65 than there were the day before, and on the average those who now reach age 65 can look forward to 15.3 more years of life. Projections indicate that the number of Americans who are 65 and over will rise to nearly 32 million by the year 2000 (in a total of 260 million population) and to a possible 55 million by 2030, when people born in the post–World War II baby boom are over 65. From 11 per cent of the population in 1977 and a projected 12 per cent in the year 2000, it is estimated that by 2030 between 20 and 25 per cent of the nation's population will be 65 and over (U.S. Bureau of the Census, 1977).

Demographic statistics show that the percentage increase in the population of the United States during this century has been 2½ times as great in the 65-and-over bracket as in the under-65 bracket. The median age was 16 years in 1790, when the first U.S. census was taken. It was 28 years in 1970, will pass 30 years in 1981, and if the present trend continues it will approach 35 years by the year 2000 and 40 years by 2030 ("The Graying of America," 1977). One reason for the steady rise in the proportion of older people in the population is the decline in deaths due to heart disorders and other killer diseases in the 45–75 year age range. For example, the death rate for people between 45 and 54 dropped six times faster and the death rate in the 65 to 74 age group more than four times faster between 1973 and 1975 than during the preceding 13 years.

The dramatic increase in the elderly population reflected by these figures amply attests to what gerontologist Robert Butler calls the "graying of America." Not only will this growth have a pronounced effect on our economic and social institutions in the years to come, but also it carries with it the challenge that these added years not be wasted, that new opportunities for personal development be provided that will add "life to years" and not just "years to life." As will be discussed in more detail in Chapter 7, the growing political power of the aged, which promises to surpass that of the black power and women's liberation movements, will exert a great deal of influence in realizing this challenge. In particular, compared with their counterparts today, the "young-old" group of people 55 and over who have retired from their first career are expected to be healthier, better educated, and more demanding of a greater variety of options in life than heretofore (Neugarten, 1975).

Longevity Throughout History

Life expectancy has increased throughout history from an estimated 20 to 30 years during the days of ancient Greece and Rome, rising very slowly to 35 years in the Middle Ages and Renaissance, to 45 years in mid-nineteenth century America, 47 years in 1900, and 70+ years in the 1970s. It is estimated that the average life expectancy in the United States will be approximately 82 years by the year 2000.

These figures, however, do not tell the whole story. Although life expectancy is much greater today than during ancient times, the oldest people living in those times were approximately the same age as the oldest people living today. Rosenfeld (1976) notes that Sophocles wrote "Oedipus Rex" at the age of 75 and won a prize for drama at 85. Marcus Seneca, the renowned Roman orator, lived for 93 years (53 BC–39 AD). Thus, the average life span has increased, but the maximum life span appears to have remained essentially the same.

Compared with the size of the population as a whole, not until the nineteenth century were there substantial increases in the number of old people. It was during the past century that the first dramatic breakthroughs in medicine and public health were made. One of the major causes of the shorter life expectancy during previous centuries was the higher rate of infant mortality rather than greater mortality among older groups. Even during our own century, infant mortality, defined as death before the age of one year, has decreased from 9990 per 100,000 population in 1915 to 1980 per 100,000 in the 1970s (Whaley, 1974). Next to infancy, the greatest decrease in death rate has occurred in early childhood, followed by a smaller decrease between the ages of 5 and 55, and an even smaller decline in the 55+ age group. Advances in the treatment of influenza, pneumonia, tuberculosis, diphtheria, and typhoid and scarlet fever have greatly reduced mortality during infancy and early childhood.

The increased proportion of older people in the general population since the late 1950s has been due in some measure to the declining fertility rate. When the fertility rate declines, the effect is to reduce the proportion of people in younger age categories while increasing the proportion of older people in the population as a whole. The U.S. fertility rate declined from 3.76 children in 1957 to 1.75 in 1976, and by the late 1970s the United States and many other countries were well on their way toward Zero Population Growth (ZPG). If the drift toward ZPG continues, and indications are that it will, it is estimated that by the year 2030 the percentage of people below 20 will have *decreased* by approximately 8 per cent, but the percentage of people 55 and over will have *increased* by the same percentage.

Other Factors In Longevity

SEX DIFFERENCES

Longevity also varies considerably with the sex of the person. Statistics on aging among women during different historical periods are more difficult to obtain than those for men, but it is estimated that the average life span of women in pre-Christian days was approximately 25 years and had reached only 30 years by the fifteenth century. Death during childbirth was a major contributory cause to the difference in longevity between the sexes in earlier times. However, by 1977 the average life span for American women was approximately 76 years, compared with 68½ years for men. Today, women tend to outlive men by about eight years, with 1 out of every 8 American women compared to 1 of 11 men being 65 years old or older (Flieger, 1976). These statistics are reflected in the fact that although the ratio of women to men in the general population is about 51 to 49, among Americans in the 65 and over bracket the ratio of women to men is 4 to 3 (Fig. 1–1). The ratio of older women to older men is projected to become even greater by the year 2000, when there will be 18.6 million women compared with only 12 million men.

The widening sex difference in longevity is due primarily to the fact that at every period of life males are more susceptible than females to disease, and especially heart disease, cancer, and respira-

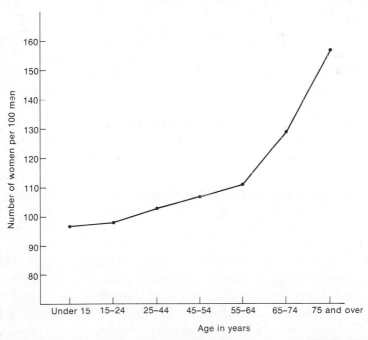

Figure 1–1. Sex ratio as a function of age. The data are from the 1970 United States Census. (Adapted from U.S. Bureau of the Census. Some demographic aspects of aging in the United States. *Current Population Reports.* Series P-23. No. 43. Washington, D.C.: U.S. Government Printing Office, 1973, Table 6.)

tory disorders. The reasons for the greater susceptibility to disease in the male are not clear, but experts point to environmental factors, stress, and hereditary differences between the sexes. Added to the greater longevity of women as a contributor to the high proportion of widows among the elderly is the fact that women usually marry men who are several years older than they.

MARITAL STATUS

It is a statistical fact that, on the average, married people live longer than unmarried people, but the reasons are not entirely clear. Several possible explanations for this fact have been offered, among them: (a) marriage selects rather than protects, in that people who are more likely to live long are also more likely to marry or stay married; (b) society views unmarried people as odd or unusual, a circumstance which places them under social stress and consequently wears them down physically; (c) close interpersonal ties, which are more likely to be absent in unmarried people, are important in maintaining a sense of well-being, which, in turn, promotes longevity (Kobrin and Hendershot, 1977).

The relationship between marriage and longevity is not a simple one, because the effects of marriage interact with those of sex. Women live longer than men, but the difference is much less for married than for unmarried people. Gove (1973) also interprets this finding in terms of social ties. He notes that unmarried women tend to have stronger ties than unmarried men to family and friends but that, compared to those of married men, the roles of married women are more confining and frustrating. As a result, from a psychological viewpoint women are seen as benefiting less from marriage and suffering less from being single than men are.

Kobrin and Hendershot (1977) tested Gove's (1973) theory concerning the importance of social ties to longevity in a national sample of people who died between the ages of 35 and 74. They found a complex interaction in the relationships of sex, marital status, and living arrangement to mortality rates. Among the men, those who were heads of families lived longest, followed by those who were living in families but not as heads. Those men who lived alone had the lowest average longevity. Among the women, those who were heads of families lived longest, but in contrast to the men, those women who lived alone had the second highest longevity.

Finally, those women who lived in families but not as heads had the lowest average longevity.

In general, the findings of Kobrin and Hendershot are consistent with those of Gove, in that close social ties and higher social status, which are more likely to be found in marriage than outside of it, favor greater longevity. However, this is truer for men than for women. Unmarried men typically have fewer social ties and less social status than married men, but unmarried women usually retain interpersonal ties and may have even greater social status than they would as dominated members of a family.

ETHNIC GROUP DIFFERENCES

Another important variable that is related to longevity is ethnic group membership. Blacks, Mexican-Americans, and American Indians, in order of decreasing life expectancy, have shorter life spans than white Americans (National Center for Health Statistics, 1974). Approximately 11 per cent of the total population is black, but only 8 per cent of the elderly are black. On the average, black men live 6½ years less than white men, and black women live 6 years less than white women. One reason for the shorter life expectancy of blacks is that hypertension is over twice as common in American blacks as in whites. But the life expectancy of black men who reach age 65 is almost equal to that of their white counterparts (Fig. 1–2). The average life spans of two other ethnic groups in the United States are even lower than that of blacks—approximately 57 years for Mexican-Americans and only 44 years for American Indians.

Some of the environmental factors associated with these ethnic group differences are poverty and lack of education and associated conditions of poor housing, poor nutrition, and poor medical care. Better social and economic conditions and the resulting greater availability of life's necessities—good housing and satisfactory working conditions, clean water and nutritious food, adequate health care—may also help to explain why people live longer in technologically more advanced societies.

NATIONALITY AND LOCALITY

During the twentieth century, the annual rate of increase in the over-65 population has been greater in the United States and

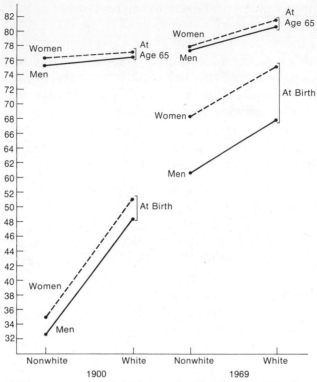

Figure 1-2. Life expectancy at birth and at age 65 in 1900 and 1969. The statistics are plotted separately by sex and ethnic group. (Adapted from U.S. Bureau of the Census. Some demographic aspects of aging in the United States. *Current Population Reports, Series P-23*, No. 43. Washington, D.C.: U.S. Government Printing Office, 1973, Table 13.)

Canada (3 per cent) than in most European countries. For example, the percentage gain in older people has averaged only 1 per cent in France and Sweden. In general, the elderly population is proportionally larger and has grown faster in highly industrialized Western countries than in the developing countries of Latin America, Asia, and Africa. The average life span in some Far Eastern countries, for example, is still only about 30 to 35 years.

Examples of very long life spans are found in sizable numbers among the Hunza people in the Karakoram Range of the Himalayas, the Abkhasia of the Republic of Georgia in the U.S.S.R. (Fig. 1–3), and the Andean "viejos" of the village of Vilcabamba in Ecuador. Nearly 50 out of every 100,000 people in the Caucasus region of the Soviet Union, compared to only 3 out of 100,000 Americans, live to be 100. Birth records of the Hunza are more difficult to obtain than those of the Abkhasians and Vilcabambans, but UNESCO data

Table 1-1.   ORDER OF TOP TEN STATES IN TERMS OF
NUMBER OF ELDERLY PEOPLE*

Rank	State	Number of People 65 Years and Over	Per Cent of State Population
1	New York	1,998,000	11.0
2	California	1,986,000	9.5
3	Pennsylvania	1,348,000	11.4
4	Florida	1,267,000	15.7
5	Illinois	1,134,000	10.2
6	Texas	1,120,000	9.3
7	Ohio	1,050,000	9.8
8	Michigan	798,000	8.8
9	New Jersey	749,000	10.2
10	Massachusetts	661,000	11.4

*After Schultz, 1976, p. 37.

indicate that the Hunza are the only totally cancer-free people in the
world.

The distribution of older people in the United States varies
with locality, but one cannot conclude from this fact that life expectancy is necessarily greater in certain sections of the country than in
others (Table 1-1). The most populous states—New York and
California—also contain the largest numbers of people who are 65
and older. Florida, several Midwestern states, and Massachusetts,
however, also have sizable older populations.[3] The great majority of
these people live in urban areas or towns, with only 5 per cent living
in rural areas.

Specific types of climate are often prescribed for patients
having certain physical disorders—for example, a warm dry climate
that is relatively free of air pollution in cases of emphysema. Tuberculosis sanitaria are frequently located at high altitudes, and altitude
is also related to heart disease. It is also noteworthy that all of the
long-living peoples of the world live in mountainous regions. Re-
viewing deaths in New Mexico between 1957 and 1970, Mortimer,
Monson, and MacMahon (1977) found 403 deaths from coronary
heart disease per 100,000 men who were living at the lowest altitude
but only 291 deaths from the same cause per 100,000 men living at
the highest altitude.

EXERCISE, DIET, AND PSYCHOSOCIAL FACTORS

The importance of exercise to long life should not be
minimized, although too much exercise may be as bad as too little.

Exercise, especially at high altitudes, causes the heart to work harder and thus become conditioned for emergencies. All three of the long-living groups of people referred to above are agrarians who get plenty of exercise, and the Vilcabambans in particular are quite explicit in attributing their good health and old age to walking.

Gots (1977) argues that perhaps even more important in contributing to a long, healthful life than such environmental factors as altitude and exercise is what one eats. The diet of the Abkhasians, for example, is quite low in calories, meat, eggs, and salt. Lowered food intake, and especially a diet low in fats and calories, has been found to be associated with a healthier, longer life in technologically advanced societies as well (Fig. 1–3). Based on a study of the diets of long-living groups of people, nutritionists are now recommending the following diet for those who desire to live long (Gots, 1977, p. 168):

(1) Lower protein intake and more protein from vegetables (grains, legumes, cereals), and less from animal products (red meat, whole milk, and eggs).
(2) Less fat, especially animal fat.
(3) Fewer calories—enough to satisfy energy requirements but no more.
(4) Skim-milk instead of whole-milk products.
(5) Chicken and fish more often and red meats only three or four times a week.
(6) Greater portions of whole grains, beans, rice, nuts, fresh fruits, and vegetables that provide essential vitamins, minerals, and fiber.

Moderation in eating, smoking, and drinking (alcoholic bev-

Figure 1–3. Shirin Gasonov, a Russian farmer who was born over a hundred years ago, inspects a vineyard near his home. (From Fantino & Reynolds, 1975, p. 366.)

erages), combined with physical activity, are significant personal habits related to a lower incidence of heart, brain, and liver disorders. Relative freedom from the pressures and worries of civilization, as in the case of the Hunza and Vilcabamba peoples, may also contribute to a long life. Psychological factors, such as maintaining an interest in one's surroundings and feeling useful and accepted by others, can be just as important as diet, nonsmoking, and exercise. Thus, from a study of factors promoting the long lives of the Abkhasians, Benet (1974, 1976) concluded that although work and diet are important, equally essential is a social structure that permits a meaningful old age and a sense of group belonging.

HEREDITY

Many biological and psychosocial factors have an influence on longevity. Children born of older mothers, for example, have a higher incidence of congenital disorders that shorten life.[4] Even more important, however, is the genetic makeup of the individual.

Certain authorities feel that the role of heredity in longevity has been overemphasized, but length of life does tend to run in families. For example, the parents and grandparents of national groups of long-living peoples also tended to live to ripe old ages. The correlation between the life spans of different people varies directly with the degree of genetic relationship, parents who live long tending to have children who also live long. Fraternal twins generally live to much the same age, but, as would be expected for a characteristic affected by heredity, the ages at death of identical twins are even closer. From a study of identical twins who were 60 years and older, Kallmann and Sander (1963) concluded that there is a substantial amount of stability in physical and mental traits throughout a lifetime. In spite of pronounced differences in environment in some instances (e.g., New York doctor vs. Western rancher, English-speaking vs. foreign-language-speaking), elderly identicals were just as difficult to tell apart as when they were younger; they had similar hair patterns and wrinkle patterns, and their energy levels were very close. A particularly dramatic example of biological similarity persisting throughout a lifetime was found in the case of a pair of twin sisters. Both became blind and deaf in the same month, both developed senile psychosis, and both died within a few days of each other.

Of course, neither heredity nor environment by itself determines aging. As implied in the following quotation from Hans Selye (1976, p. 82), heredity and environment interact in their effects on longevity:

It is as though, at birth, each individual inherited a certain amount of adaptation energy, the magnitude of which is determined by his genetic background, his parents. He can draw upon this capital thriftily for a long but monotonously uneventful existence, or he can spend it lavishly in the course of a stressful, intense, but perhaps more colorful and exciting life. In any case, there is just so much of it, and he must budget accordingly.

ATTITUDES TOWARD OLD AGE

It has been said that, next to dying, the realization that one is aging is the most shocking event of one's life. This is probably more likely to be true in a youth-oriented culture such as ours, where people spend a great deal of time and money attempting to slow down or at least camouflage the effects of aging. Many elderly people attempt to conceal their ages not only from others but even from themselves. Some never come to use the word "old" as self-descriptive, even when they are in their 70s (Taves and Hansen, 1963). Whether one's personal conflict between denial and acceptance of aging and old age is weak or strong, the attitudes of other people definitely influence it.

Attitudes toward old age vary considerably with time, place, and person. Even the intellectual elite of the same society can have differing viewpoints toward old age. Robert Browning, in his 1864 poem "Rabbi Ben Ezra," extended an invitation to

Grow old along with me!
The best is yet to be,
The last of life, for which the first was made.
Our times are in His hand
Who saith "A whole I planned,
—Youth shows but half;
trust God;
see all nor be afraid."

The response of Matthew Arnold, in his 1867 poem "Growing Old," was

What is it to grow old?
Is it to lose the glory of form?
The lustre of the eye?
Is it for beauty to forgo her wreath?
—Yes, but not this alone.

Cultural Differences in Treatment of the Aged

Some primitive societies respect and even revere the aged. For example, the Jivaro Indians of the Andes believe that old people have supernatural powers which increase with age. In poorer tribal groups, however, the elderly are viewed merely as a burden and are sometimes killed. Other primitive peoples, such as the Eskimos and certain American Indian and African tribes, respected the experience and wisdom of the elderly but left them to die when they could no longer take care of themselves. Usually the older person accepted the necessity of his demise and sometimes even assisted in it. For example, old people in certain South Sea island native groups, seeing themselves as no longer useful or wanted, paddled away from their families to die. Similarly, after deciding that he was prepared to die, an old American Indian warrior might tie himself to a stake in hostile territory and then fight off braves and warriors of the hostile tribe until they eventually killed him.

One would expect a more humane approach to the elderly in modern society, but according to some observers old people are not invariably treated as human beings. The fear of aging and dying may cause younger people to be defensively afraid of and even hate the old. To de Beauvoir (1972), it is Western society that truly degrades the old. Sometimes an old man is a respected, venerated sage, but more often he is viewed as a ridiculous, doddering old fool and mocked by the young. Neugarten (1971) takes a somewhat more optimistic point of view but still recognizes the tendency of American society to stereotype the old as poor, isolated, sick, and unhappy on the one hand or as powerful, rigid, and reactionary on the other. Neugarten points out that these stereotypes influence our behavior and make the prospect of old age very unattractive to us.

Stereotypes and Misconceptions

Robert Butler (1974, 1975), who coined the term *ageism* to refer to the social stereotyping of older people as well as the social discrimination against them, cites many examples of negative attitudes. Future physicians, whose first encounter with an older person in medical school is in the form of a cadaver, may engage in gallows humor and refer to older patients as "crocks," "turkeys," or even "dirt-balls." Alex Comfort (1976) reports knowing licensed physicians who ridiculed and psychologically castigated older people whom they viewed as insulting to their medical skills.

All in all, health professionals are significantly more negative in their attitudes toward treating older people than they are toward treating younger people (Spence, Feigenbaum, Fitzgerald, and Roth, 1968). Another example of prejudice toward the elderly in a professional person was the university professor who maintained that "The old, having no future, are dangerously free from the consequences of their own political acts, and it makes no sense to allow the vote to someone who is actually unlikely to survive and pay the bills for (what) he may select" (Tiede, 1970). It has been suggested that the stereotyping of older people by professionals may serve as a kind of justification for inattentiveness to their needs. Personnel directors, for example, may use stereotypes as a rationalization for ignoring older workers (Pines, 1976).

To quote Butler (1974, p. 11): "Ageism can be seen as a process of systematic stereotyping of and discrimination against people because they are old—just as racism and sexism can accomplish this with skin color and gender. Old people are categorized as senile, rigid in thought and manner, old fashioned in morality and skills. Ageism allows the younger generations to see older people as different from themselves. Thus they subtly cease to identify with their elders as human beings." This quotation refers to several stereotypes pertaining to the aged. Among the other stereotypes, myths or misconceptions cited by Butler and others (Comfort, 1976; Perry, 1974; Verwoerdt, 1969a) are the following:

1. Most old people are ill or in poor health.
2. Most old people are senile or in their second childhood.
3. Most old people are rigid or inflexible.
4. Most old people can't do a good job and should retire.
5. Most old people have no sex life.
6. Most old people want to disengage or gradually withdraw from active participation.
7. Most old people live alone, abandoned by their families and other relatives.
8. Most old people do live or should live in institutions (homes, hospitals, etc.).

There are other myths or misconceptions, for example the myth that conceives of old age as a magic land where everyone is a happy retiree from the worries of the world and the myth that people automatically start going downhill at chronological age 65.

RESEARCH ON MISCONCEPTIONS AND STEREOTYPES OF OLD AGE

The results of several older research studies with subjects from age eight to college level substantiate the fact of a negative image of the elderly. Kogan and Shelton's (1962) sample of college students tended to downgrade the appearance of old people, felt that the old resent the young, and stated that they preferred to avoid direct personal contact with old people. Kastenbaum and Durkee (1964) also found that the adolescent has little regard for the elderly.

More recent studies with children (Hickey and Kalish, 1968; Serock, Seefeldt, Jantz, and Galper, 1977) have substantiated the observation that children have a generally unpleasant image of growing old and old people. Serock et al. (1977), in studies conducted at the University of Maryland's Center on Aging, found that most of the 180 children (ages 3 to 11) whom they studied described the elderly in a negative way as "wrinkled, short, and gray-haired," they "chew funny," "don't go out much," "sit all day and watch TV in their rocking chairs," and "have heart attacks and die." When asked how they felt about growing old themselves, all but a few of the children stated that they simply did not want to do it. Such stereotypes and attitudes, communicated by parents, teachers, and peers, appear in many famous books and plays and are even shared by professional people. In fact, as Butler (1975) points out, old people frequently look at themselves in a negative light, thereby perpetuating and reinforcing the social stereotypes of old age.

Indirect evidence of the negative image of old age in the elderly themselves was obtained by Kastenbaum and Durkee (1964), who found that people over 70 consistently classified themselves as middle-aged. These findings confirm those of Phillips (1962) in a study of 346 people who were 60 years old and above. Sixty-one per cent of Phillips's group classified themselves as middle-aged, 67 per cent thought that other people viewed them as middle-aged, and 62 per cent stated that they felt younger than most people their age.

Does direct personal contact with the elderly help to change negative attitudes toward them? Yes, to some extent, particularly if the contacts are spontaneous and if the elderly are not ill (Tuckman and Lorge, 1953; Spence, Feigenbaum, Fitzgerald, and Roth, 1968; Steinbaum, 1973). Although exposure to the aged and knowledge of the aging process do not necessarily have positive effects, courses in gerontology can help to change attitudes when supplemented by positive contacts with the elderly. Summarizing the findings of a number of studies on this topic, Bennett (1976) concluded that negative attitudes toward the elderly are very difficult to change. Consequently, she anticipates a continuation of the fear and even denial of one's own aging and a reluctance to work with old people. Denial of aging and the aged is, however, a two-edged sword, because in so doing we ultimately deny ourselves. As Butler put it, "We don't all grow black or Chinese, but we do grow old."

The results of a Harris survey conducted for the National Council on the Aging (1975) make abundantly clear that adult Americans harbor many misconceptions about what old age is really like. This survey, some of the results of which are summarized in Figure 1–4, compared the general public's expectations of the "serious" problems of old age with the personal experiences reported by the elderly themselves. Half or more of the general adult group that was surveyed expected poor health, insufficient money to live on, and loneliness to be very serious problems, but one fourth or less of the elderly sample actually reported these as problems. It is interesting that many of the old people who were questioned gave different answers when asked about other people than they did when asked about themselves. They tended to see themselves as having fewer problems than other old people such as the "old fogey" or "old biddy" down the street. Harris concluded that the elderly do have problems—inadequate money, poor health, loneliness, poor medical care, fear of crime, and difficulties in getting from place to place. These problems, however, are not as pervasive as the general public believes, and perhaps the greatest problem of the elderly is the attitude of the public toward them.

PROFESSIONAL INTEREST AND RESEARCH

As is true today, people in ancient times were aware of the effects of time on their physical and mental abilities. Attempting to reverse or postpone these effects, they consulted magicians, priests, physicians, or anyone purporting to have a remedy or palliative to combat the ravages of time.

The ancient Romans looked upon old age itself as a disease, and stemming from this belief was the search for a way to "cure" the

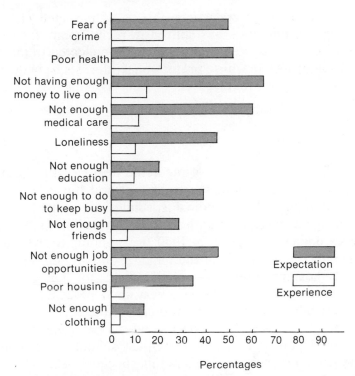

Figure 1–4. Selected results of a Harris survey comparing the general American public's expectations of the serious problems of older people with the personal experiences reported by a sample of older people themselves. (Adapted from Moore, 1975; after National Council on Aging, 1975.)

disease and find the secret of eternal life. Efforts to discover this secret and the related searches for the philosopher's stone and the fountain of youth occupied the time and energies of many brave and brilliant men. Needless to say, their quest was unsuccessful, although it has not been abandoned even today. Public attention and support have shifted, however, to attempts to make old age more pleasant rather than indefinite in length.

Although the Social Security Act of 1935 arbitrarily defined "old" as age 65 and above, several divisions can be identified in the developmental period known as "old age." Barrett (1972) makes a case for three subperiods in the gerontological (old age) period. He labels ages 58 to 68 as the "Period of Later Maturity," ages 68 to 78 as the "Early Longevous Period," and age 78+ as the "Later Longevous Period." Dividing old age into subperiods, similar to developmental stages at the other end of the life scale, reflects the growing professional interest in problems of the aged. To some extent, research emphasis has shifted in recent years from early childhood to later life. Researchers who have elected to make the shift have joined others whose professional interests lie in the fields of geriatrics and gerontology.

Geriatrics

Geriatrics is a branch of medicine dealing with the health problems of the aged, both the treatment and the prevention of disease and injury. This medical specialty was founded by an American, Ignaz Nascher, and the first geriatric clinic in the United States was opened in Boston in 1940. Responding to the fact that older people constitute one of the major groups requiring medical care, many hospitals now have special clinics for the aged.

According to Butler (1975), a very small percentage of medical school faculty are experts in problems of the aged. Butler, who has continually stressed the need for greater interest and research in geriatric medicine, believes that medical schools have failed to motivate students toward careers in this specialty because they are not exposed to healthy older people. He recognizes that if a sufficient number of trained geriatricians were available, the diseases of old age could be made less debilitating, less burdensome, and hence less costly.

In any event, medical schools are expanding their research and training programs in this area as professional interest grows. The growth of interest in problems of the aged is indicated by the increasing membership in professional organizations and the growing number of publications on geriatrics. The major professional organization of physicians who specialize in geriatrics is the American Geriatrics Society. From its beginning in 1950 as a society of only 352 members, it has grown to over 7000 today. Three American medical journals in the field of geriatrics are the *Journal of the American Geriatrics Society; Geriatrics;* and the *Journal of Geriatric Psychiatry.*

Being practical people, medical scientists will probably discover additional ways to slow down aging long before they understand the process itself (Comfort, 1972). To date, they have succeeded in increasing the average life span, but as indicated earlier in the chapter this has been accomplished mainly by saving the lives of infants and young people rather than prolonging the lives of the

very old. A dozen years ago, Brown (1966) cited a number of research directions that may help to prolong life, among them being
organ transplants, control of cells and tissues so damaged organs
and limbs can be regenerated, and the development of virus cells or
cells with special inhibitors or stimulator substances. As we shall
see in the next chapter, this list has been extended in the intervening
years.

Gerontology

Interest in sociological and psychological research on aging
was encouraged by various writings and activities in the late
nineteenth and early twentieth centuries. Noteworthy among these
were the writings of the Frenchman Frederic Le Play, the surveys of
the Briton Charles Booth, and statistical studies concerning the
relationships of age to crime rates and suicide that were initiated by
the Belgian Adolphe Quetelet. The psychologist G. Stanley Hall
wrote the first important American book on aging, *Senescence,* in
1922—when Hall himself was in his eighth decade of life. However,
a Russian, V. Korenchevsky, is considered to have been the father
of gerontology.

The science of *gerontology,* which grew out of these early
efforts, is the study of biological, psychological, medical, sociologi
cal, and economic factors having a bearing on old age. The gerontology of today is an interdisciplinary field, based on the premise that
solutions to the problems of aging require the cooperative efforts of
specialists in many fields. Biologists contribute their knowledge and
research concerning the biological processes involved in aging;
psychologists study changes in mental abilities, personality, and
behavior with age; sociologists study the social roles and status of
older people and other aspects of group behavior in old age. Obviously, there is a great deal of overlap among the activities of the
various specialists, a fact that is recognized and accepted in the
multi- or inter-disciplinary approach.

The International Association of Gerontology, a worldwide
organization of gerontologists, with branches in many countries,
originally focused on medicine and biology but expanded its professional activities in the 1950s to include the social sciences. The
primary professional association of gerontologists in the United
States is the Gerontological Society, which has divisions of Biological Sciences, Clinical Medicine, Psychological and Social Sciences,

and Social Research, Planning and Practice. Together with several other professional and governmental organizations, the Gerontological Society promotes interdisciplinary research on aging. Research studies and position papers on topics in gerontology are published in the *Journal of Gerontology* and *The Gerontologist*.

Longitudinal and Cross-Sectional Research Methods

Psychologists and other social scientists who receive a substantial amount of training in research methodology have devoted considerable attention to developmental research methods. The measuring instruments or tests employed in developmental investigations suffer from problems of reliability, validity, and adequacy of standardization. In addition, the decision of what kind of research design to employ is seldom easy to make.

Because of the high cost of research, especially long-term longitudinal research, advances in our knowledge of developmental psychology and sociology are often difficult to achieve. In a *longitudinal investigation,* the same individuals are followed up and reexamined over a period of several months or many years. But most behavioral research on aging is based on *cross-sectional investigations,* in which different age groups of people are compared on some characteristic to determine how that feature varies with age. Cross-sectional studies are less expensive than longitudinal studies and, with effort, can be completed in a relatively short period of time. They do not require long-term commitments on the part of researchers, and subjects are not so easily lost as a result of moving away, dying, or loss of interest in the project. A possible shortcoming of cross-sectional studies is that they necessitate some kind of initial matching of the different age groups. For example, in studying the relationship of intelligence to age, one would certainly want to match the various age groups on education before comparing them on intelligence. The problem is that matching is often difficult to accomplish, and even so differences in educational *opportunity* could still affect the results of the investigation. The main difficulty in interpreting the results of a cross-sectional study is that the investigator cannot be certain whether the observed differences among age groups are produced by the aging process itself, by generational or cultural differences *(cohort differences),* or by time-related changes in the attitudes and values of society.

With regard to the validity of research findings, both cross-sectional and longitudinal studies have limitations. Since a person's age is related to the cultural context in which he or she was brought up, cross-sectional studies confound (i.e., mix up) the effects of age and cohort differences. Longitudinal studies, on the other hand, tend to confound the age of the person with the time at which the behavioral or other measurements are made. Time of measurement is an important variable because the physical, social, and psychological context in which the measurement takes place changes with time. Furthermore, changes in scores on the same tests administered to the same individuals at different times may be the results of practice effects or increasing familiarity of the material rather than to age per se.

What is needed in order to obtain a clearer picture of the effects of age, apart from cohort and time-of-measurement differences, is a combination of the cross-sectional and longitudinal approaches. Arguing in this vein, Schaie (1967) proposed a three-component model that includes three types of comparisons (Table 1–2). A simple cross-sectional study would involve the three times of birth (cohort) comparisons in any column of Table 1–2 (cells A-D-G, B-E-H, or C-F-I). A simple longitudinal study involves the three comparisons in any row of the table (cells A-B-C, D-E-F, or

Table 1–2. REPRESENTATION OF CROSS-SECTIONAL, LONGITUDINAL, AND TIME LAG DESIGNS FOR DEVELOPMENTAL RESEARCH*

Time of Birth (Cohort)	Time of Measurement		
	1960	1970	1980
1930	30 / A	40 / B	50 / C
1920	40 / D	50 / E	60 / F
1910	50 / G	60 / H	70 / I

Time Lag

Ages in years are above letters in cells of table

*Adapted from Botwinick, 1973, p. 296. (See text for explanation of table.)

G-H-I). In a third type of age-related comparison, the *time lag design,* several cohorts are examined, each at a different time period. As depicted by the three boxes in the lower left to upper right diagonal of Table 1–2 (cells G-E-C), the subjects in a time lag study are all of the same age at the times of measurement, but they were born at different times (i.e., they belong to different cohorts) and are measured or examined at different times.

In summary, a cross-sectional study confounds age and cohort differences, a longitudinal study confounds age-related differences with differences due to time of measurement, and a time lag study confounds cohort differences with differences related to time of measurement. Only by the combined use of all three types of studies can one hope to unravel the true effects of age on human characteristics, free of the confounding effects of cohort differences and the time at which the measurements are made.

Research Agencies

Private foundations provide some financial support for research on aging, but the greatest amounts of money and other assistance come from governmental organizations and agencies. Until fairly recently, federal support of research and research training concerned with the biological, medical, psychological, and sociological aspects of aging was the responsibility of the Adult Development in Aging Branch of the National Institute of Child Health and Human Development. A very small percentage of the budget of the National Institute of Mental Health was also allocated for research on the psychiatric and psychological problems of old age.

Currently, many federal agencies are involved in research and training programs that benefit the elderly. The research and training programs on aging of four agencies located in the Department of Health, Education, and Welfare—the Administration on Aging, the Office of Nursing Home Affairs, the National Institute on Aging, and the Office of Education—are described in Table 1–3. The newest of these federal agencies, and the one concerned primarily with research, is the National Institute on Aging. In 1975 this agency took over the Gerontology Research Center in Baltimore as its internal program and assumed the aging grants functions of the National Institute of Child Health and Human Development. Dr. Robert Butler, whose eminent career in gerontology was motivated

Table 1-3. DEPARTMENT OF HEALTH, EDUCATION, AND WELFARE TRAINING AND RESEARCH PROGRAMS BENEFITING THE ELDERLY*

Administration on Aging	
Multidisciplinary Centers of Gerontology	Grants to public and private nonprofit agencies and institutions to establish or support centers for such activities as training personnel, research and demonstration projects, and consultation services.
Personnel Training	Project grants for training persons employed or preparing for employment in gerontology and for publicizing available career opportunities in the field of aging.
Research and Demonstration Programs	Project grants for established research and demonstration projects involving the living patterns and living standards of the elderly and delivery of services to them, and to help identify and meet transportation problems of the elderly.
Office of Nursing Home Affairs	
Nursing Home Care, Training and Research Programs	Project grants and contracts to provide short-term training for employees of long-term care facilities and for supporting studies of long-term care. Office of Nursing Home Affairs responsible for training nursing home inspectors and certifying nursing homes participating in Medicare and Medicaid programs.
National Institute on Aging	
Research on Aging Process and Health	Conducts and supports research relating to biological, behavioral, and sociological aspects of the aging process and the special health problems of the elderly.
Office of Education	
Research on Problems of the Elderly	Federal grants to institutions of higher learning to plan, develop, and implement programs specifically designed to apply the resources of higher education to the problems of the elderly.

*Adapted from Select Committee on Aging. *Federal responsibility to the elderly.* Washington, D.C.: U.S. Government Printing Office, 1976, p. 13.

to some extent by the fact that he was reared by his grandparents, became the first director of the National Institute on Aging in May, 1976.

Among the activities that the National Institute on Aging is pursuing in the area of biology are research on senility, untoward drug reactions in the elderly, osteoporosis (see Chapter 2), and

Figure 1–5. Robert N. Butler, M.D., the first Director of the National Institute on Aging of the National Institutes of Health. (Reprinted by permission of Harper & Row.)

prosthetic devices for the elderly. The Institute's research support is, of course, not limited to biology, and an effort is being made to strike a balance between support of biological and social science research on aging. The research budget of the National Institute on Aging was approximately $30 million in 1977, which may seem like a great deal but is small compared to the $685 million authorized in the same year for the National Cancer Institute.

Other nations are apparently following the lead of the United States in supporting research on aging. For example, the British Council for Aging is enlisting the cooperative efforts of experimental and behavioral gerontologists, geriatricians, and caring agencies in basic research on aging.

SUMMARY

Old age is generally considered to begin in the early to middle sixties, a viewpoint which neglects the fact that people age at different rates and that physical and psychological factors must be taken into account in defining old age. For a number of reasons, primary among which is the reduction in infant mortality but also a decline in deaths caused by certain disorders of adulthood, life expectancy has risen steadily during the present century. The increase in average longevity has resulted in a greater proportion of elderly people in the population and an attendant shift in the social status of and concern about this group. All people, of course, do not age at the same rate. A number of variables—heredity, marital status, ethnicity, nationality, locality, diet, exercise, psychological characteristics, and the sociocultural environment—have been found to be related to longevity.

Attitudes toward old age and the aged vary with the culture, social group, and age of the person. Modern society harbors many misconceptions and stereotypes pertaining to the aged, misconceptions that lead to responding toward elderly people as odd or even nonhuman. Even young children express negative attitudes toward the elderly, attitudes that are frequently supported by parents and other authority figures. Although the elderly themselves may share the overall negative social perception of old age, they do not necessarily agree with the general public about what problems are most serious in old age.

The two professions that are most concerned with the processes and problems of aging are geriatrics and gerontology. Geriatrics is a medical specialty that deals with health and disease in old age, whereas gerontology is an interdisciplinary field encompassing all aspects of knowledge about aging.

A variety of methodological approaches—longitudinal, cross-sectional, time lag—have been applied in developmental research on aging. These different research methodologies are necessitated by the fact that many variables other than the process of aging itself, in particular differences in cohorts and times of measurement of the criterion variable, affect the outcomes of a developmental investigation.

Research and training programs to benefit the elderly have received increased support from the public and private sector during the past decade. The National Institute of Aging is the newest of the federal agencies that screen and support research projects concerned with aging and the aged. Interest in the biological, psychological, and sociological problems of aging is international in scope, and research on these problems is being actively pursued throughout the world.

suggested readings

Benet, S. *Abkhasians: The long-living people of the Caucasus.* New York: Holt, Rinehart & Winston, 1974.

Butler, R. N. *Why survive? Being old in America.* New York: Harper & Row, 1975.

Curtin, S. R. *Nobody ever died of old age.* Boston: Little, Brown, 1972.

de Beauvoir, S. *The coming of age.* (Trans. Patrick O'Brian.) New York: Putnam, 1972.

Hendricks, J., and Hendricks, C. D. *Aging in mass society: Myths and realities.* Cambridge, Mass.: Winthrop Publishers, 1977.

Serock, K., Seefeldt, C., Jantz, R. K., and Galper, A. As children see old folks. *Today's Education,* 1977, 66(2), 70–73.

notes

[1] Some animals, such as fishes, continue to increase in size throughout their lives.

[2] The immature larvae and pupae of these insects, however, may live for months or even years.

[3] According to state-by-state figures provided by the National Center for Health Statistics, average life expectancy in 1971 was highest in Hawaii and lowest in Washington, D.C.

[4] Interestingly enough, women who bear many children tend to live longer than those who bear fewer children. One wonders if this is related to the fact that having a good marriage and being sexually active are also associated with a longer life.

Chapter 2

Biological Factors in Aging

If one accepts the assertion that personality and behavior are the joint products of biological structure and the particular experiences of a person, then it is important to learn something about the biological processes of aging in order to understand better the psychology of later life.

PHYSICAL APPEARANCE AND PHYSICAL DISORDERS

The thriving mass market for skin creams, scalp preparations, dental adhesives, cleansers, and assorted cosmetics is a testimony to the changes in physical appearance that accompany aging. The preoccupation of our culture with youth is motivated by the same desire for long life as "inhaling the breath of young girls" and the search for the fountain of youth during former times (Sinick, 1976). Many people continually attempt to slow down or hide the process of aging by special diets and vitamins, face lifts, and cosmetics to cover up wrinkles in the skin.

Decreases in the natural moisture and elasticity of the skin with aging are matters of great concern to older people. As a person ages, the fibrous protein material (collagen) of which skin is primarily composed disappears, causing a diminution in the total amount of skin. Consequently, by examining a two-millimeter sample of skin, a dermatologist can usually estimate a person's age within a range of five years. Also quite common in old age are "liver spots" (*lentigo senilis),* darkly pigmented areas that occur on the back of the hands and wrists but actually have nothing to do with the liver. Treatments for aging, wrinkling skin—which are expensive and only temporarily effective—involve the injection of silicon under the skin or mildly wounding the skin to induce it to lay down more collagen material.

Among the other noticeable signs of aging are graying and thinning hair, loss of teeth, and increased hair on the chins of women. The eyelids thicken, the eye sockets develop a "hollow" appearance, and a cloudy ring *(arcus senilis)* forms around the cornea of the eye. The hips become broader and the shoulders narrower, and height decreases. The bowed spine and shrinking height with aging, which are especially noticeable in old women, are caused by a loss of the fibrous protein collagen between the vertebrae of the spinal column.

The magnitude of these changes varies greatly from person to person and is influenced by environmental conditions such as exposure to sun, air and water pollution, and diet. Owing to a lifetime of deprivation and to a culturally conditioned diet, black people are more susceptible to the physical signs of old age than whites. Lacking hormonal treatments during menopause, older black women tend to manifest symptoms of aging much sooner than white women (Perry, 1974).

Age-related physical changes are overwhelming and even disastrous to the self-images and security of some people, whereas other individuals are able to transcend their physical disabilities and be happy in spite of their altered appearance and health (Shanas et al., 1968). Because of the greater cultural expectations of beauty in the female sex, the physical manifestations of aging seem to be of greater concern to women in general than to men (Nowak, 1974). Changes in bodily appearance can also affect a person's social and occupational—and hence economic—status, especially when the individual continues to pursue an occupation in which physical attractiveness is very important.

HEALTH AND DISEASE

Physical appearance and attitude are obviously affected by physical health. If one is healthy, old age can be another interesting period of life; if one is ill, it can be terrifying and depressing. One might suppose that, because of advances in medicine and living conditions, old people of today would tend to be healthier than those of yesteryear. However, as the high incidence of disability and poor health among the aged suggests, this is not necessarily correct. Ten per cent of the American population is over 65, but this group occupies more than 30 per cent of the hospital beds. In spite of gains in average longevity during the past century, the incidence of heart disease and cancer during later life has not declined. Consequently, it is debatable whether older people of today are healthier than were those during times past. It has even been suggested that medical science, by interfering with the Darwinian principle of survival of the fittest, has succeeded merely in creating a numerous but relatively weak population.

As was implied in the last chapter, the expected life span of a 65 year old American is close to what it was in 1900. At age 65, one could expect to live 13 more years in 1900, compared to 15 more years today—an increase of only 2 years. If cancer, one of the major causes of death in the aged of today, were completely eliminated, the average life span would rise by only 1.5 to 2.3 years. But if all cardiovascular and kidney diseases were conquered, the average life span would be increased by approximately 7 to 10 years (Butler, 1975; Myers and Pitts, 1972). These are significant, if not dramatic, increases in longevity.

It is a truism that most people do not die of the "natural causes" of old age but rather from the diseases accompanying it. Not only is the frequency of illness and accidents greater but also recovery is usually slower among the old than the young. The number of days in bed, number of visits to the doctor, and number and length of hospital stays all increase as a person grows older. In fact, aging can be defined biologically as a decline in the body's ability to avoid or combat the effects of disease, accident, and other stressors (Timiras, 1972). The diseases of old age are expensive to treat, accounting for 25 per cent of health insurance payments in the United States. Preventive maintenance and good health management during young adulthood and especially middle age are, however, cheaper and better insurance for a healthy old age. One important principle of longevity is health care between the ages of 25 and 50 when people are at their full strength and decisions concerning physical care depend primarily on the individual himself rather than the physician.

Cardiovascular Disorders

Of the various diseases, cardiovascular disorders, cancer, and hypertension are major causes of death in old age. Of course, cardiovascular disorders, including heart attack and stroke, are not limited to the old. Substantial numbers of middle-aged and even young people (mostly men) are also victims. Heart attacks in young and middle-aged adults are most often due to the clogging of blood vessels by fatty deposits. In old people, however, they are more often caused by calcium lining the blood vessels or by a thickening of cardiac valves with the fibrous protein collagen.

Collagen, the chief constituent of connective tissue fibers, accounts for the difference in texture between a tough old bird and a succulent spring chicken. This material, which as noted previously, decreases with aging in the skin and between spinal vertebrae, increases with age in certain internal organs. The elasticity of arteries is so affected by collagen that the arteries of an octogenarian (80+ years) may be nearly as solid as metal. Collagen also affects the increased rate of aging observed in diabetes and a number of other diseases. Unfortunately, medical science has not yet discovered a way to reverse the gradual infiltration of collagen molecules into body tissues.

Most body structures decrease in weight as a person ages. For example, there is a loss of fat in the legs and forearms and a decrease in the mass of bone and muscle. Because of the tendency of body cells to reproduce themselves imperfectly and in smaller numbers, there is a decline in the number and quality of cells in most organs. Contrary to this general rule, the weight of the heart actually increases with age. It loses some of its resiliency, however, making the number of heartbeats fewer and more irregular. The capacity of the heart decreases by about 30 per cent from maturity to old age, and it takes longer to return to its normal pumping and beating levels after excitement or exercise. These changes in the heart (and in the coronary arteries as well) result in a reduced blood flow through the body, and consequently decrease the oxygen and nutrients to the cells and the rate at which waste products are carried away. The reduced oxygen supply is one reason why older people usually fatigue more rapidly than the young.

A heart attack, which is clearly an anxiety-arousing experience, may have profound psychological effects on the victim. A person who suffers a severe heart attack requires not only medical treatment and a curtailment of activities but also psychotherapeutic measures. Some heart patients develop *angor anima*, a fear of impending death, which can precipitate another attack. In any event, there are important physical and psychological reasons for keeping the heart patient relaxed and untroubled.

Great strides have been made in the treatment of heart disease and other cardiovascular disorders during the past few years, and breakthroughs in the treatment of cancer, arthritis, and other crippling diseases are expected at any time. The fact that pacemaker, artificial valve, open-heart surgery, and heart transplant are household terms attests to the progress in treating cardiac disorders and the education of the public about these matters.

Chronic Disorders

As is true of the heart, the functioning of other internal organs is affected by age. The organs of the body, however, do not age at an equal rate. The heart and blood vessels age at one pace, the liver at another, the nervous system at a third rate, and so forth. The effectiveness of the lungs and kidneys diminishes even more rapidly than that of the heart. The vital capacity of the lungs and their oxygen uptake, as well as the number of functioning excretory units in the kidneys, decrease markedly with age. In general, the digestive and eliminative processes do not function as well in the old as in the young. A decline in bladder capacity and enlargement of the prostate gland are responsible for many of the urinary problems of older men.

Not only are the elderly as a whole more susceptible to diseases than younger people, but also they typically have a greater number of diseases. The wide range of interacting symptoms and the ambiguity of certain physiological indicators in the elderly make medical diagnosis difficult. Diabetes is sometimes diagnosed when it is not present, and heart disease and cancer often go undetected in their early stages. The physician must also be careful that the treatment of one disorder does not cause another problem to become more severe. Modern antibiotics, surgical methods, and physical therapy techniques have greatly improved the fight against disease in the elderly. Still, physicians must take special care with drug dosages; the elderly have less tolerance for drugs than younger people.

Older people are also more susceptible to the more common chronic disorders, including arteriosclerosis, diabetes, arthritis, rheumatism, gastrointestinal problems, renal disease, and endocrine imbalance. Only a minority of old people are infirm, but approximately three fourths of those who are over 65 have one or more chronic conditions that place restrictions on their activities. Even when these diseases do not kill, they can make life extremely unpleasant for oneself and others. Arthritis, an inflammation of the joints accompanied by pain and stiffness that result in movement difficulties, is especially common in old age. The arthritic individual experiences problems in getting around and engaging in the heretofore routine movements of pleasurable activities. Although there is no cure for rheumatoid or spinal arthritis, the symptoms can be relieved by drugs and other treatments. Most of the other chronic conditions can also be treated, if not cured, and some of them can possibly be prevented.

As a person ages the dense part of bone structure becomes spongier and more fragile, causing vertebral, rib, and hip fractures, pain in the joints of the lower spine and hips, and a loss of several inches in height. A common cause of these changes is *osteoporosis,* a gradual long-term loss in the mass of the bones. In this disorder, which is four times as common in women as in men, the bones become less dense and more porous. Women who have gone through the menopause are often given estrogens to control osteoporosis, in addition to large doses of calcium, vitamin D, fluoride, and perhaps growth hormones. Jowsey and Holley (1973) maintain that the degenerative changes of osteoporosis are triggered by a decrease in the calcium/phosphorus ratio rather than by the total amount of calcium in the body. Consequently, they advocate treating osteoporosis by increasing the amount of phosphorus in the patient's diet. Other physicians have prescribed exercise to help relieve the pain and muscle spasms and possibly even reduce the bone loss of postmenopausal osteoporosis. In a study at the Mayo Clinic, however, little relationship was found between loss of muscle strength and loss of bone mineral (Sinaki, Opitz, and Wahner, 1974). This finding casts doubt on the value of muscular exercise in combatting the bone mineral loss of osteoporosis.

SENSATION AND MOVEMENT

The functioning of the human body becomes less efficient in old age, and its ability to cope with physical stress and to adapt to environmental change declines. Any change, including aging itself, is stressful, and hence poses a problem of adjustment for the elderly. But reductions in the efficiency of functioning and adaptability are far from entirely determined by heredity, nor are they inevitable. The individual's previous history of injury and disease, and the kind of life that he or she has lived, play important roles in determining the magnitude and rate of functional deterioration with age. These factors also affect a person's ability to compensate for declining sensory and motor abilities.

Vision

Aging is accompanied by modifications in the structure and functioning of all of the sense organs. Most of these changes are gradual, beginning in the 30s and 40s but becoming pronounced only after age 60 or so. Visual acuity, the ability to see small details, shows a pronounced decline after age 65 or 70. A part of this loss is due to a decline in the size of the pupil, the result of which is that less light reaches the retina. Another change that produces problems with detail vision, especially at near distances, is a disorder known as *presbyopia* (from the Greek *presbys,* meaning old, and *ops,* meaning eye). Presbyopia, which is correctable with "reading glasses" or bifocals, is not considered a "severe" visual impairment, however. The more severe losses of visual ability in old age are usually produced by cataracts, degeneration of the macula, or glaucoma (Moorehead et al., 1969). Most common among the severe visual disorders is the decrease in lens transparency known as cataracts. Even more severe than most cataracts is glaucoma, an increase in intraocular pressure that damages the optic nerve and eventually produces blindness. A number of diseases (e.g., diabetes) can also produce disorders of the retina and hence interfere with vision.

The process of aging also causes the eyes to lose some of their ability to adjust to darkness, necessitating a brighter light for reading and other close work. The capacity to distinguish color (especially greens and blues) and brightness of objects decreases. The rapidity with which visual stimuli can be detected, especially when stimuli are presented in quick succession, also declines. A reduction in the rapidity with which the pupil of the eye reacts to light affects the speed of detecting visual stimuli. Smaller changes in the environment become more difficult to detect and must be repeated or intensified for the individual to perceive them. Older people also tend to be less receptive than young adults to certain perceptual illusions and aftereffects (e.g., the Necker cube illusion, Ebbinghaus illusion). However, they are even more receptive than younger adults to other illusions (e.g., the Müller-Lyer illusion) (Fig. 2–1).

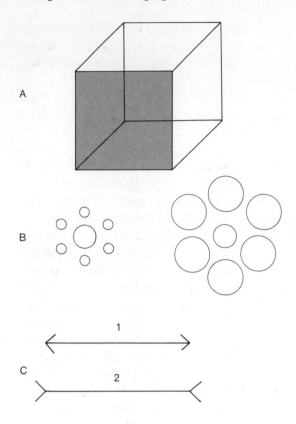

Figure 2–1. (A) Necker cube illusion, devised by L. A. Necker in 1832. The shaded surface can be made to appear on the front or back surface of the cube. (B) Ebbinghaus illusion, devised by H. Ebbinghaus. The circles in the middle of the two patterns are of equal size, but the one in the left pattern appears larger than the one in the right pattern. (C) Müller-Lyer illusion, devised by F. Müller-Lyer in 1889. Line 1 appears shorter than line 2, although they are the same physical length.

Certain researchers have attempted to find general principles to account for perceptual changes with age. One of these principles, known as *stimulus persistence theory,* has been formulated as follows (Axelrod, Thompson, and Cohen, 1968, p. 193):

In the senescent nervous system, there may be an increased persistence of the activity evoked by a stimulus, i.e., . . . the rate of recovery from the short-term effects of stimulation may be slowed. On the assumption that perception of the second stimulus as a discrete event depends on the degree to which the neural effects of the first have subsided, the poorer temporal resolution in senescence would then follow.

This theory has been used to explain why older people react more slowly than younger ones to a series of stimuli presented in rapid succession. According to the principle stated above, it takes longer for an old person to recover from the effects of one stimulus before he or she is ready to respond to a second stimulus.

Stimulus persistence theory is consistent with many but not all of the research findings on perception in the aged. Even less tenable, however, is the "common-sense" hypothesis that diminishing vision is a cause of the older person's retention of a more youthful view of himself!

As any pilot knows, vision sometimes conflicts with the gravitational sense, a situation that can have disastrous consequences. In an experimental arrangement introduced by Witkin (1959), the subject is placed in a darkened room and assigned the task of aligning an illuminated rod, which is surrounded by a tilted square frame, to the true vertical upright position. In this situation, elderly people, relying more on visual cues than on their sense of body position, tend to line up the rod with the frame rather than the true vertical. Using Witkin's term, they show more *field dependence* than younger adults and are similar to children in this regard.

Hearing

Beginning as early as the third or fourth decade of life, sensitivity to sound, particularly sounds of high frequency, begins to diminish. Referred to as *presbycusis,* and produced by degenerative changes in the middle ear, inner ear, and auditory nerve, this disorder is even more common in the aged than visual impairment. It affects the hearing of sibilants such as *s, sh,* and *ch,* which are carried by speech frequencies of over 3520 hertz (Shock, 1952b) (Fig. 2–2). Since discrimination among higher-pitched sounds is

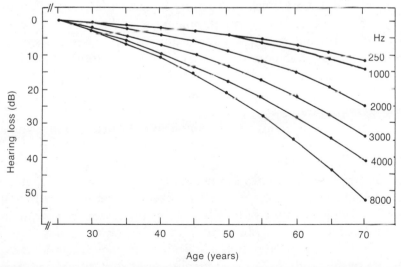

Figure 2–2.   Hearing loss as a function of age for tones of various frequencies. (After Botwinick, 1973. Data from Spoor, 1967.)

particularly affected, it is recommended that the speaker lower the pitch of his voice when speaking to persons with presbycusis. Barrett (1972) notes, however, that a hearing loss need not affect an old person's appreciation of familiar music, since auditory memory can fill in the tonal gaps and lead one to "hear" frequencies to which he or she is no longer sensitive.

Older people often experience difficulty in understanding rapidly spoken words, caused perhaps by a combination of problems in hearing and processing information rapidly. Deterioration in hearing, of course, is due not only to the aging process itself but also to the structural damage inflicted by years of noise bombardment and accidents involving the ears.

Psychological factors also play a role in hearing, as indicated by the popular saying that people hear what they want to hear. Savitz (1974) maintains that, in many instances, the "hard of hearing" complaint of the elderly is really a "hard of listening" problem. Loquacious elderly people constantly recount the activities and deeds of their younger days and may not listen closely to the statements of other people. Savitz recommends to a talkative elderly person that "he lend his ears to his neighbor's tales as his neighbor does to his."

Semantic problems are also involved in communicating with the elderly. As we grow old we appear to lose some of our ability to stretch the meanings of words, and this impairs our understanding of the total idea that is being communicated. Consequently, speech therapists who work with the elderly suggest that special care be taken when talking to very old people, so that they can both understand what is said to them and be understood themselves. The speaker should make certain to face the older person to whom he is talking and to speak louder than normal. Getting the person's attention by touching or gesture is also recommended.

It is commonly accepted in psychiatric circles that the hard of hearing are especially prone to paranoid symptoms.[1] Cooper and his co-workers (Cooper, Curry, Kay, Garside, and Roth, 1974) obtained evidence that this may be true of elderly people in particular. A study was conducted of 132 mental hospital patients averaging 68 years of age. None of the patients had been mentally ill before the age of 50, but at the time of the study 65 of them were paranoid, and 67 (the "control group") had other psychiatric problems. Over 46 per cent of the paranoid patients had a hearing loss, compared to 38 per cent of the controls—a statistically significant difference. Since the deafness of the paranoid patients was of a long-standing, bilateral nature, usually produced by chronic middle-ear problems, deafness had begun long before the onset of the mental disorder. It was concluded that the existence of a long interval between the onset of deafness and of the paranoid psychotic condition provides an opportunity for prevention of the mental disorder.

Other Senses

Taste, smell, touch, pain, and temperature sensitivity also decline with age. Over half of the taste buds are lost in later life, but taste sensitivity does not greatly diminish until the late 50s. Odor sensitivity declines markedly with age (Barrett, 1972), although the individual may not be aware of it. The diminution in smell and taste is signaled by a preference for stronger essences and, notwithstanding digestive upsets, for spicier foods. However, learning can apparently compensate for the loss of smell and taste receptors, as witnessed by the fact that wine tasters and gourmets are frequently elderly. Touch and the other skin senses also show diminished sensitivity with age. The ability to experience pain is only about one-third as great in an average 70 year old as in an average 20 year old (Arehart-Treichel, 1972), but subjective complaints of pain are still common. Temperature sensitivity is also affected, with poor circulation making it more difficult for an older person to adjust to cooler temperatures.[2] This is especially true in cases of arteriosclerosis, in which the increase in blood pressure produces both poor circulation and headaches.

Movement

Owing to decreased strength and energy level and increased stiffness in the joints, movement becomes more difficult with age. On visits to the doctor, older people frequently complain of weakness and fatigue, but four fifths of those over 65 manage to get around from place to place fairly satisfactorily. When the individual suffers from arthritis or another chronic disorder, however, physical activity can be quite troublesome.

Speed of responding on tasks requiring fast reflexes or reactions, especially reaction-time situations in which the person must choose among several alternatives, shows an age decrement. The ability to coordinate various movements, fine muscle movements in particular, also declines (Botwinick, 1970; Shock, 1952a). Although some slowing of movement always occurs in old age, practice, motivation, and physical exercise affect speed and skill in psychomotor tasks. In any event, the range of individual differences in the motor abilities of older people is quite large. For example, it has been found that superbly healthy men in their 70s and 80s perform as well as normal men of 20 (Birren, Butler, Greenhouse, Sokoloff, and Yarrow, 1963; Botwinick and Thompson, 1968). The study by Birren et al. (1963) compared the physical and mental abilities of healthy men in the 65–91 age range with those of a group of young men whose average age was 21. It was found that the older men were as good as the younger ones on several measures. There was, for example, no difference between the two groups in blood flow to the brain and the consumption of oxygen during exercise.

In spite of declining sensorimotor abilities, nearly 60 per cent of older Americans have valid driver's licenses. Recognizing that because of disease or disability many older drivers pose a danger for themselves and others, a special screening examination for the aged has been advocated (Butler, 1975). The examination, which would have to be passed every year after age 50, would consist of visual, auditory, and reaction-time tests, as well as measures of judgment in driving situations. Combined with certification that the person is in good physical condition, such an examination could appreciably lower the high accident rate of elderly drivers (Fig. 2–3). Since losing one's driver's license is a discouraging experience to anyone who values the speed and convenience of automobile transportation, a person who failed any part of the test battery would be given an opportunity to make up the deficiency. Refresher courses, such as the one developed at the University of Michigan's Institute of Gerontology, have been designed to assist older people in overcoming just such driving deficiencies.

Getting Inside an Older Skin

Researchers at the University of Michigan's Institute of Gerontology have devised a special method for studying the sensorimotor problems associated with old age and creating understanding in younger people (Pastalan, 1974). Labeled the Empathic Model, the researchers have used mechanical devices to simulate the loss of sensation and movement that people experience as they grow older. Some of these devices are coated lenses, nose plugs and

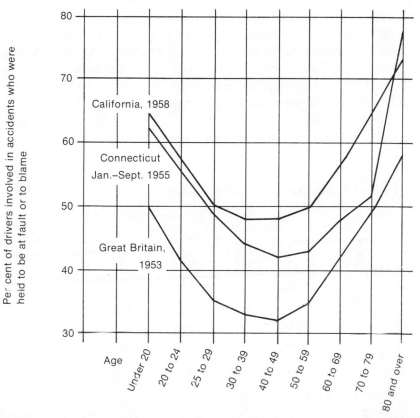

Figure 2–3. Drivers of different ages involved in accidents and held to be at fault. According to these statistics, the safest drivers are in the age range 30–60. (After McFarland, Tune, and Welford, 1964. Reprinted with permission.)

ear plugs, and fixatives or gloves to densensitize touch. Among the lessons that a younger person who dons these gadgets learns are the difficulties that older people experience in seeing traffic signs and distinguishing words from background noise.

Using the Empathic Model, investigators have pinpointed several sources and types of perceptual problems: difficulty seeing in natural and unbalanced artificial light because of glare; the fading of colors, greens and blues most and reds least; poorer depth perception and slower visual recovery in moving between brighter and darker places; the blurring of sounds, especially those containing high frequencies, by background noise. Other sensory and motor problems revealed by the Empathic Model are the facts that food doesn't taste as good as it formerly did (and therefore many old people don't eat well), degrees of temperature are more difficult to distinguish (posing potential hazards in bathing and in washing dishes), and fine muscular control declines (making the turning of pages and dials difficult). As a result of their findings, the investigators have recommended changes in lighting and color combinations and other environmental modifications that take into account the skills and abilities of older people. Among their recommendations for driving are to make road signs larger and more distinctive and to remove unnecessary lights, signs, and other roadside distractions.

Report 2–1

SAGINAW, Mich. (AP)—Four junior high students became old people for a day to see how they felt and how others acted toward them.

"I found myself getting very irritable because I couldn't get around as well as I normally do," said 13-year-old Mike Russell of Zilwaukee.

He and others are students at Saginaw's North Intermediate School. Their health education teacher, Albert Garcia, helped apply the bandages, earplugs and splints to simulate physical handicaps.

The experiment was similar to those conducted at the University by Dr. Tamerra Moeller's students in her class on the psychology of aging.

"We tend to forget all of the adjustments a person must make as a result of the physical processes of aging," Dr. Moeller said. "Declining vision or hearing, chronic illness, memory loss—these processes are painful and unnerving."

Armed with this information, the students and their teacher devised ways to experience for a few hours some of those same physical ailments.

They used earplugs to reduce hearing, noseplugs to stifle smell, gloves to make hands slow and awkward, as they might be with arthritis, and bandages or splints to make arm and leg movements difficult.

A couple of them also put patches on one eye. They had first tried to use crinkled plastic wrap to get the impression of eyesight blurred by cataracts, but the paper kept slipping.

"The eyepatch was the biggest problem," said Mike. "I kept misjudging distance. The first surprise was that I couldn't catch a table tennis ball. Then I tried to pick up a pencil and missed. I even misjudged steps."

Terry Colby, 13, said: "When I went home at noon my mother said, 'You're not coming to the table with those gloves on.'

"I told her I had to, it was part of an experiment for health class. The gloves really cut down on movement, and even though I was slow and careful, I still spilled my glass of Kool-Aid."

Thirteen-year-old Holly Neuman had a plastic bag over her right hand and a bandage on the left.

"I couldn't turn the pages of my books," she said. "I also found the eye that wasn't covered got tired."

Ray Lucas, 13, spent the day with tape across his nose, and that helped him discover how closely the sense of taste is linked to the sense of smell.

"At noon, I had a deviled egg sandwich that tasted blah," he said. "Even the water tasted funny. My candy bar wasn't too good, either."

THE NERVOUS SYSTEM AND SLEEP

There is some dispute over the matter, but it is a generally accepted fact that human beings are born with essentially all of the brain neurons (approximately ten billion) that they will ever have.

The size and complexity of these neurons increase as the individual grows, but unlike neurons outside the central nervous system, those in the brain and spinal cord do not regenerate when destroyed by injury or disease. It has been reported that by age 75, brain weight has declined by an average of 44 per cent and the number of axons in the spinal cord by 37 per cent (Barrett, 1972). This phenomenon is due to a decrease in the number and size of neurons with aging. Previous estimates that 100,000 brain neurons are lost each day after age 30 are undoubtedly exaggerations, and most authorities now agree that in the absence of disease the brain's ability to function may not be greatly impaired in old age. Nevertheless, the ability of the brain to process information is affected by a decrease in the number of neurons, a measurable loss in the velocity of nerve impulses, and a reduction with aging in the blood supply to the brain. It is estimated, for example, that the cerebral blood supply of a 75 year old is 10 per cent less than that of a 30 year old.

Age-related changes in the brain have an effect on the sleeping-waking cycle, although environmental and psychological factors also play important roles in sleep. Many older people sleep poorly at night, while catching up by means of "cat naps" during the day. Not only do older people get less sleep but also the sleep they get is not as deep as that of younger people.

William Dement and his associates have shown that sleep actually consists of four stages, ranging from light sleep to very deep sleep. The cycle from light to deep sleep and back again to light sleep takes about 1½ hours on the average. It is during Stage 1, the stage of lightest sleep, that the rapid eye movements (REMs) indicative of dreaming occur. The intermediate stages, Stages 2 and 3, comprise about 60 per cent of sleep time and Stage 4—the stage of deepest sleep—about 20 per cent of sleep time. Some dreaming without REMs does occur in Stages 2, 3, and 4, but much less than in Stage 1. It has been found that the REM period of sleep (Stage 1) shortens somewhat and Stage 4 (deepest sleep) shortens appreciably in old age. During the later hours of night sleep, old people typically alternate between Stage 2 and REM (Roffwarg, Muzio, and Dement, 1966).

RESEARCH ON THE BIOLOGY OF AGING

As is true of different body structures and systems, people also age at greatly different rates. At the other end of the spectrum from the centenarians of Abkhasia, Hunza, and Vilcabamba (see Chapter 1) are the victims of a rare childhood disease known as *progeria*. Even in early childhood, a victim of this disorder shows signs of premature senescence and dies of "old age" as a young teenager. Similar to progeria is Werner's syndrome, a disease that has its onset in the late teens. Like progeria victims, but at a later age those with Werner's syndrome suffer from arrested growth (Rosenfeld, 1976). Progeria, Werner's syndrome, and hypothyroidism are said to "mimic aging," since their victims are not truly old but show many of the signs of senescence.

Theories of Aging

Scientists who study the process of aging have taken a special interest in both long-livedness and short-livedness in an effort to discover clues to the biology of aging. Various hypotheses or theories that serve as guides to research in this area have been proposed. One theory attributes aging to an increased breakdown in the homeostatic, or self-regulatory, mechanisms of the body that control the internal environment. Related to this view is the *autoimmune hypothesis,* which maintains that the immunological defenses of a person diminish with age, causing an increase in autoimmune diseases such as arthritis as the body turns upon itself. A breakdown in the body's immunological system could, it is believed, be the result of a reduction in a hormone such as thymosin, a secretion of the thyroid gland that decreases during ages 25 to 45.

Another theory of biological aging is the theory of cross-linkage. *Cross-linkage* is the inadvertent coupling of large intracellular and extracellular molecules that causes connective tissue to stiffen. It has been suggested that cross-linkage of DNA molecules prevents the cell from reading the genetic information properly (Pye, 1977). As a consequence, enzymes that are sufficiently active to maintain the body and its functions are not produced. Some authorities believe, however, that although cross-linkage is associated with aging, it is an effect or correlate rather than a cause of aging. Another possible cause of aging at the cellular level is an accumulation of chemical "garbage," such as free radicals, in the cells. *Free radicals* are broken-off parts of molecules, or molecules with an electron stripped off, that connect to and damage other molecules.

Following Selye (1976), many researchers have become convinced that there is an "aging clock"—a genetically determined aging program—somewhere in the body. The aging clock presumably dictates the rate and time at which, barring physical mishap, one can expect to age and die. Some authorities believe that the aging clock is in the brain, perhaps in the hypothalamus. Others maintain that the evidence points to the existence of aging clocks in the body cells. A proponent of the individual cell theory is Leonard Hayflick, whose experiments demonstrated that there is a built-in limit to the number of times that individual cells can subdivide before they die. Tortoise cells divide 90 to 125 times, human cells 40 to 60 times, and chicken cells 15 to 35 times (Hayflick, 1970).

An acceptable theory of aging need not be of an all-or-none quality, and there is evidence of multiple sites or causes of aging. Aging can occur at the tissue level, the cellular level, or in the cell nucleus. At the tissue level aging is related to an increase in collagen; at the cellular level, to a deterioration of mitochondria—the little energy machines in the cytoplasm of the cell; and at the nuclear level, to mutations of DNA and the cross-linkage of molecules within the cell nucleus (Anderson, 1974).

In addition to multiple sites, the evidence points to at least two kinds of processes in aging. The first of these is accidental damage to the molecules, membranes, or parts of the body. The second process is the "wired-in," genetically programmed "aging clock" referred to above. Such a clock probably consists of a series of special on-off gene "switches," which, when the organism has reached maturity, turn off certain cell activities while turning on new cells that cause the destruction of the body's protein building blocks. Belief in the existence of such a genetic program has resulted in increased research directed at the DNA and RNA molecules that are responsible for cell replication. In addition, research on the role of the hypothalamus and endocrine glands—the pituitary and thymus glands in particular—continues.

Prolonging Life

Whether the social and economic problems that would be posed by a greatly extended average life span could be solved is of concern to many gerontologists, but scientists and laymen alike remain quite receptive to efforts to prolong life. C. S. Lewis once asked: "Why this preoccupation with squeezing out more spatio-temporal existence? Could it be a lack of confidence in what comes hereafter?'' Whatever the answer to Lewis's question may be, the number of diets, drugs, surgical procedures, and other methods that have been tried to obtain longevity is legion. One approach that works to a degree in lengthening the lives of small animals is calorie restriction begun around the time of birth. However, it appears that, while lengthening life, underfeeding results in animals that are less resistant to stress than normally fed ones (Anderson, 1974). Another experimental method for lengthening life is hypothermia—lowering the body temperature by 2 to 3 degrees Celsius, a procedure that can extend the lives of small animals by 20 to 25 per cent.

It is a sensible idea to eat lightly but nutritiously at any age, but caloric restriction and body cooling will not dramatically increase the longevity of humans when initiated after puberty. Consequently, most people who are preoccupied with living longer, and looking and feeling better as well, have turned to dieting, drugs, and other methods. Unfortunately, these procedures are not always effective, or they can have double-edged effects. For example, many people who were concerned about the role of cholesterol in arteriosclerosis and heart attacks switched from saturated to polyunsaturated fats. But as Rosenfeld (1976) points out, polyunsaturated fats increase the oxidation reactions of cells, thereby creating more free radicals and hence more cellular damage of the sort associated with aging.

The situation with drugs and vitamins is not much clearer. One drug—Gerovital—is purported by its advocates to be able to treat a host of old age afflictions, including angina pectoris, arteriosclerosis, arthritis, gray hair, high blood pressure, and wrinkled skin, as well as depression and other psychological disorders. The difficulty is that Gerovital is prepared from procaine hydrochloride, commonly known as Novocain, which has been shown to have no significant effect on the physical or psychological problems of old age.

Reasoning that aging is associated with too much tissue or cellular oxygen, researchers have reported some success in prolonging the life spans of animals by the use of dietary supplements of antioxidants such as vitamins C and E.[3] For example, there is some evidence that doses of vitamin E in the diets of rats can increase the life spans of these animals by 39 per cent or more (Harman, 1972). In an experiment by Packer and Smith (1974), human cells that were treated by vitamin E were found to be significantly more resistant to the physical stress produced by exposure to oxygen and visible light. The experimenters attributed their results to the fact that, as a natural antioxidant, vitamin E countered the oxygen and light before they could oxidize (damage) the molecules in the body cells. Unfortunately, Packer and Smith themselves, in addition to other investigators, have been unable to reproduce their own initial findings (Packer and Smith, 1977).

Summarizing the results of his experiments with vitamin E and those of others, Harman (Harman, Heidrick, and Eddy, 1976) concluded that the decline in the immune system with age is the result of the degrading action of free radicals on the body cells. Therefore, he maintains, the antioxidant abilities of vitamin E can help retard the decline of the immune system by protecting the cells from free radicals. But as Packer and Smith discovered, vitamin E, in its role as an antioxidant, does not always increase the life spans of cells. Rather, they speculate, when vitamin E does extend cellular life span, the results are produced by the interaction of vitamin E with some as yet unidentified chemical or chemicals.

SUMMARY

Age-related changes in the skin, muscles, and bones of the human body, and the consequent altered appearance of the individual, represent a source of stress that may be weathered well or poorly. Changes in the physical structure of the body are also associated with disease in old age, cancer and cardiovascular disorders being the biggest killers of the aged. Other troubles, even if not as lethal, are chronic disorders such as osteoporosis, arthritis, rheumatism, digestive and eliminative problems, and diabetes. Osteoporosis, a gradual loss of bone mass which is more common in women than in men, can lead to painful fractures of the spine, hips, and rib cage.

Presbyopia is the most common visual disorder of aging, but more serious are cataracts and glaucoma. Other age-related changes in the eye necessitate stronger light and larger print. A gradual loss of sensitivity to high and middle pitches (presbycusis) is also observed in old age. Declining sensitivity to sound can usually be helped by a hearing aid, although psychological factors play a role in the understanding of speech and the appreciation of music. Taste, smell, touch, pain, and temperature sensitivity also decline with age.

Movement becomes more difficult and reaction time slower with aging, but there is a wide range of individual differences in motoric functioning. The use of mechanical devices worn by younger observers (the "Empathic Model") can assist in understanding the sensorimotor deficits associated with aging.

Decreases in the quantity of brain neurons and in the speed of nerve impulses affect the capacity of the brain to process information in old age. The sleep pattern is also affected, the elderly sleeping not only less but also not as deeply as younger people.

Among the various explanations that have been offered to account for biological aging are the autoimmune hypothesis, the theory of cross-linkage, and the accumulation of free radicals in cells. A comprehensive theory of aging needs to take into account at least two processes: accidental damage to molecules, membranes, or body parts; and the functioning of a wired-in, genetically programmed "aging clock."

Experiments in lengthening the lives of animals have involved caloric restriction, hypothermia, and various drugs. Antioxidants such as vitamins C and E have received particular attention, and some success reported. However, the overall experimental results permit no definitive conclusions regarding the effects of these vitamins or other chemicals on the aging process.

suggested readings

Bergman, M. Changes in hearing with age. *The Gerontologist,* 1971, *11*(2), Part I, 148–151.

Birren, J. E. and Schaie, K. W. (eds.) *The handbook of the psychology of aging.* New York: Van Nostrand Reinhold, 1977.

Cherry, L., and Cherry, R. Slowing the clock of aging. *The New York Times Sunday Magazine,* May 12, 1974, pp. 20, 78ff.

Dibner, A. S. The psychology of normal aging. In Spencer, M. G. and Dorr, C. J. (eds.), *Understanding aging: A multidisciplinary approach.* New York: Appleton-Century-Crofts, 1975.

Rosenfeld, A. *Prolongevity.* New York: Alfred A. Knopf, 1976.

Timiras, P. S. Developmental physiology and aging. New York: Macmillan, 1972.

notes

[1] Paranoid conditions are mental disorders characterized by systematic delusions of grandeur or persecution, or by ideas of reference. Delusions are firmly held beliefs that the patient will not relinquish even in the face of contrary evidence.

[2] Because of their vulnerability to accidental hypothermia—a loss of body heat that is potentially fatal—it is recommended that temperatures in homes and facilities for the elderly be kept above 65° F.

[3] Dietary supplements of other antioxidants—Santoquin (a quinoline derivative), 2-MEA (2-mercaptoethylamine), and BHT (butylated hydroxytoluene)—have also been found to increase the life spans of experimental animals ("How does Vitamin E . . . ," 1977).

Chapter 3

Mental Abilities

A popular view of old age is that it is a time when abilities decline, activities become more restricted, and one is forced to depend more on other people. It is often incorrectly held that old people have poor memories, cannot think clearly, and undergo a general decline in mentality. As discussed in Chapter 2, sensorimotor abilities usually show a marked decline in old age. But as we shall see in the present chapter, mental abilities do not deteriorate quite so rapidly, and judgment and wisdom can compensate for the losses in physical and mental abilities that do occur. Certainly, many very old people remain independent and active almost until the time of death, adapting successfully and maintaining their level of mental ability.

CREATIVE PERFORMANCE

Evidence that creative production does not necessarily decline in old age can be found by analyzing the biographies of famous artists, scholars, and scientists. Pianist Artur Rubinstein was still playing brilliantly at age 89, some say with greater sensitivity and skill than ever. Many famous men—Goethe, Picasso, Edison, and Burbank—continued their highly creative endeavors into the ninth decade of life. Giuseppe Verdi produced the joyous, exuberant opera "Falstaff" at age 80, and Justice Oliver Wendell Holmes, Jr. formulated many of his most impressive legal opinions while in his 90s.

Old people learn new things, develop new skills, and may become truly creative for the first time during later life. Grandma Moses was 73 when she started painting, and held her first exhibition at age 80. By the time of her death at 101 she had achieved international fame as an artist. One may argue, however, that these are exceptions and that creative performance typically peaks much sooner than old age. An early study found that the period of peak productivity in the arts was 30 to 39 years and that productivity declined thereafter (Lehman, 1953). Likewise, chess masters tend to reach their peak in their 30s, although they typically show little decline until their 50s. A dramatic illustration of a continuing high level of mental functioning in chess is that of the chess master Blackburne, who gave nine exhibitions between the ages of 76 and 79, averaging 21 games at each exhibition and winning 86 per cent of them (Buttenwieser, 1935).

A problem with Lehman's (1953) conclusion that creativity usually peaks in the 20s and 30s is that many of the people who were studied died when they were still fairly young. This circumstance produced a bias favoring early peak creativity, a methodological shortcoming which Dennis's (1966) study attempted to correct. Dennis's investigation of 738 people who lived to age 79 or beyond reported comparative longitudinal data on the productivity of three major groups—scholars, scientists, and artists (art, music, and literature). People in the fine arts and literature tended to produce more in their 20s than scholars and scientists, but the period of greatest output for all three groups was in the 40s or shortly thereafter. The performance of scholars declined little after age 40, but the output of artists and scientists decreased appreciably after age 60. Other studies have found that inventors and historians tend to reach maximum productivity around age 60.

Differences in the period of peak productivity of various groups depend not only on individual creativity but also on the length of the training period. This period is longer for scientists and scholars than for artists (Dennis, 1966). Productivity in the arts seems to depend more on individual creativity than experience and therefore peaks early. Creative production in scholarly or scientific endeavors, on the other hand, demands a longer training period, and consequently creativity in these fields shows a later peak. In any event, the great variability in creativity during old age leads one to question the advisability of setting a fixed age for retirement from a specific vocation.

GENERAL INTELLIGENCE

In addition to curiosity, motivation, and flexibility, an extremely important factor in creativity at any age is ability. Of the many efforts that psychologists have made to measure general and specific mental abilities, research and application in the area of intelligence testing have been in the forefront. Unlike creative performance, which is actually a criterion variable, measures of general intelligence and specific mental abilities have been used primarily as predictors of future performance. The instruments employed to measure these variables attempt to assess maximum mental performance—what a person is capable of achieving with adequate motivation and opportunity.

Wechsler Adult Intelligence Scale

Traditional intelligence tests, which are loaded with school-type tasks, were not designed originally to assess the abilities of older people. Early tests such as the Stanford-Binet Intelligence Scale were directed primarily at school-age children, the major purpose of the tests being to determine the abilities of children to profit from scholastic work. The first individual tests of intelligence constructed specifically for adults were the Wechsler-Bellevue Intelligence Tests, published originally in 1939 and revised as the Wechsler Adult Intelligence Scale (WAIS) in 1955. The WAIS, which consists of 11 subtests and is scored for verbal, performance, and full scale intelligence quotients (IQs), was standardized on a wide age range of adults. The old age sample consisted of over 50 men and 50 women in each of four age groups (60–64, 65–69, 70–74, 75 and over), but the number of cases in each age/sex group on which the IQ tables were based was considerably smaller than this. All of the old-age groups were selected by quota sampling procedures from metropolitan Kansas City, which was taken as a typical American city. For a number of technical reasons, the sample used in computing the IQ tables on the WAIS turned out not to be truly representative of older Americans in general.

A graphic plot of the average WAIS subtest scaled scores for the four old-age groups is presented in Figure 3–1. It will be noted that the average scaled scores for these four groups are higher on the first six subtests (the Verbal Scale) than on the last five subtests (the Performance Scale). Since the mean subtest scaled score for people in general is 10, the old-age sample scored below the general population mean on all subtests, but particularly on Digit Symbol (DS)—a speeded test. It will also be observed that there is a general decline in the average scaled scores on all subtests after ages 60–64.

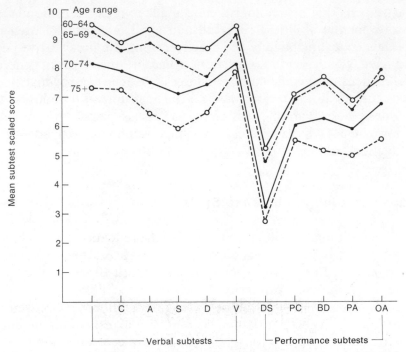

Figure 3–1. Mean WAIS subtest scaled scores for the four subgroups of the old-age standardization group. (Adapted from Doppelt and Wallace, 1955.)

Testing Older Adults

In addition to difficulties of score interpretation posed by inadequate norms, there are special problems in administering intelligence tests to older people. To begin with, it is often questionable whether a young examiner can establish sufficient rapport with an older examinee so that the latter will be motivated to do his or her best. Sometimes older people would rather not try at all than try and fail. Older adults, to an even greater extent than young adults, do not relish performing tasks which they can see as having no bearing on their lives.

Other problems encountered in administering psychological tests to older persons are the speededness aspect of many tests, the distractibility and easy fatigability of many older people, and the presence of sensory defects. Old people are usually at a disadvantage on timed tests, but they frequently show little or no inferiority compared to younger people when time is not limited. Also, as indicated in Chapter 2, sensory defects in old age can interfere with performance. Occasionally, however, an alleged sensory defect may actually be a problem in reading or auditory comprehension. The writer has had the experience of preparing to examine a functionally illiterate elderly man who "conveniently" forgot his eyeglasses and was therefore unable to read the test items.

Even when all goes well with the testing procedure, the examiner must be careful not to confuse scholastic intelligence with everyday mental functioning. Many older (and younger) people who do poorly on intelligence tests manage to cope satisfactorily with the demands of everyday living. From a practical viewpoint, how well a person functions in everyday life is the best measure of his or her abilities. This has led some authorities to suggest that tests for older people would have greater validity if they consisted of problem situations specific to the lives of the elderly.

Cross-Sectional and Longitudinal Studies

The results of earlier studies of changes in general intelligence with age were almost always based on cross-sectional data (Yerkes, 1921; Jones and Conrad, 1933; Doppelt and Wallace, 1955). From his analysis of scores on the Army Alpha Test administered to American Army officers during World War I, Yerkes (1921) found that average scores on this early group-administered test of intelligence decreased steadily from the late teens through the sixth decade of life. A similar trend was observed by Jones and Conrad (1933) in a study conducted in 19 New England villages. An analysis of the relationship of mean Full Scale scores on the Wechsler-Bellevue Form I (Wechsler, 1958) showed that mean standard scores peaked in late adolescence, remained fairly constant from that point until the late 20s or early 30s, and subsequently showed a steady decline through old age (Fig. 3–2). A composite picture of the findings of cross-sectional investigations through 1960 indicates that scores on general intelligence tests reach a maximum during the late teens or early twenties, show little appreciable further change until ages 30 to 35, and then decrease steadily through old age.

The problems encountered in interpreting the results of cross-sectional studies were described briefly in Chapter 1. Cross-sectional investigations compare people of different cohorts; that is, a group of people brought up in one kind of sociocultural climate is compared to a group brought up in another sociocultural climate. Differences among cohorts in factors such as educational opportu-

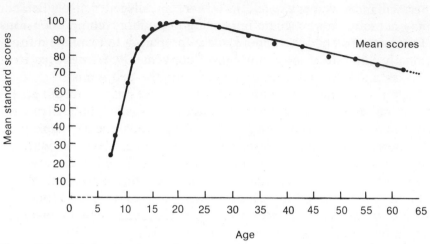

Figure 3–2. Relationship of mean Full Scale scores on the Wechsler-Bellevue Form I to age (7–65 years). (After D. Wechsler, *The measurement and appraisal of adult intelligence,* 4th ed., 1958. Baltimore: Williams and Wilkins © 1958.)

nity, which is closely related to intelligence test scores, and the selective migration of brighter people away from home make it difficult to match people of different ages.

Over the past half-century there has been a steady rise in the average socioeconomic and educational levels in the United States. The fact that intelligence test scores are positively related to both educational level and socioeconomic status has the effect that older cohorts, who grew up during less affluent times and had less formal education, score significantly lower than younger cohorts. This result may be misinterpreted as demonstrating that intelligence declines with age, rather than showing that the increase in test scores has been produced by improvements in education and socioeconomic status.

In contrast to cross-sectional studies, the findings of several longitudinal investigations indicate that intelligence test scores may actually increase after early adulthood. It can be argued that since these longitudinal studies have most often been conducted on college graduates or other intellectually favored groups, the increases with age do not necessarily apply to the general population (Bayley and Oden, 1955; Nisbet, 1957; Campbell, 1965; Owens, 1953, 1966). However, longitudinal investigations with people of average intelligence (Charles and James, 1964; Eisdorfer, 1963; Tuddenham, Blumenkrantz, and Wilkin, 1968) and with noninstitutionalized mentally retarded adults (Baller, Charles, and Miller, 1967; Bell and Zubek, 1960) have yielded similar findings. Botwinick (1967) interpreted these results as suggesting that intelligence continues to increase by small amounts during adulthood, reaching a plateau between the ages of 25 and 30. Subsequently, people who are below average in intelligence decline somewhat, but above-average people manifest no decline or even improve until age 50. Furthermore, a recent study by Baltes and Schaie (1974) found that intelligence may continue to increase even after age 70. As the results of longitudinal investigations make clear, intellectual decline with aging is by no means inevitable, varying with the task and the individual. But as Baltes and Schaie (1974) have observed, there is evidence that intelligence drops significantly during the months or years just prior to death.

Intellectual Decline with Age: A Debatable Issue

It is not a simple matter to decide whether the research evidence warrants any firm conclusions regarding the alleged decline in intelligence during old age. As two recent papers, one by Horn and Donaldson (1976) and the other by Baltes and Schaie (1976), amply demonstrate, even authorities—depending perhaps on their particular theoretical biases—disagree on the matter. Horn and Donaldson (1976) maintain that decrements in at least some of the important abilities constituting intelligence are likely to occur if one lives long enough. Based on their own data, Baltes and Schaie (1976) do not reject this conclusion in toto. But they maintain that the data on wide individual differences in intelligence, together with its multidimensionality, modifiability, and the interaction between age and cohort, lead one to the conclusion that intelligence is a very plastic variable. Consequently, they feel that psychologists should give more attention to the matter of changing intelligence in a changing world. Efforts must be made to modify behavior, rather than being resigned to its seeming fixedness or inevitable decline in old age.

Whether intelligence test scores rise or fall during adulthood is affected by the kinds of experiences that a person has which are similar to the tasks on intelligence tests. One must also consider the appropriateness of traditional intelligence tests for older adults. Wesman (1968) argues, for example, that older adults are not necessarily less intelligent than younger ones simply because they do not do as well as the latter on tests designed primarily for younger people. Older adults may possess highly specialized knowledge and skills in areas that are not included in traditional tests of intellectual abilities.

Biological Variables

Not only have genetic differences been implicated as important in determining the level of one's intelligence, but heredity also appears to influence the changes in mental ability with age. Other biological variables known to affect a person's mental status are nutrition, medical care, and associated health-related factors. Thus, studies of people in their 70s, 80s, and 90s have found a higher correlation between health and intelligence than between age and intelligence (Birren, 1968; Palmore, 1970). Generally speaking, brighter people are healthier in old age, and they live longer. Neugarten (1976) suggests that the relationship between intellectual decline and mortality may be reflective of personality adjustment, the better adjusted being both brighter and healthier.

One health-related factor that affects only a small percentage of older people but that interferes with efficiency of intellectual functioning is chronic brain syndrome and associated brain damage (Ben-Yishay, Diller, Mandelberg, Gordon, and Gerstman, 1971; Overall and Gorham, 1972). A relatively common condition is high blood pressure (hypertension), which may be accompanied by cardiovascular disease and stroke. And a serious stroke, which is related to an insufficient flow of oxygen to the brain, can affect both intellective functioning and those motor skills that are required for speaking and walking.

The results of an investigation by Wilkie and Eisdorfer (1971) indicate that when intelligence does decline during old age, it may be caused not by aging itself but rather by high blood pressure. Over a 10 year period, these researchers observed 202 men and women who were in their 60s and 70s. The participants were divided into three groups according to their blood pressure—normal, borderline, and high—and were given a complete battery of psychological tests. The relationship between blood pressure and intellectual changes was seen by the end of the tenth year to be a complex function. Participants whose blood pressure was normal showed no significant change in intelligence, whereas those with high blood pressure showed a drop of almost ten points on the intelligence test. The third group (those with borderline blood pressure) actually increased their score on the test by an average of several points. This last finding was interpreted as support for the theory that slightly elevated blood pressure is needed to maintain good circulation in the brains of old people.

SPECIFIC MENTAL ABILITIES

General intelligence tests measure a combination of several mental abilities, and the pattern of change in performance with age depends on the specific ability being measured. For example, cross-sectional data on the WAIS subtests reveal that scaled scores on the subtests of the Verbal Scale remain fairly constant, but that scaled scores on the Performance Scale subtests decrease more significantly with age (Wechsler, 1958; see Fig. 3–1). The findings of other cross-sectional studies are similar in that vocabulary and information scores typically manifest no appreciable change, but perceptual-integrative abilities and comprehension of numerical symbols decline more rapidly.[1]

A classical longitudinal study of age changes in mental abilities was that of Owens (1953), who compared the Army Alpha scores of a group of middle-aged men with their performance on the same test 30 years earlier. It was found that the men scored higher in middle age than as youths on every subtest except arithmetic. Related investigations point to the conclusion that an older person's verbal ability stays fairly constant and may even improve as long as he or she remains in good health. Experience undoubtedly plays a role in determining which abilities decline and which do not, in that well-rehearsed verbal abilities involving vocabulary usage and verbal comprehension show little or no decrease with age (Arenberg, 1973).

As one ages it may become increasingly difficult to understand new ideas, make complex decisions, master new concepts, or solve laboratory-type problems. But whether these changes are due to a decline in mental aptitude, the interfering effects of prior learning, physical and mental inactivity, loss of motivation to perform various tasks, or some other factor is not clear. Gergen and Back (1966) maintained that, as a result of a limited time perspective, old people prefer short-range rather than long-range solutions to problems. Furthermore, the limited time perspective of the elderly may be complemented by a limited space perspective, in which the

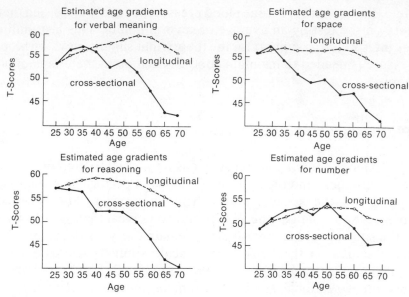

Figure 3–3. Standard scores on four subtests of the SRA Mental Abilities Test as a function of age in cross-sectional and longitudinal studies. (From Schaie and Strother, 1968, pp. 675–76. Copyright 1968 by the American Psychological Association. Reprinted by permission.)

individual considers only those factors that are physically close to him. Also related to problem solving is the shift in sex differences in some abilities with aging. The superiority of young men to young women on laboratory-type problems undergoes a change with aging, in that there is no sex difference in this skill during the 50s and women are superior to men in the 60s (Young, 1971). In fact, the data point to a greater overall age-related decline in the mental abilities of men than in those of women (Neugarten, 1976). However, just how much of this difference is due to the highly verbal nature of the tests employed is not clear. Certainly, throughout the life span males tend to score lower than females on verbal-type tasks.

The most comprehensive studies of the differential effects of aging on mental abilities have been conducted by Warner Schaie and his associates (Baltes and Schaie, 1974; Schaie and Labouvie-Vief, 1974; Schaie and Strother, 1968). The results of the investigation by Schaie and Strother (1968), which employed both cross-sectional and longitudinal methods, are illustrated in Figure 3–3. Fifty people in each five-year age interval from 20 to 70 years were tested with the SRA Mental Abilities Test, and as many as could be located were retested seven years later. The results varied with specific abilities, but some decline was noted using both cross-sectional and longitudinal approaches. Figure 3–3 indicates that the cross-sectional approach revealed the greatest decline in abilities with age, and the decline began at an earlier age than with the longitudinal approach. A later longitudinal study (Baltes and Schaie, 1974) found a decline in the mental factor of "visuo-motor flexibility" but no significant change in "cognitive flexibility" with age. However, increases in the factors of "crystallized intelligence" and "visualization" were observed in the later years. The former term is Raymond Cattell's label for intelligence that is specific to certain fields, such as school learning or tasks in which habits have become relatively fixed. In contrast to fluid intelligence (g_f), which is general to many different fields and depends primarily on heredity, crystallized intelligence (g_c) depends more on environment.

MEMORY AND LEARNING

A well-known saying is that "old age is the mother of forgetfulness," and a common complaint of the aged is loss of memory (Savitz, 1974). It might appear that memory is a single specific ability, but research has indicated that there may be several kinds of memory. *Short-term memory* (STM) is defined as the ability to retain information from a second to a few minutes at most, and *long-term memory* (LTM) as retention for at least 10 to 20 minutes. Very long-term memory was involved in Kastenbaum's (1966) study of the earliest memories of 276 centenarians. Many of these people were quite engrossed in their memories of the distant past, to a much greater degree than their memories of more recent events. Another illustrative study of very long-term memory was conducted by Smith (1963) with a sample size of one, in an attempt to recall verbal materials learned 30, 40, and 50 years before. It was found that forgetting was most rapid after 63 years of age and that more difficult material that had not been overlearned originally or practiced subsequently was most difficult to recall.

Beginning with the classic work of Hermann Ebbinghaus, most laboratory experiments on learning and memory have employed special materials such as nonsense syllables, simple perceptual configurations, or meaningful verbal materials. The majority of these investigations have been concerned with remembering over several days or at least a few hours, but recent research has focused on short-term memory. People use short-term memory in recalling unfamiliar telephone numbers or other information needed for only a short time.

Short-Term Memory

Psychologists have been aware of short-term memory for over a half-century, since many intelligence tests contain items (digit span, for example) that measure the examinee's immediate memory span for numbers or words. But systematic investigation of the characteristics of short-term memory and the factors that affect it began only about 20 years ago (e.g., Peterson and Peterson, 1959; Welford, 1958). A typical experiment consists of showing the subject a very short list of letters, words, or numbers, and immediately thereafter requiring him or her to perform some unrelated activity to prevent rehearsal of the material. Then after a few minutes the subject is asked to recall the original list. The results of experiments of this sort have revealed how quickly people can forget information when enough time is not provided for the information to be integrated or consolidated into the existing mental framework. It has also been found that short-term memory behaves very similarly to long-term memory. For example, the amount of material that is recalled decreases progressively with time since original learning.

Numerous investigations have been concerned with the relationship of short-term memory to age. In one of these (Inglis, Ankus, and Sykes, 1968), 240 people between the ages of 5 and 70 were tested on a rote learning task and a short-term auditory memory task. On both tasks, performance rose until adulthood and then fell in old age. The investigators interpreted the findings as indicating that short-term memory storage is involved in many learning tasks and may be the cause of wide variations in performance across individuals. A similar conclusion was arrived at by Welford (1958), who maintained that short-term memory is involved in several types of learning processes that are affected by aging.

Certain psychologists have concluded that the similarity between the behavior of short-term and long-term memories indicates that there is no meaningful distinction between the two phenomena. Other psychologists believe, however, that there are two qualitatively distinct processes having different physiological storage mechanisms. Bower (1966), for example, postulated a two-stage theory of memory, the first stage (short-term memory) involving a temporary memory-storage mechanism and the second stage (long-term memory) a more permanent storage mechanism. According to Bower's theory, perceived information first goes into temporary storage and must then be coded in some way by means of a mnemonic (memory-facilitating) operation in order to be placed in permanent storage.

Recognition vs. Recall Memory

Another distinction between types of memory is recognition versus recall. Recognition memory is used when one is required to select the correct response from a list or group, whereas recall memory is used when material must be learned "by heart" and the correct response given without using prompts. Schonfield (1965) was interested in determining whether the difficulty that old people appear to have in learning new material is due to a problem of absorbing (storing) the material or of recalling it once it has been stored. His experiment consisted of presenting two lists of 24 words each on a screen at intervals of 4 seconds between words. Immediately after the last word was presented, memory was tested by the recall method for one list and by the recognition method for the other list. The participants were 134 people between the ages of 20 and 75, half of whom performed the recognition test first and half the recall test first. The results, which are illustrated in Figure 3–4, revealed no age deterioration in average recognition scores but a consistent drop in recall scores. The investigator concluded that older people do show a defect of memory, but this appears to be a loss of ability to retrieve memories rather than a deficiency in the storage system itself. One can also interpret these results as demonstrating that older people acquire and store information less well than younger people, and as a consequence have an incomplete knowledge of it. This incomplete knowledge is sufficient for them to recognize the learned material but not to recall it.

Interference and Arousal

Loss of memory in old age has traditionally been attributed to a decline in the number of brain neurons and to large accumulations of *plaque*—collections of altered dendrites and axons in the brain. Decrements in performance with age cannot, however, be explained entirely in terms of structural changes in the nervous system. Moti-

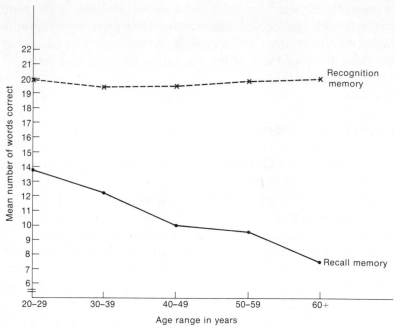

Figure 3–4.   Mean scores on recognition and recall tests as a function of age. (Adapted from Schonfield, 1965.)

vation and other psychological factors play important roles in both learning and memory. For example, an older person is less likely than a younger one to attempt to learn something that is meaningless or seemingly useless to him—the kinds of tasks that psychologists frequently devise for their research. As the following two investigations demonstrate, interference, which causes attention to shift, and arousal are also significant variables in learning and memory.

Data obtained by Kirchner (1958) indicate that the older person's problem with remembering is due not so much to simple recall failure but rather to the difficulty of retaining information in the presence of interference or shifting attention. Older people seem to take longer to consolidate new information, and they are more susceptible to the interfering effects of other stimuli. Kirchner's experimental task consisted of a row of twelve lights that went on and off at random; each light had a switch just below it. The older subjects did as well as the younger ones when the task was to press the switch below the light that had just gone off, but they did progressively worse than the younger ones when required to press the switch below the next-to-the-last light to go off, the switch below the next-to-the-next-to-the-last light to go off, and so on. The poorer performance of the older subjects was interpreted as a difficulty in retaining information in the face of interference or shifts in attention rather than as a failure of recall.

Explanations of an age-related decrement in learning and memory must also take into account the fact that older people often fail to respond when a rapid response is called for. However, as noted previously, older people tend to be generally slower than younger age groups, both in learning and in performing. When elderly people are given more time in which to respond, their performance improves significantly. Another finding is that older people show heightened, prolonged arousal of the autonomic nervous system during learning. Presumably the heightened arousal causes them to commit more errors of omission when the learning situation is rapidly paced. Consequently, if autonomic arousal during learning could be controlled by an autonomic-blocking drug such as propranolol, perhaps elderly people would learn more quickly.

Arguing in this manner, Eisdorfer, Nowlin, and Wilkie (1970) paid 28 men volunteers in the age range 60–78 years to have a drug (or placebo) administered to them and subsequently to learn a list of eight high-association words by the method of serial anticipation. Thirteen of the men (the experimental group) were chosen at random to receive the drug propranolol hydrochloride; the remaining 15 men (the control group) received a saline solution. Heart rate, plasma free fatty acid, and the galvanic skin response were monitored to measure autonomic activity during the learning task. As indicated by these physiological measures, propranolol was at least partially effective in reducing arousal. Furthermore, the men who received the drug performed significantly better on the learning task than the controls.

Effects of Drugs and Other Chemicals

It is possible that certain drugs or chemicals can improve the efficiency of learning and memory, and many drugs have seemed at first to have this effect. The change, unfortunately, is usually short-lived or is produced by improvements in motivation and general health or is attributable to a placebo effect. A few years ago interest was shown in ribaminol, a compound based on the RNA (ribonucleic acid) molecule. This drug, which appeared to speed up protein synthesis in the brain, was tested on hospitalized senile patients and college students. Initial results indicated that the drug had some effect on short-term memory, but the results were not confirmed by further tests.

One physiological theory of age decrement in memory holds that hardening of the arteries starves brain cells of oxygen-bearing blood, causing the cells to stop receiving and processing information. For example, Jacobs, Winter, Alvis, and Small (1969) found that daily breathing of 100 per cent oxygen at high atmospheric pressures ("hyperoxygenation") prevented a loss of memory in the old people whom they studied. The benefits of hyperoxygenation reportedly lasted at least two weeks. The results were interpreted as being caused by improvement in the functioning of brain tissues that were deficient in oxygen rather than a reversal of the degeneration process in neurons.

In a further investigation of hyperoxygenation and memory, Boyle ("Can oxygen fight . . .", 1972) oxygenated patients at three atmospheres for 30 minutes—a higher pressure than Jacobs et al. (1969) employed, but for a shorter period of time. As a result of these investigations and several others, many researchers became quite enthusiastic about the procedure, and especially its apparent ability to improve memory of recent events. Attempts to replicate these findings, however, have not been uniformly successful, and the earlier investigations have been severely criticized. It has been suggested, for example, that the care and attention which older people receive while they are being treated by hyperoxygenation may be sufficient to stimulate their brains and motivate them to remember better (the Hawthorne effect again). In any event, hyperoxygenation is not a procedure that will cure memory disorders or empty all institutions for the elderly.

EDUCATION FOR THE ELDERLY

Any evaluation of the results of studies relating mental abilities to age should take into account the fact that elderly people as a group are less energetic, weaker, and slower in their responses than younger people. Perhaps the most characteristic thing about being older is being slower. As we have seen, however, the intellects of older people are not generally impaired, and they are quite capable of new learning.

Learning and Characteristics of the Elderly

Returning to the matter of cohort differences that affect performance on psychological tests, laboratory tasks, and behavior in general, it is significant that elderly people as a group have less formal education than younger adults. Furthermore, younger people have an advantage in that during the past generation or so, radio, television, and other media and improved transportation facilities have increased the amount of information that is available during a person's formative years.

As indicated throughout this book, there are wide individual differences among older people in motivation, experience, and test performance. The reader must realize that our discussion of many topics deals with the "generalized" older person, and a specific elderly individual may be quite different from the hypothetical average. People who maintain an interest in their surroundings and those who are required to keep using their problem-solving capabilities decline less rapidly with age. Education is especially important, since highly educated individuals tend to show greater resistance to intellectual decline. The restricted time perspective to which Gergen and Back (1966) refer also seems less evident in older people who have more education. Nevertheless, as these investigators also noted, even those older people who have more education prefer short-range solutions over long-range solutions to problems.

It is frequently alleged that older people are rigid or "set in their ways" and have difficulty learning new things, not because of reduced learning capacity but because old knowledge and habits get in the way of new learning. Although there is some evidence in support of such "interference effects" in laboratory-type tasks (Kirchner, 1958), educational psychologists now emphasize the modifiability of behavior at any stage of life. It is realized that continued learning and problem-solving in later life can sustain and even improve intellectual abilities, attitudes, and interests—all of which interact to influence performance. Even with people of limited abilities, special techniques, coupled with enthusiastic, patient instruction, can sometimes work wonders.

Among the instructional techniques that are recommended when teaching the elderly are:[2]

(1) Provide ample time for students to master the lesson or task.
(2) Repeat the material to be learned several times if necessary.

(3) Employ a generous amount of positive reinforcement, providing for success experiences as needed.
(4) Set short-term goals that students are capable of attaining within a reasonable period of time.
(5) Since older people are more easily fatigued than younger students, use shorter practice periods than with the latter group.
(6) When demonstrating a physical skill, verbalize what you are doing and have the learners do so also.
(7) Be aware of and make provisions for those students having visual or auditory defects (e.g., sufficient illumination, books with large print, tape recordings, louder than normal speech).

Formal Education Programs

Directed specifically toward helping those elderly retirees who must live on a subsistence income to become more self-sufficient is the job training provided by such organizations as the Senior Skills Center at Santa Rosa, California. Enrollees at the Center can choose training in office skills, home maintenance, small appliance and electronics repair, or offset printing. There are also classes in home health care, horticulture and gardening, arts and crafts, and English as a second language (Brown, 1977).

The stimulation provided by an educational atmosphere is an enriching experience for many elderly people, and thereby important to their physical and mental health. Recognition of this fact has been demonstrated by programs such as Fordham University's College at Sixty and the Third Age College in Toulouse, France. For several years now, New York City residents who are 65 or older have been enrolled "tuition-free" in any undergraduate course at CUNY in which space is available. As one Columbia University dean stated, "Older people are good people to teach. We find them very highly motivated, very thoughtful people and usually highly intelligent. Their life experience is rich."

Community colleges, such as Los Angeles City College and New York City Community College, both with several hundred students over 60, have been especially forward-looking in addressing themselves to the needs of senior citizens. The Institute for Retired Professionals of The New School for Social Research has also

Report 3-1

FAYETTEVILLE, N.C. (AP)—An 80-year-old grandmother is attending Methodist College, where her son is president and one of her 12 grandchildren is a student.

Alice Pearce, who dropped out of Indiana University 59 years ago, is taking three classes. Her attendance this semester was a last-minute decision.

Her son, Dr. Richard W. Pearce, is president of the college. Her grandson, Ed, is a sophomore on the 700-student campus.

Ed first encountered his grandmother on campus when she walked into his history class with an armload of books.

"All I could think to say was 'What on earth are you doing here?'" he said. She replied, "Well, you can't sit around doing nothing or you'll go crazy."

Mrs. Pearce plans to enroll fulltime next semester in order to earn a bachelor of arts degree in English, hopefully within three years.

She said she has noticed only a few changes from the 1917–18 school year at Indiana. "I really can't see that much change because the core requirements are very similar," she said. "One difference I do note is that now when we discuss ancient history in Western civilization, I remember the events firsthand."

In 1920, Mrs. Pearce married and dropped out of Indiana University.

"It was just as well," she said, "because I was completely lost on that campus of 1,500 students." The university now has an enrollment of 31,000.

"Another difference," Mrs. Pearce said, "is that there seems to be so much more to learn now. But the freshman class of 1976 is just as wonderful as the freshman class of 1917."

Dr. Pearce, asked what he thinks about his mother attending the college, said it's great but laughed and added, "I want her grade reports sent to me."

developed a program of course work for retired persons. Every term, these institutions and many others throughout the nation register people of 70, 80, 90, and even 100 years old for courses dealing with such complex topics as "Illusions of Peace in the Middle East." It is anticipated that in the future more and more elderly people will be signing up for college courses, and that a semester of art history or English literature will become an educational and recreational experience for increasing numbers of them. Older students are taking courses not only in traditional academic subjects but also in practical topics such as living on a fixed income, coping with illness, and adjusting emotionally to old age. Among the other course offerings aimed specifically at older people are "Sex Over 65," "The Psychology of Dying," and "Film Time: Oldies But Goodies."

Student comments about specific courses and their college experiences are enlightening. One older student at Mercyhurst College in Erie, Pennsylvania, stated that she hoped a course on fixed income would teach her to live within her budget ("I know it's late, but I'm still going to try"). A second student gave a more political reason for attending the class: "We have to find out if our Social Security payments are too low for a decent life and whether we should fight for more" ("Learning for the Aged," 1972). Concerning the interrelationships of older and younger students, an elderly man felt that he had finally been accepted by his youthful fellow students when they asked him if he was interested in marijuana. Another was delighted at being asked out by three young coeds, but disappointed that "nothing came of it."

Educational Statistics and Organizations

It would be misleading to present an overly optimistic picture of education for the aged. Whereas 6 per cent of people over 65 have graduated from college, 15 per cent are functionally illiterate (Butler, 1975). The fact remains that the vast majority of adult students in American educational institutions are young, and only about 400,000 older Americans are enrolled in courses. More specifically, the results of one recent survey (Quirk, 1976) gave the following percentages of adults in various age brackets who state that they are enrolled in an educational institution or taking courses: 34 per cent of those 18 to 24 years old, 15 per cent of those 25 to 39, 5 per cent of those 40 to 54, 5 per cent of those 55 to 64, and only 2 per cent of those over 65. Thus, education for the elderly is still a relatively modest enterprise. Furthermore, although the majority of elderly people are alert and intellectually capable, they often discover on returning to school after a long absence that they must spend time relearning how to learn or redeveloping the needed study skills and routines. It is sometimes difficult to pick up the books again and break through the nonscholarly habits of a lifetime.

There are several professional organizations that provide educational information and services to retired persons. The Institute for Retired Professionals of The New School for Social Research paved the way in the area of educational opportunities and activities for the elderly. The largest organization in this category is The Institutes of Lifetime Learning, a combined effort of the National Retired Teachers Association and the American Association of Retired Persons. As the members of these organizations well recognize, not only should opportunities be provided for retired persons to take course work and training but also their services as teachers of the young should be utilized to a greater extent.[3] Much of our culture, which is not communicated very well by most courses in history and the social sciences, could probably be taught more effectively by knowledgeable elderly people. More generally, many qualified older persons could serve as professional aides, tutors, and advisors to the young (Odell, 1976).

Figure 3–5. An important but frequently overlooked role of the elderly is teaching and guiding the young. (Joel Gordon.)

SUMMARY

The popular view of old age as a time of declining mental abilities is certainly not true of all old people, and in any case it requires considerable qualification. Although the period of peak productivity among scholars, scientists, and artists is typically reached before later life, many famous people have continued their creative endeavors into their seventh, eighth, and even ninth decade of life.

Testing older adults poses particular problems of test administration and interpretation that can affect the validity of the test results. The old age norms on the WAIS and other intelligence tests are not truly representative of the American population. The findings of developmental studies of general intelligence depend significantly upon the research methodology employed. In general, the results of cross-sectional studies reveal a decline in overall mental ability after the late 20s or early 30s. However, cross-sectional studies do not adequately control for cohort differences. In any case, the findings of longitudinal studies indicate little or no decline in general mental ability after early adulthood. The entire question of age-related changes in mental abilities is still very much open and will require the application of a combination of methodological approaches to answer satisfactorily.

Among the specific mental abilities that have been found to decline with age are the ability to understand new ideas and short-term memory. The ability to recall learned material from mental storage appears to be affected more than the ability to recognize learned material. Evidence also indicates that older people take longer to respond and to consolidate new information, are more susceptible to interference or distraction, and show heightened and prolonged autonomic arousal during learning.

Some of the biological variables that are known to affect mental ability are heredity, nutrition, and health. Various chemicals and treatments (ribaminol, hyperoxygenation, etc.) have been alleged to improve memory in the aged, but the findings of research with these chemicals have been criticized because of inadequate controls and other methodological shortcomings.

Education and training programs for the elderly are receiving increased attention, and many educational institutions have designed specific courses of study and training for this age group. To be sure, the elderly constitute a relatively small percentage of the American student population, but the success of educational programs for them indicates that many old people can and want to continue learning. This is especially true when the particular assets and limitations of older learners are taken into account in the instructional process. A number of organizations provide educational information and services to the elderly, who can perform not only in the role of students but also as teachers.

suggested readings

Botwinick, J. *Cognitive processes in maturity and old age.* New York: Springer, 1967.

Boyarsky, R. E., and Eisdorfer, C. Forgetting in older persons. *Journal of Gerontology,* 1972, *17,* 254–258.

Costa, F., and Kastenbaum, R. Some aspects of memories and ambitions in centenarians. *Journal of Genetic Psychology,* 1967, *110,* 3–16.

Dennis, W. Creative productivity between the ages of twenty and eighty years. *Journal of Gerontology,* 1966, *21,* 1–8.

Mead, M. Grandparents as educators. *The Saturday Evening Post,* 1977, *249*(2), 54–59.

notes

[1]An exception is the task of detecting a simple figure in a complex one, a skill that improves with age.

[2]Adapted from "Implications for Teaching," the third in the filmstrip series *Perspectives on Aging* (Concept Media, 1500 Adams Ave., Costa Mesa, CA 92626).

[3]A step in the direction of providing more education and training for the elderly would be passage of a federal bill such as the Lifetime Learning Act (S.2497), which was proposed by Vice President Mondale when he was a senator. This bill, an amendment to Title I of the Higher Education Act of 1965, would establish an Office of Lifetime Learning within the Office of Education.

Chapter **4**

Personality Development and Sexual Behavior

Personality is the unique organization of traits and patterns of behavior that typify an individual and make him psychologically different from other people. As with all human characteristics and behavior, personality is a product of the continuous interaction between heredity and environment. Consequently, the personality does not stop developing when physical growth ceases. From beginning to end, human personality is the result of coping with changes in the environment. Just as infancy, childhood, adolescence, and early and middle adulthood pose certain developmental tasks that must be mastered, so the period of later maturity brings its own challenges and crises.

DEVELOPMENTAL TASKS AND CRISES

Problems of adjustment during later life are caused not so much by the fact that one is old or retired but rather by the stress of *transition* to old age and retirement. In addition to adapting to decreased strength and to disease, older people must adjust to changes in sexual behavior, greater dependence on others, and possibly to the deaths of family and friends. Among some of the more stressful experiences that could affect one's outlook and expectations at this time are altered physical appearance, serious illness, retirement, and the death of a spouse. The physical changes are especially difficult to cope with, since the appearance and feelings of one's body affect the self-concept. There is a tendency for older and younger people alike to minimize their physical and mental shortcomings or disabilities, but this is a normal ego-protective reaction. Most people do not like to think of themselves as old, because such thoughts produce feelings of discomfort and anxiety. Whether we like it or not, we do age, and aging affects our personalities. Also, our personalities can affect the rate at which we age.

Some people are overwhelmed by the changes produced in their bodies by aging, and they literally "grieve" for the physical and psychological losses that they have suffered. Others are able to transcend or overcome these physical changes and find satisfaction in spite of declining strength, appearance, and health.

Coping with Old Age

In order to compensate for a changing body and sociovocational roles, older people adopt new diets, develop new occupational skills, and find new ways of using their increased leisure time. Considerable readjustment to changing social values and mores is required, and many people experience a loss of status and self-satisfaction. To the extent that it can be measured, reported overall satisfaction and happiness with one's life appear to decline gradually after the late 20s. Morgan (1937) and Landis (1942), in two separate surveys of elderly people, found that approximately 50 per cent of the respondents reported that the years of young adulthood seemed happiest in retrospect (Table 4-1). The stage of life that is perceived as having been the "happiest," however, varies considerably from

Table 4-1. PERIOD OF LIFE THAT SEEMED HAPPIEST IN RETROSPECT TO TWO SAMPLES OF ELDERLY PEOPLE

	Percentage of Respondents	
Happiest Period	SAMPLE 1*	SAMPLE 2**
Childhood (5 to 15 years)	15	11
Youth (15 to 25 years)	19	19
Young adulthood (25 to 45 years)	49	51
Middle age (45 to 60 years)	12	6
Later life (60 years and over)	5	5
Undecided	0	8

*After Morgan (1937). Respondents were 370 New York residents between the ages of 70 and 90.
**After Landis (1942). Respondents were 450 Iowa residents between the ages of 65 and 98.

individual to individual, and the common assumption that old people "live in the past" is an inaccurate generalization (Cameron, 1972).

Integrity vs. Despair

In contrast to Sigmund Freud, who considered sexual factors to be of primary significance in personality development, modern psychoanalysts and psychologists place greater emphasis on learning and culture as determinants of personality. Illustrative of the importance given to social factors in personality development in more recent psychoanalytic writings is Erik Erikson's descriptive taxonomy of the crises (conflicts) and goals in eight stages of life. According to Erikson (1963), the psychosocial development of a person can be described in terms of eight progressive stages. During each stage a particular crisis or conflict comes into prominence and must be resolved if psychological development is to proceed normally. Thus, as indicated in Table 4–2, the crisis of trust vs. mistrust in infancy must be resolved by acquiring a basic sense of trust. And the major crisis of early childhood—autonomy vs. shame and doubt—is resolved by attaining a sense of individuality.

Middle age is the time of life when most people take an inventory of their lives and, spurred on by anxiety stemming from the imminence of death, come to the conclusion that if they are going to make a radical change in life style it should be now. This is the point at which a person's time perspective begins to shorten, because he realizes that his personal future is limited. Erikson refers to the major crisis of middle age as "generativity vs. self-absorption," and the goal of middle age as the development of an interest in future generations.

The major crisis of old age is "integrity vs. despair," and the primary goal is to become an integrated and self-accepting person. The way in which the individual handles this crisis depends not only on personality characteristics that have been developing for years but also on one's physical health, economic situation, and the meaningfulness of his social roles. The despairing person views life with a feeling of regret that greater use has not been made of his or her assets, that potential has not been realized, or goals that were set originally have not been attained. Such a person is keenly aware of old age as the "no-solution problem" about which gerontologists have written. Feeling that time is now too short to begin anew or to try different approaches to achieving a happy, integrated per-

Table 4-2. ERIKSON'S STAGES OF PSYCHOSOCIAL
DEVELOPMENT*

Stage	Crisis (Conflict)	Goal (Resolution)	Description
Infancy	Trust vs. mistrust	Acquire a basic sense of trust	Consistency, continuity, and sameness of experience lead to trust. Inadequate, inconsistent, or negative care may arouse mistrust.
Early childhood	Autonomy vs. doubt	Attain a sense of autonomy	Opportunities to try out skills at own pace and in own way lead to autonomy. Overprotection or lack of support may lead to doubt about ability to control self or environment.
Play age	Initiative vs. guilt	Develop a sense of initiative	Freedom to engage in activities and parents' patient answering of questions lead to initiative. Restrictions of activities and treating questions as a nuisance lead to guilt.
School age	Industry vs. inferiority	Become industrious and competent	Being permitted to make and do things and being praised for accomplishments lead to industry. Limitations on activities and criticism of what is done lead to inferiority.
Adolescence	Identity vs. role confusion	Achieve a personal identity	Recognition of continuity and sameness in one's personality, even when in different situations and when reacted to by different individuals, leads to identity. Inability to establish stability (particularly regarding sex roles and occupational choice) leads to role confusion.
Young adulthood	Intimacy vs. isolation	Become intimate with someone	Fusing of identity with another leads to intimacy. Competitive and combative relations with others may lead to isolation.
Middle age	Generativity vs. self-absorption	Develop an interest in future generations	Establishing and guiding next generation produces sense of generativity. Concern primarily with self leads to self-absorption.
Old age	Integrity vs. despair	Become an integrated and self-accepting person	Acceptance of one's life leads to a sense of integrity. Feeling that it is too late to make up for missed opportunities leads to despair.

*After Erikson (1963), as adapted by Biehler (1976), p. 150.

sonality, this person finds it difficult to accept the inevitability of death. Eventually the person's life is ended not with a bang but with a whimper of despair, demonstrating through this attitude the errors in his or her philosophy of life.

Portrait of a Well-Adjusted Older Person

The person who has developed an effective set of solutions to the major tasks and crises during the preceding stages of life can look forward to old age as the capstone of a life well lived. Such a person has no overwhelming regrets and would be willing to go through it all again, but thinks less about the past and more about using the remaining time wisely. Having come to terms with personal goals and achievements, the integrated person is self-accepting and lives hopefully rather than helplessly. Old age is welcomed as an opportunity to take stock of and clarify a lifetime of experiences. Finding his or her responses to them satisfactory, this person is in a much better position to cope with the inevitable changes and losses.

A New Identity and a New Definition

It is often said that the satisfied elderly person has a clear sense of his or her own identity, but one must be cautious about viewing old age as merely a "summing up" period of no further development. Self-development and the search for identity—Erikson's major goals of adolescence—continue throughout life. As Butler (1971, p. 51) phrases it: "When identity is established or maintained, I find it an ominous sign rather than a favorable one. A continuing life-long identity crisis seems to be a sign of good health." An individual's new identity in old age comes from finding new uses for what has been learned during the previous years and developing new ways of coming to terms with reality. That reality consists of personal strengths and weaknesses as well as a changing world that is not always to one's liking.

Furthermore, Rappoport (1976) takes exception to the practice of referring to old age as a "natural" stage or phase in human development. As he points out, almost all of the characteristics that our society has come to associate with old age are now seen to be the results of physical or emotional stress. The process of aging is the joint result of the deterioration of the body and the attitudes of society, and the symptoms of oldness are the consequences of internal and external stress. But as observed in victims of famine, war, and other human tragedies, severe stress can age a person at any period of life. The effects of social expectations and cultural practices on aging are seen in the fact that a physically and mentally healthy environment—one in which the person has an adequate diet, sufficient exercise, good medical care, meaningful activities to perform, and social acceptance—can go far in delaying or coping with the "natural" process of aging. The gradual erosion of the effects of traditional stereotypes about aging and senility is becoming more and more evident in our society, because people are living not only longer but also more energetically and happily.

PERSONALITY TRAITS AND THE ELDERLY

A variety of procedures and instruments—observations, ratings, personality inventories, and projective techniques—have been used in the study of personality. Unfortunately, unlike the WAIS and a few other cognitive tests, little interest has been shown in standardizing personality assessment instruments for older groups. It is much easier and less expensive to develop tests and determine norms on large captive audiences of young students. Consequently, we must frequently generalize about personality in old age from small samples of people who may or may not be representative of the groups of older peole in whom we are interested.

One reason for the paucity of data about personality in old age is that the field of later life counseling has not been very popular, and funds for research on the psychology of old age have not been plentiful. However, as witnessed by the expansion of centers for the study of aging at the University of Chicago, the University of Maryland, Duke University, and other locations, increasing information regarding the affective characteristics of older people is becoming available. Several professional journals and popular magazines have recently published issues devoted to or featuring the elderly. For example, the November, 1976, issue of *The Personnel and Guidance Journal* dealt almost entirely with adult development and gerontology.

Continuity of Personality

The unique pattern of traits and behaviors that characterize a person as a special human being manifests a great deal of continuity throughout life. One such manifestation is seen in the fact that people who have been most active and interested during their earlier years tend to remain so in the later years of life. Neugarten (1971) found that if we know about an individual's personality in middle age and how events in earlier life have been dealt with, we can make broad predictions about how the person will react to old age. Likewise, from her talks with older people, Curtin (1972) concluded that those who were maladjusted had usually been uninvolved, passive, or unhappy when they were younger. They did not become radically different personalities on the day that they turned 65; rather, they had much the same temperament as when they were 30, 40, or 50. She also observed that aging does not solve but rather compounds one's personal problems. People who have difficulty coping with life at age 30 will most likely have similar problems at 65.

The observations of Neugarten and Curtin are supported by the findings of an extensive investigation by Reichard, Livson, and Peterson (1962, p. 171):

With the exception of the mature group, many of whom had reported difficulties in personal adjustment when younger, these personality types were relatively stable throughout life. Poor adjustment to aging among the angry men and the self-haters seemed to stem from lifelong personality problems. Similarly, the histories of the armored and rocking chair groups suggest that their personalities changed little throughout their lives.

Thus, whether or not an individual adapts successfully to later life is determined to a large extent by how well-adjusted he or she already is upon reaching old age. Nevertheless, human personality is not static; it is modified to some extent by the very process of aging and the success of one's reactions to the problems that it presents.

Self-Acceptance and the Self-Concept

As people develop and become aware of the differences between their own aims and those of others, they usually come to behave in more realistic and socially appropriate ways. The reactions of other people to an individual's presence and behavior not only cause the person to modify that behavior but also affect his view of himself. These reflected evaluations from people who are significant to the individual, in addition to successes and failures in dealing with other aspects of the environment, result in the acquisition of a self-concept. The self-concept includes the overall value that one places on oneself as a personality, as well as evaluations of one's own body and behavior. Biological factors such as physical appearance, health, innate abilities, and certain aspects of temperament are important in determining the frequency and kinds of social experiences that a person has and the degree of social acceptance that is attained. But these biological factors interact in complex ways, and they always operate in a social context. Therefore, the social evaluations placed on the physical and behavioral characteristics of an individual who possesses a particular biological makeup—and consequently his evaluation of himself—depend on the specific sociocultural group to which the person belongs.

The results of a number of investigations have provided insight into self-concept and self-acceptance in old age. Referring to Kuhlen's (1956) finding that the degree of personal happiness in most people reaches a maximum in the middle adult years, Bloom (1961) speculated that self-acceptance would follow a similar trend. The hypothesis was confirmed in an investigation of male surgery patients, ranging in age from 20 to 70 years, at a New York Veterans Administration hospital. Degree of self-acceptance increased steadily from age 20 until the middle to late 50s and then declined. Caution must be exercised in generalizing from Bloom's study, because different results are obtained with different samples. Kaplan and Pokorny (1969), for example, suggest that it is not age per se that affects the self-concept but rather the events occurring in later life. Thus, these investigators found that a more negative self-concept was associated with having a lower standard of living than one had hoped for, and living alone or with relatives rather than as a couple.

Destiny Control and Self-Confidence

If a person feels weak and powerless—characteristics considered by many people to be earmarks of old age—he will tend to resign himself to a poor socioeconomic and physical condition. In fact, it has been shown that both the physical and the mental health of older people are influenced by the feeling of having some control over the important events in their lives. People who feel they have outlived their options and must submit blindly to whatever fate holds in store become easily depressed or angry. That this sense of "destiny control'' changes with age was documented in a longitudinal study by Gutmann (1964). It was found that the typical 40 year old man, seeing himself as energetic and the environment as within his control, was willing to take risks and accept challenges. In contrast, the typical 60 year old tended to see the world as more dangerous and complicated and no longer as likely to be within his control.

Obviously, both the active, assertive orientation of the average middle-aged man and the more passive, conforming orientation of the older man represent seemingly realistic attempts to accommodate to the environment. As the investigations of Gutmann (1964) and others make clear, during the period between 40 and 60 an individual's perception of himself in relation to the environment gradually shifts from seeing himself as generally strong and capable of overcoming risks to viewing the world as a complicated, dangerous place in which conformity and accommodation are the best policy. Thus, at age 60 or 70, a formerly bold, outer-directed orientation may have changed from involvement with people and things to an increasing preoccupation with the inner life (Ullmann, 1976).

Interiority and Loneliness

During the fifth and sixth decades an individual's life space and interests tend to shrink, producing a tendency toward ''increased interiority,'' or introspection (Neugarten, 1968). This turning inward of the personality, signaling a decreased interest in external things, may have either a positive or a negative effect. A normal coping response to the stress accompanying aging, introspection and the resulting re-evaluation of the self can lead either to feelings of greater self-reliance or to a sense of inadequacy and depression.

Loneliness and the feeling of not being wanted or needed can occur when one's family and friends begin to die or move away, and children and grandchildren—who typically live within only an hour's distance—visit dutifully but briefly. Coupled with the fear of loneliness and the loss of health in later life is a concern about being a burden on one's children. Most older people have a strong desire for dignity and independence, but this comes into conflict with feelings of loneliness and rejection. Actually, there should be and frequently is an interchange of social and emotional support between elderly parents and their adult offspring, as well as between grandparents and grandchildren. And even when social contact between generations is minimal, loneliness and the sense of loss—of youth, physical attractiveness, and opportunities—are not so severe in people who have been successful and feel self-fulfilled.

Rigidity and Flexibility

Older people sometimes appear to be easily annoyed with the ways of the younger generation. One study of men 70 years and older found that older men are frequently annoyed by the behavior of teenagers, as well as by heavy drinking and intolerance in others. Their own inability to accomplish things, their feelings of helplessness and aloneness, were found to be other common sources of annoyance to older people (Barrett, 1972). Younger adults might attribute such annoyances to inflexibility, and the personality dimension of flexibility vs. rigidity has indeed received a great deal of attention from gerontology researchers. Older people are sometimes said to be less adaptable, less willing or able to change their ways of doing things. They are allegedly more reluctant to try new approaches to social problems, preferring to stick to the tried and true old ways.

Robert Butler (1974) refers to the so-called inflexibility of older people as a myth. To Butler, the structure of a person's character seems to be fairly well established by the time of old age. But unless one is severely hampered by brain damage, low mentality, or lack of education, people can and do change right up to the time of death. Perhaps the word "cautious" is a better description of the elderly than "inflexible" or "rigid." A lifetime of experience has taught them not to expect miracles and to become more suspicious about what can be accomplished by physicians, politicians, social planners, and other members of the power elite.

It is probably correct that older people are less likely to risk being wrong for the sake of being right or fast, but if the directions and structure of a task are clear the older person will usually do his best (Barrett, 1972). It is also true that old people are sometimes reluctant to make complex decisions in ambiguous situations, but the flexibility with which they respond depends upon lifelong habits and behaviors. Some people, young and old, can absorb new information more readily than others, and consequently they manifest less resistance to change. Those with higher intelligence and greater self-confidence are more willing to accept reasonable risks rather than rigidly adhering to what has worked in the past. In contrast, the senile patient is more likely to be rigid and unadaptable in the face of environmental change.

Time Perspective

The "Empathic Model," which was discussed in Chapter 2, can also be applied to help understand the personalities and emotional reactions of older people. The frustrations, social roles, mourning, joblessness, sexual behavior, and political attitudes of the elderly have all been simulated by placing younger people in a variety of contrived situations typical of those encountered by the elderly. This procedure should serve to give the participants greater insight into the situations faced by elderly people and why they react as they do (Kastenbaum, 1971; Kastenbaum and Durkee, 1964).

Other approaches to comparing the perceptions and attitudes of young and old have also been devised. In studying the time perspective of the elderly, the participant is asked to select from the past, present, and future the three years which are the most important to him or her. The results of this procedure reveal that, regardless of the person's actual age, the time span between the earliest and latest "most important years" is approximately 30 years. As one grows older, however, this 30-year range shifts backward, signaling an increase in the number of past-oriented people with aging. It has been found that most people are past-oriented by age 40, and that by age 50 nearly all are (Kastenbaum, 1971).

INDIVIDUAL DIFFERENCES IN PERSONALITY

Personality is concerned as much with differences among people as with their biological, psychological, and social similarities. The uniqueness of personality is especially pronounced in old age. Elderly people manifest an even wider range of individual differences in personality than young adults. For example, in a study of 70 year olds (Neugarten, Havighurst, and Tobin, 1968), the researchers were more impressed with the variations than the similarities among personalities. Thus, aging is not a leveler of differences among individuals, and people continue to change as they grow older.

Sex Differences

Although a certain amount of deviant behavior in the old is tolerated by society, behavior that seems normal in younger people

Figure 4–1. Changing sex roles in old age. (H. Armstrong Roberts.)

is often viewed as abnormal in an elderly person. The modification of personality as a function of age also interacts with gender. In some ways the sexes become more alike with age: both men and women are somewhat more eccentric and preoccupied with their own lives and personal needs. But after retirement the role relationships between the sexes may reverse, with women becoming more aggressive or assertive and men more submissive and nurturant. This pattern is the opposite of typical sex-role behavior during the early adult years (Neugarten and Gutmann, 1958). Gutmann (1964, 1967) argued that the relatively greater aggressiveness manifested by elderly women is not developed suddenly in old age; it results from the release of aggressive urges that have been there all the time. During the years when they are rearing their children, women typically suppress their aggression, as is required by the nurturant, mothering role. But when the children have grown up and moved away, the woman feels free to express her aggressiveness with impunity.

Types of Adjustment

Considering personality characteristics as a whole, various patterns of coping and defensive behavior are observable in old age. In a study of aging and personality, Reichard, Livson, and Petersen (1962) obtained 115 ratings of the personal characteristics of 40 well-adjusted and 30 poorly adjusted older men. Evidence was obtained for five personality types or clusters—mature (constructive), rocking chair (dependent), armored (defensive), angry (hostile), and self-hating. These five types represent fairly specific methods of coping with the problems of old age. The *mature* men, who were relatively free of neurotic conflicts, could accept themselves and grow old with few regrets. Also fairly well adjusted were the *rocking chair* type, who viewed old age in terms of freedom from responsibility and as an opportunity to indulge their passive needs. The *armored* type, which was somewhere in the middle in terms of adjustment, defended against anxiety by keeping busy. The first of the poorly adjusted types, the *angry* men, expressed bitterness and blamed other people for their failures. Also maladjusted were the *self-haters,* who, depressed rather than angry, blamed themselves for their disappointments and misfortunes. These people, hating themselves and old people in general, viewed later life as a useless, uninteresting period.

Personality, Activity, and Happiness

Further evidence for the variety of individual differences in personality and adjustment in old age was obtained in a study by Neugarten, Havighurst, and Tobin (1968). The study was concerned with the relationships of long-standing personality characteristics and social activity to happiness in a sample of people aged 70 to 79. The four major personality traits, derived from an assessment of each person on 45 dimensions, were: integrated, armored-defended, passive-dependent, and unintegrated. The life satisfaction of each person was rated according to the extent to which the person appeared to take pleasure in daily activities, regarded life as meaningful, accepted responsibility for his past life, felt successful in having achieved his major goals, had a positive self-image, and was generally optimistic about life. A measure of role-activity consisted of observers' ratings of the extent and intensity of the social roles of parent, spouse, grandparent, kin-group member, and church

Figure 4-2. Bernice L. Neugarten, a prominent researcher in the field of personality development in middle and late life.

member. A wide range of activity patterns and life styles, depending on the type of personality possessed by the individual, was noted.

Among the *integrated* personalities, who functioned well and had complex inner lives as well as intact intellective abilities and egos, were three patterns of role activity. The *reorganizers* engaged in a wide variety of activities, the *focused* types devoted most of their energies to a few important roles, and the *disengaged* people possessed high satisfaction with their lives but had voluntarily moved away from role commitments.

The men and women who were labeled as *armored-defended* personalities were striving, achievement-oriented poeple who pushed themselves. The two patterns of aging that were observed in this group were the *holding-on* people, who believed that they would be all right as long as they kept busy, and the *constricted* individuals, who reduced their involvement with other people and experiences and defended themselves against aging by concentrating on losses and deficits.

Two patterns of aging were also found in the *passive-dependent group—succor-seeking* people with strong dependency needs who expressed medium satisfaction with life as long as they had at least one or two people to lean on, and *apathetic* people, who were passive individuals with few activities or social interactions and little interest in their surroundings.

The fourth main type of personality observed in this investigation was the disorganized or *unintegrated,* who had serious psychological problems.

The overall results of this investigation support the common observation that whether a person becomes active or disengaged during later life depends upon personality characteristics as much as anything else. Well-integrated personalities tend to adjust well to old age, whereas people who are dissatisfied or unhappy with themselves and their previous experiences have adjustment difficulties. Level of activity is also important to life satisfaction: those who keep a young, active, problem-solving attitude are better adjusted. Furthermore, activity and motivation are interacting variables, motivation for living and orientation toward others being affected by whether or not a person is engaged in useful activities.

SOCIAL STATUS AND ROLES

Personality and behavior are the products of both inborn propensities and experience, and the environmental factors—especially economic and social ones—that affect experience continue to influence personality in old age. It is no accident that well-adjusted older people are more likely to be in the higher socioeconomic bracket and to possess good health, a good education, and close family and friendship ties. People who are reasonably well off both physically and financially tend to cope better with the debilities and changing roles of old age than those who are in poor health and have little money or education. Near-poverty, or even merely reduced financial circumstances, affects a person's self-esteem and can lead to feelings of depression. If an individual's past attempts at coping with environmental and personal stress have not been successful, the economic and social problems of old age may be sufficient to cause him to become one of Reichard's (1962) angry or self-hating personalities.

Blau (1973) has decried the tendency of some writers to deny or gloss over the fact that many older people in our society live useless, meaningless lives. He points out that, given the option, people usually prefer to live their lives with the meaning and purpose that comes from having personally and socially significant roles to play. Eleanor Maxwell notes that in certain primitive societies, old people keep young in spirit by "starring" in specific social rituals. For example, an elderly Eskimo woman in the Canadian Arctic may give her all in a tug-of-war contest, while elderly Apaches bless babies, and senior members of the Bakongo tribe of Africa train youngsters for adult life. Although the setting up of rituals in which older people can play leading roles would not be easy in our society, Maxwell suggests that if the elderly are encouraged to participate in a variety of social groups they will find leading roles to play ("Aging . . .", 1976).

Changes in social roles are inevitable as one grows older, but for older and younger people alike rewarding interactions with others are important for positive mental health. Among the types of social roles that give meaning to one's life in old age are those stemming from relationships with family and friends, in addition to vocational/avocational, political, and religious activities.

Family and Friendship Roles

During the age range of 45 to 65, which may be referred to as the postparental phase of the family cycle, the children are grown and often have married and moved away from home. Some women experience a profound depression (the "empty nest" syndrome) at this time, whereas others find more time to devote to and achieve satisfaction from their marriage. In some instances, old age may be a time of role-reversal with respect to one's children—the aged parent now playing the role of the nurtured one and the son or daughter the role of caretaker.

For the majority of elderly, the new social role of grandparent emerges, with its negative connotations of growing old or, alternatively, the pleasure and excitement of a new personality and the continuity of generations. The tendency in our society to segregate the generations has reduced the degree of social interaction and emotional interchange among different age groups, an important function of the extended family of yesteryear. This is unfortunate, because children need their grandparents just as much as their grandparents need them. Maintaining too much psychological distance between the young and the old because of some irrational fear of old age is a disservice to both groups. Curtin (1972, p. 36) expresses the fear of many adults that

mine will be the last generation to know old people as friends, to have a sense of what growing old means, to respect and understand man's mortality and his courage in the face of death. Mine may be the last generation to have a sense of living history, of stories passed from generation to generation, of identity established by family history. It is such an unholy waste.

Grandparents, who can add a sense of identity and stability to the family and society as a whole, vary extensively in the perceptions of the grandparent role. On the one hand are those who see themselves as mere babysitters for someone else's children and on the other hand are those who relate to their grandchildren with joy and love. The latter group, and grandfathers in particular, often find that the role of grandparent is even more emotionally gratifying than that of parent. To these people the grandparent role involves its traditional elements of teacher and advisor to the young. The age of the grandparents also has some relationship to the way in which they react to their grandchildren. Younger grandparents are more likely to be somewhat fun-seeking in their role, as if they were the child's playmate. Older grandparents tend to be more distant and formal in their behavior toward their grandchildren, becoming close only on special occasions (Christmas, birthdays, etc.) (Neugarten and Weinstein, 1964).

For those older people with a living spouse, the marital relationship is still of primary importance, and many couples experience great pleasure in just being alone with each other. Marriage, in old age as at other times of life, does not guarantee happiness, but older people who remarry after the death of a spouse tend to be happier than those who remain unattached. This is perhaps truer for men than for women, since many single women make better adjustments in later life than married women.

Although they are usually less important than close relatives, friends and neighbors complement the family relationships of the elderly. Older people tend to have friends who are similar to themselves in status, values, and interests. Friends usually live close by, but easily available transportation can extend the friendship circle beyond the immediate neighborhood. Elderly friends meet in their homes, at church, in community centers, and many other places within traveling distance.

Religious Roles

Just as in younger age groups, there are religious fanatics, atheists, and moderates among the aged. Older people as a whole are not doctrinaire, but they do attach more importance to religion than younger people. The elderly reportedly pray, read scriptures, and are involved in religious organizations to a greater degree than other age groups. It is not clear, however, whether this is caused by age per se or cohort (generational) differences. The older people of today grew up during a time when families stressed religious observances more strongly than they do now, and that early training has persisted throughout life. Whatever their religious beliefs may be, most elderly people consider their personal moral values to be quite high.

SEXUAL BEHAVIOR

The reproductive capacities of both sexes diminish during later life, but there are authenticated instances of men in their tenth decade siring children and women as old as 57 giving birth. Even more startling is the feat reportedly accomplished by Rustam Mamedor (142 years) and his wife (116 years), who live in the Caucasus region of the U.S.S.R.: Their youngest son was born when Rustam was 107 and his wife 84 years old (Gots, 1977)! These, of course, are very rare events, and normally women lose the capacity to reproduce sometime between the ages of 45 and 50. This is the period of life when ova are no longer regularly released from the ovaries, and the corpus luteum fails to form.

It was formerly believed that aging of the reproductive system was caused directly by a decrease in the sex hormones, testosterone and estrogens, produced by the male and female gonads. Subsequent research, however, implicated insufficient pituitary or hypothalamic sex hormones in reproductive aging. Now it is believed that reproductive aging is caused by defects in the production of chemicals (neurotransmitters) that assist in the release of sex hormones by the hypothalamus. Since the blueprint for production of these neurotransmitters presumably exists at the cellular level, we are back once more to an individual-cell explanation of aging—this time aging in the reproductive system (Arehart-Treichel, 1976).

Incidence of Sexual Activity

A definition of old age as "the time when a man flirts with girls but can't remember why," the description of sexual life in the elderly as "tri-weekly, try weekly, try weakly," and one-liners such as "What do you do with a dirty old man? Introduce him to a dirty old woman'' suggest the mixture of humor and disapproval with which society views sexual activity in the aged (Puner, 1974). Whatever the attitudes of society may be, reference to the "sexless older years" is a social stereotype contradicted by research findings.

The results of research, from Kinsey to Masters and Johnson, point to only a slight decline in sexual interest with age. The findings of a 20-year study conducted by Eric Pfeiffer and his associates at Duke University (Pfeiffer, Verwoerdt, and Wang, 1968, 1969) showed that two thirds of the men who were followed up were sexually active after age 65, and one fifth were active during their 80s. In fact, more than 20 per cent of the elderly men in this investigation reported an *increase* in sexual activity as they grew older. This phenomenon, which was more common among unmarried men, is dramatic evidence that sexual desire does not automatically terminate at age 65. One 73 year old man in another investigation expressed his attitude toward sex as follows (Vinick, 1977, p. 12):

> I don't know if I'm oversexed, but I'm a lover. I like to pet, kiss, hug. I have more fun out of loving somebody I love than the ultimate end. You know, some people—and this is the failure of sex, too—some people want sex and forget the rest of it—the hugging and the petting and I think that's wrong. People say, "What will happen to me when I get older?" Well, I'm still alive! There's no thrill like that today. People try dope, they try smoking, they try drinking. This is the one thing that's good for the body.

Whereas being a widower or otherwise unmarried reportedly did not decrease the sexual activity of the older men who were interviewed by Pfeiffer et al. (1968, 1969), 90 per cent of the elderly women stated that they stopped having intercourse when their husbands died or became impotent or ill. One third of the women septuagenarians in this study reported an interest in sex, but only 20 per cent were actually having intercourse. Rather than a difference in desire, the lower rates of sexual activity in women were attributable to a lack of available men, a reluctance to engage in sex out of wedlock, concern over personal appearance, and a belief that sex should cease after the menopause.

The investigations of Pfeiffer et al. (1969) and others (e.g., Newman and Nichols, 1960) also indicate that older people in lower socioeconomic groups are more sexually active than those in upper socioeconomic groups. However, the findings of studies of ethnic-group differences in sexual behavior are conflicting. Whatever the gender or socioeconomic or ethnic group of a person, research findings underscore the truism ''Use it or you'll lose it.'' Continued sexual activity is most important for the ability to function sexually in old age. As documented by the fact that people who are more sexually active in their youth are also more active in old age, human sexual behavior is a lifelong habit pattern (Newman and Nichols, 1960).

Psychophysiology of Sex

Whereas the Kinsey reports (e.g., Kinsey, Pomeroy, and Martin, 1948) and the Duke University studies have helped to dispel the myth that sexual activity in old age is abnormal, precise information regarding the physiology of sex in the elderly was lacking prior to the investigations of Masters and Johnson (1970). In these studies, elderly people were interviewed and their performance during the sexual act was monitored. One finding concerning sexuality in older women, of which laymen and health professionals alike should be aware, is that menopause does not eliminate sexual need or functioning, especially when hormones are used, and sometimes increases it. The postmenopausal aging process does reduce the size of the cervix and uterus, and it causes the vaginal walls to become thinner. Also the degree of vasocongestion of the breasts, clitoris, and vagina is affected, and vaginal lubrication is reduced. Sex hormone replacement therapy can help to control these effects, as well as the attendant vaginal discomfort that older women sometimes experience.

With respect to the physiological effects of old age on male sexuality, Masters and Johnson observed that there is a decline in the male sex hormone testosterone, the testes shrink, fewer and less fertile sperm are produced, and the volume of ejaculate decreases. Older men take longer to achieve an erection, which may be incomplete but sufficient for vaginal penetration. There are fewer genital spasms, the force of the ejaculate is reduced, and after ejaculation it takes longer to have another erection. For both sexes, all phases of sexual excitement (excitement, plateau, orgasmic, resolution) are prolonged. However, none of these changes need detract from sexual appreciation, and the enjoyment of intercourse is usually retained by both men and women.

Masters and Johnson have joined many gerontologists in proposing a program of sex education for the aged. Such a program should include information on techniques of intercourse specific to the needs of the elderly, in addition to ways of coping with fears of sexual inadequacy, the reputed dangers of sex to health, and the disapproving attitudes of relatives and the larger society (see Butler and Lewis, 1976).

Widowhood, Divorce, and Unmarriage

It has been mentioned previously that the percentage of women (57 per cent) substantially exceeds the percentage of men in the over-65 age bracket. Over 52 per cent of these women are widows, which is 3 to 4 times the number of elderly widowers (Table 4–3). An interpretation of these statistics is that a widow's sexual activity is greatly limited by her ability to find an available partner, a situation that is less likely to occur with a widower. Also, it is more socially acceptable for an older man to marry a younger woman than for an older woman to marry a younger man.

Divorce among late middle-aged and older people who have been married as long as 30 to 50 years is not as rare as it once was. Occasionally, a couple will remain incompatible but unseparated for decades, finally "making the break" after their children have grown up and moved out. Being able to stay happily married into old age is attributable to a combination of affection, habit, and a respect for the individuality of one's spouse. As is true of social adjustment in

Table 4–3. MARITAL STATUS OF PERSONS
AGE 65 AND OVER*

	Per Cent		
Group	1965	1970	1975
MEN			
Single	6.6	7.8	4.6
Married	71.3	71.8	78.9
Widowed	19.5	18.1	14.4
Divorced	2.6	2.4	2.2
WOMEN			
Single	7.7	7.7	6.3
Married	36.0	35.5	38.7
Widowed	54.4	54.6	52.4
Divorced	1.9	2.3	2.6

*After Schultz (1976), p. 38.

general, marital happiness in old age is positively related to marital happiness during the earlier years. Happy couples tend to remain happy, while unhappy couples tend to become even unhappier as they age. In any event, the divorce rate among older people is significantly lower than average, and most people who get divorced remarry sooner or later. These remarriages, which are usually successful, are more common in older men, although the number of 65-and-over women who marry—most for the second time—has doubled during the past decade. Among the reasons that older women give for marrying are companionship, a desire to take care of someone, and intimacy (Vinick, 1977).

There is a road sign at Sun City, near Tampa, Florida, that says: DRIVE SLOWLY. GRANDPARENTS PLAYING. For a number of reasons, one being the reduction in Social Security benefits when retired people marry,[1] the elderly sometimes engage in what geriatric counselors refer to as "unmarriages of convenience." These are companionable, sexual relationships not formalized by a license or ceremony. Certain older people, especially men, also confess to enjoying the secretive, "swinging-singles" experience of living together without benefit of clergy.

Indications of the growing public acceptance of sexuality among the aged are also found in the mixed reactions to the recommendations of several gerontologists and laymen that private rooms be provided in nursing homes so that patients can have sex with each other and/or visitors. It has been suggested that the chronic anxieties of nursing-home patients could be alleviated by sexual intercourse. Although most nursing homes do not publicly sanction conjugal visits and other sexual arrangements among patients, they have begun to show a greater tolerance toward sexual contacts.

Sexual Problems and Deviations

Among the cruelest misconceptions of older people are the notions that elderly men are either impotent or "dirty old men" and that postmenopausal women who express an interest in sex are "frustrated old women." Even old people confess that when they were young they also believed that old men who were interested in sex were lechers. To counter this tendency on the part of society—

Figure 4–3. Kissing on a park bench and holding hands in a shopping center. (Richard Ferro.)

young, middle-aged, and old—to label any older person who is interested in sex as a D.O.M. ("dirty old man") or an F.O.W. ("frustrated old woman"), one elderly Californian responded with a bumper sticker on his sports car that declared: "I'm not a dirty old man; I'm a sexy senior citizen" (Lobsenz, 1974).

It should be clear by now that sex in old age is not a perversion, although some old people do have sexual problems or express deviant sexual behavior. One sexual problem in old age of which many elderly men are afraid is impotence. When impotence does occur in the aged, it is usually caused not by a permanent loss of the sex drive but by overeating, excessive drinking, medications, fatigue, boredom with the sexual partner, emotional stress, or mental disorder. As documented by Kinsey (1948) and other researchers, masturbation is fairly common in both youth and old age. On the other hand, there is no evidence that sexual disorders (exhibitionism, child molesting, etc.) are anything but rare exceptions among the elderly. There are no adequate statistics concerning the incidence of homosexuality in old age, but its occurrence in the elderly produces the same intense social reaction as it does at any age. Indicative of our politically active times are recent efforts in both the United States and the United Kingdom to obtain public acceptance and support of older, especially "widowed," homosexuals.

Sex Therapy

Masters and Johnson (1970) have pioneered in the rapid but effective treatment of cases of sexual inadequacy. Many of their patients, and those of their associates, have been elderly people who had stopped having sexual relations because of misunderstandings concerning the natural physiological changes with age. Report 4–1 describes one such case. It required approximately one week of therapy to restore the sexual functioning of this couple. They regained their confidence, and the sexual dysfunction disappeared when they came to realize that the symptoms they were experiencing—increased time to attain an erection and reduced seminal fluid in the man, decreased vaginal lubrication in the woman—were not abnormal in any way and that they could continue to enjoy sexual relations in spite of these age-related changes.

Report 4–1*   *Sexual Inadequacy*

Mr. and Mrs. A were 66 and 62 years of age when referred to the Foundation for sexual inadequacy. They had been married 39 years. . . .

They had maintained reasonably effective sexual interchange during their marriage. Mr. A had no difficulty with erection, reasonable ejaculatory control, and. . . had been fully committed to the marriage. Mrs. A, occasionally orgasmic during intercourse and regularly orgasmic during her occasional masturbatory experiences, had continued regularity of coital exposure with her husband until five years prior to referral for therapy. . . .

At age 61, . . . Mr. A noted for the first time slowed erective attainment. Regardless of his level of sexual interest or the depth of his wife's commitment to the specific sexual experience, it took him progressively longer to attain full erection. With each sexual exposure his concern for the delay in erective security increased until finally . . . he failed for the first time to achieve an erection quality sufficient for vaginal penetration.

When coital opportunity [*next*] developed . . . erection was attained, but again it was quite slow in development. The next two opportunities were only partially successful from an erective point of view, and thereafter he was secondarily impotent.

After several months they consulted their physician and were assured that this loss of erective power comes to all men as they age and that there was nothing to be done. Loath to accept the verdict, they tried on several occasions to force an erection with no success. Mr. A was seriously depressed for several months but recovered without apparent incident. . .

The marital unit . . . accepted their "fate." The impotence was acknowledged to be a natural result of the aging process. This resigned attitude lasted approximately four years.

Although initially the marital unit and their physician had fallen into the sociocultural trap of accepting the concept of sexual inadequacy as an aging phenomenon, the more Mr. and Mrs. A considered their dysfunction the less willing they were to accept the blanket concept that lack of erective security was purely the result of the aging process. They reasoned that they were in good health, had no basic concerns as a marital unit, and took good care of themselves physically. . . . Each partner underwent a thorough medical checkup and sought several authoritative opinions (none of them encouraging), refusing to accept the concept of the irreversibility of their sexual distress. Finally, approximately five years after the onset of a full degree of secondary impotence, they were referred for treatment.

SUMMARY

People vary extensively in their ability to cope with the tasks and problems of later life. Declining health and physical appearance, the loss of employment and loved ones, and erosion of the sense of significance and meaningfulness of one's life can lead to depression and despair. On the other hand, more integrated persons who possess effective mechanisms for coping with the stresses of aging and who are willing to search for a new identity in old age can find new challenges and sources of gratification at this period of life.

Personality, the unique organization of abilities, traits, and behavior patterns that characterize an individual, manifests a sub-

---

*From Masters and Johnson (1970), pp. 326–328.

stantial degree of consistency across the life span. People who are well-adjusted in youth and middle-adulthood tend to remain so in later life; people who are maladjusted in earlier life continue to have adjustment difficulties in old age. Although the self-concept may decline in later life, rather than being a function of age per se the decline is related to lowered socioeconomic security and other events occurring in old age.

In general, older men are somewhat more passive and less willing to take chances than younger men. Also of interest is the sex-role reversal observed in many elderly couples, with the husband becoming more nurturant and affiliative and the wife more aggressive and self-centered. An age-related trend toward interiority or introspection, which is perhaps a normal coping response to the stresses of aging, has also been observed. Increased rigidity or inflexibility is said to characterize the aged, but it is more accurate to describe this age group as "realistically cautious" rather than "rigid."

Reichard and his colleagues found evidence for five types of reaction patterns in older men: mature, rocking chair, armored, angry, and self-hating. Similarly, in a study of the relationships of personality and social activity to happiness in older people, Neugarten and her colleagues described four major personality types—integrated, armored-defended, passive-dependent, and unintegrated, with two or three subcategories under each of the first three types. A well-integrated personality and an active, problem-solving attitude were found by Neugarten to be associated with better adjustment. Having socially meaningful roles to play is also related to adjustment in old age. Among the various types of roles that provide satisfaction for the elderly are those involving family, friends, religion, and sex.

Many people continue to be sexually active well into their 70s and 80s, thus disproving the myth of the "sexless older years." Studies by Pfeiffer and his colleagues have provided data relating to the incidence of sexual activity in old age, and the pioneering investigations of Masters and Johnson have done much to clarify the psychophysiology of sex in old age. For a variety of reasons, elderly men are more sexually active than elderly women, but sex is becoming more socially acceptable for both of these groups. Sexual problems and deviations occur among the elderly, as with all age groups. Owing to the efforts of Masters and Johnson, Butler and Lewis, and other therapists, progress has been made in the treatment of sexual disorders in old age.

suggested readings

Huyck, M. H. Sex and the older woman. *In* Troll, L. E., Israel, J., and Israel, K. (eds.), *Looking ahead*. Englewood Cliffs, N.J.: Prentice-Hall, 1977.

Masters, W. H., and Johnson, V. E. Sex after sixty-five. *The Saturday Evening Post,* 1977, *249*(2), 48–52.

Peterson, J. A., and Payne, B. *Love in the later years*. New York: Association Press, 1975.

Saul, S. *Aging: An album of people growing old*. New York: Wiley, 1974.

Sheehy, G. *Passages: The predictable crises of adult life*. New York: E. P. Dutton, 1976.

Turnstall, J. *Old and alone*. London: Routledge & Kegan Paul, 1966.

notes

[1]Under the provisions of recent Congressional legislation, newlyweds who are 60 or over lose none of their Social Security benefits.

Chapter 5

Mental Disorders

Almost as serious as the many chronic physical disorders that occur in old age are the mental disturbances that affect the elderly. Documenting the pronounced decline in mental health after young adulthood are the results of Meltzer and Ludwig's (1971) cross-sectional study of 143 industrial workers in five age groups: 20–29, 30–39, 40–49, 50–59, and 60–69. As illustrated in Figure 5–1, the "mental health index" is highest in the 30–39 age group, shows a marked decline in the 40–49 age group, and then levels off until the 60–69 age range. The more negative mental health index in the older groups is a reflection of the lower self-confidence, greater sense of failure, weaker resistance to stress, and lesser orientation toward reality than in younger adults.

Figure 5–1. Changes in mental health with age. (Adapted from Meltzer and Ludwig, 1971.)

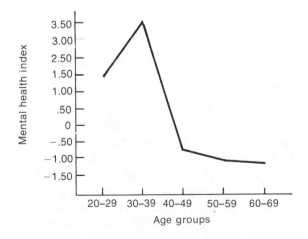

THE MEANING AND FREQUENCY OF MENTAL DISORDERS

To a great extent, normality and abnormality of behavior are statistical concepts that vary in meaning with culture and time. Sociocultural factors, such as the attitudes and tolerance of others, are important in determining what is normal or acceptable behavior. These factors are emphasized when we define as *abnormal* a person who has poor interpersonal relations, displays socially inappropriate behavior, and has no acceptable goals. According to this definition, if one repeatedly violates social norms, he or she is considered to be abnormal. But whether abnormal behavior is punished, ignored, treated, or even praised depends upon society's interpretation of the value of the behavior and the extent to which other people are willing to accept it.

Most psychologists are not content with a purely cultural or statistical definition of abnormality. They look further into the personal experiences of the individual, studying the satisfactions that are attained, the tension, anxiety, depression, and sense of isolation that are felt, and the amount of effort that is expended, in determining whether one is mentally disordered. Thought processes, perceptions, and attitudes are also important. Society may be willing to tolerate strange behavior or even be unaware of a person's problems, and he may continue to function fairly effectively over a lifetime while experiencing invisible anxieties and insecurities.

Statistics

Only about 10 per cent of the people in the United States and other industrialized Western nations are considered to be sufficiently disturbed in thought processes, emotion, or behavior to be classified as mentally disordered. This includes both the milder mental disorders (psychoneuroses, psychosomatic disorders, personality disturbances), the incidence of which remains fairly constant into old age; and the more serious psychotic conditions, which appear to be somewhat more common after age 50. People with severe mental disorders, both the young and the old, occupy about 50 per cent of the hospital beds in the United States.

It is frequently maintained that the "stress of modern living" is responsible for the high incidence of mental illness in the twentieth century. Since diagnostic criteria and other factors affecting mental hospital admissions statistics vary with time and place, the question of whether a person is more likely to become mentally ill in contemporary society than in the past is difficult to answer. However, the available data indicate that the twentieth century has not produced a greater proportion of most mental disorders (see Goldhamer and Marshall, 1953). It is true that the *number* of first admissions to mental hospitals has gone up, but the *rate* has not changed, and the average length of residence in the hospital has decreased.

Although the rate of serious psychotic disorders in men under 40 and women under 50 has not changed appreciably since 1885 (Goldhamer and Marshall, 1953), there has been an increase in mental disorders associated with old age. This increase is interpreted as being due in large measure to the fact that people are living longer and therefore are more likely to develop symptoms of mental disorder produced by changes in the brain that accompany old age. The particular physical and interpersonal stresses to which older people are subjected should also not be overlooked as causative factors. Whatever the reasons may be, approximately 3 million elderly Americans are considered to be moderately to severely mentally disordered. Over 500,000 of these individuals are sufficiently disturbed to have been placed in nursing homes or mental hospitals. In the latter facilities, people who are 65 and over account for approximately one fourth of all first admissions (Coleman, 1976).

Age differences also interact with sex, socioeconomic status, and geography in affecting the type and severity of mental disorder. For example, the rate of severe mental disorders is higher in urban areas—where the majority of older people live—than in the suburbs and rural areas. Severe mental disorders are also more common in lower socioeconomic groups, which again include a larger number of elderly people.

Classification of Mental Disorders

Normal personality changes that occur with age are exaggerated in people who become mentally disordered, with disturbances running the gamut from transient situational problems to severe psychotic reactions. The trend today is to avoid assigning nonuseful diagnostic labels to mental disorders whenever possible and to attempt to identify causes of disordered behavior. Consequently,

Table 5–1. MAJOR CATEGORIES IN THE APA
CLASSIFICATION OF MENTAL DISORDERS*

I. Mental retardation
II. Organic brain syndromes
   A. Psychoses associated with organic brain syndromes
   B. Nonpsychotic organic brain syndromes
III. Psychoses not attributed to physical conditions listed previously
IV. Neuroses
V. Personality disorders and certain other nonpsychotic disorders
VI. Psychophysiologic disorders
VII. Special symptoms
VIII. Transient situational disturbances
IX. Behavior disorders of childhood and adolescence
X. Conditions without manifest psychiatric disorder and nonspecific conditions

*American Psychiatric Association (1968).

the labels that are employed in this chapter should in no way be viewed as either completely descriptive or explanatory of the behavior of the disordered person in question. The American Psychiatric Association's classification system for mental disorders has been criticized extensively, but it is still used for purposes of record-keeping and for want of more generally accepted diagnostic categories (Table 5–1). This system, which is described in detail in the *Diagnostic and Statistical Manual of Mental Disorders* (American Psychiatric Association, 1968), separates mental disorders into psychotic vs. nonpsychotic and organic vs. nonorganic (functional) categories.[1]

FUNCTIONAL DISORDERS

When an animal or human being is under long-term stress, the level of norepinephrine in the blood becomes so low that it is difficult to behave in an organized, adaptive manner in frustrating or conflict situations. At the human level this is what is meant by anxiety, which results in efforts on the part of the individual to defend himself against further emotional stress or personality disintegration.

Reactions to Stress

Many types of psychological reactions to stress, some adaptive and others maladaptive, occur in old age. Among the maladaptive responses are denial, anger, withdrawal, and dependency. In denial, the person simply denies the seriousness of a problem or that it even exists. Another reaction to stress is becoming angry at someone or something, perhaps someone other than the direct cause of frustration. This is the case in displaced aggression, in which the victim has nothing to do with the frustrating circumstance but is merely a convenient scapegoat.

Elderly people may also withdraw in potentially threatening situations, feeling that being close to others is too risky and that self-isolation or retreat into fantasy is the best way to cope. Another type of reaction to frustration and conflict is to become helpless or overly dependent on other people. Old people with strong dependency needs may also exaggerate and exploit a physical illness and associated depression. Dependency is often fostered by well-meaning people who respond to older people as if they were unable to do anything for themselves and were in constant need of assistance.

All of these *defense mechanisms,* which are discussed in detail by Verwoerdt (1969), are maladaptive because they are not permanent solutions to problems and usually create further difficulties for the individual. Used to excess, many defense mechanisms can lead to more serious mental disturbances, e.g., paranoia as a result of excessive anger or senile regression as a result of withdrawal.

Depression and Suicide

Perhaps the most common of all reactions to stress in old age is depression. The loss of friends and family, isolation from other people, physical problems, financial insecurity, and being placed in an institution are some of the most common precipitating factors in depression during old age.

A person who is suffering from depression feels miserable and unworthy and has difficulty sleeping. Suicide attempts are an ever-present danger, showing a sharp increase during the 40–50 age period. Although the rate of attempted suicide is reportedly lower among older people, they are apparently more successful when they make the attempt. The high incidence of suicide among the elderly is reflected by statistics kept during the nineteenth and twentieth centuries. Current estimates are that 50 per cent of all suicides in the United States are committed by people over 45, and 25 per cent are committed by those who are over 65. The magnitude of the latter figure becomes more meaningful when one recalls that people over 65 constitute 10 per cent of the total population of the U.S. Even so, the 25 per cent figure is probably an underestimate, since many of the fatal "accidents" of old age are probably disguised suicides.

Suicide rate varies not only with age but also with sex and ethnic group. As illustrated in Figure 5–2, after age 25 the suicide rate increases with age for white males only. Regardless of ethnic group, however, the suicide rate is significantly higher for men than for women. For women in general and for nonwhite males the rate is fairly stable until age 75, at which time it declines. Among the factors responsible for the high rate of suicide among the elderly, and older white males in particular, are the feelings of uselessness and depression resulting from social isolation, inactivity, and loss of status. Some other causes are fear, fatigue, and a desire not to be a burden on others. One tends to think of "suicide pacts" as a

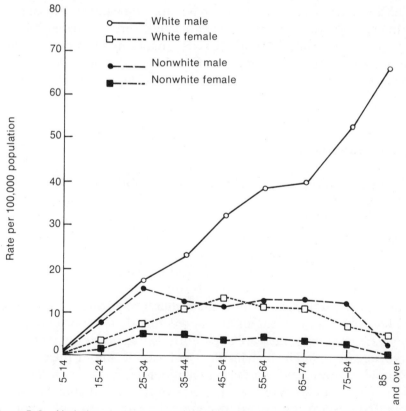

Figure 5–2. Variations in American suicide rates as a function of age and ethnic group. (Adapted from National Center for Health Statistics, 1967, p. 5.)

phenomenon of romantic youth, but double suicide also occurs among elderly couples. The newspapers occasionally carry stories of elderly couples who, because they have been the repeated victims of crime, feel unwanted, or are seriously ill, become wearied of life and decide to end it all.

Psychophysiological Reactions

Unresolved hostility and anxiety, by keeping the autonomic nervous system in an almost constant state of activation, can produce structural changes in bodily organs. According to psychodynamic theory, chronic hostility and anxiety in highly dependent personalities result in psychophysiologic autonomic and visceral (psychosomatic) disorders. The "target organ" affected by prolonged emotional disturbance may be a part of the musculoskeletal, respiratory, cardiovascular, hemic and lymphatic, gastrointestinal, genitourinary, endocrine, sensory, or nervous system. Although peptic ulcers and other gastrointestinal reactions are the most publicized types of psychophysiologic disorders, the course and severity of migraine headaches, skin conditions, backache, and bronchial asthma are also related to the patient's emotional condition. In fact, it is generally recognized that almost all physical illnesses and success or failure in treating them are affected by the personality of the patient.

Psychoneuroses and Personality Disorders

The psychodynamic explanation of neurotic behavior is that it serves to control the anxiety caused by the threatened breakthrough of unacceptable unconscious impulses. While recognizing the fact that neurotic symptoms serve to control anxiety, behavior-oriented psychologists emphasize the learned nature and anxiety-reducing function of such symptoms rather than their unconscious origin. Among the neurotic symptoms are conversion hysteria (sensory or motor disturbances of psychogenic origin), dissociative conditions (psychological amnesia, fugue, multiple personality), obsessions, compulsions, phobias, hypochondriasis, and depression. Especially common are anxiety reactions, in which anxiety is not reduced or controlled by another neurotic symptom.

Maladaptive personality patterns or character disorders may

also persist into old age. There are elderly alcoholics, drug-dependents, and sexual deviates, although these conditions are more common in younger age groups. Antisocial (psychopathic) personalities—individuals with little conscience or regard for the feelings of others—are also less common in old age. Most psychopaths appear to "burn out" by their 40s, their antisocial behavior decreasing markedly by then. Even though they can benefit from treatment and sometimes require hospitalization, individuals classified as having a psychophysiologic reaction, a psychoneurosis, or a personality pattern disturbance do not manifest the severe distortion of reality and extensive personality disorganization seen in psychotics.

Psychoses

It is expected that by 1980 over one million old people in the U.S. will be hospitalized for psychoses (Ford, 1970; Jarvik, Yen and Goldstein, 1974). *Psychoses* are disorders in which the ability to recognize reality is severely distorted and may include deficits in perception, language, and memory and alterations in mood. Approximately one half of the patients in this category are diagnosed as *functional* psychotics, which means that there is no known organic impairment or damage to the brain (Kisker, 1972).

SCHIZOPHRENIA

The two major types of functional psychoses are the schizophrenias and the affective psychoses. The schizophrenias, which compose the largest category of functional psychoses, involve severe disturbances in thinking and sometimes perception. There is a withdrawal from contact with reality and a consequent loss of empathy with others; disturbances in concept formation occur, together with regressive, bizarre behavior. Hallucinations (false perceptions) and delusions (false beliefs) may also be present. Delusions of grandeur and persecution are most common in paranoid conditions, which may or may not be accompanied by a schizophrenic process. On rare occasions, two or more people share the same delusional system, as in folie à deux ("madness of two") or, even more rarely, folie à trois ("madness of three") (see Report 5-1).

Report 5-1 Folie à Trois*

Three elderly spinster sisters, aged 72, 68, and 65, were admitted to a psychiatric hospital after a neighbor called the police to report that one of them threatened to "slit the throat" of a 10 year old neighbor boy. These sisters had worked, eaten, and lived together for more than 40 years.

When interviewed in the hospital, each of the sisters told an almost identical story about how this 10 year old boy had been "sent by them" to remove the NO TRESPASSING sign from their front lawn. Close questioning revealed that many years earlier these women had posted such a sign on their lawn because both of their neighbors "were spying" on them by coming on their lawn and looking through the front window. It was also learned that these sisters had sued one of their neighbors with regard to a boundary dispute about their property lines. They lost the suit and attempted to find another lawyer to take up their case again, but no lawyer would do so. The boy they had threatened was the grandson of their neighbor, and they described him as "rotten to the core from the day he was born."

The two younger sisters also related that they and their sister had a good deal of trouble at vacation spots, usually rooming houses near resort areas, because other people were after their money and belongings. The oldest sister vehemently denied having had such difficulties and explained that her younger sisters occasionally "told such lies," but that she would "set them right" as soon as she saw them on the ward.

When the younger sisters were again interviewed several days later, they both volunteered the information that their story about their rooming house troubles was untrue and that their neighbor had a way of influencing them to tell such stories. They then disclosed that they thought the doctor was conspiring with their neighbor against them and that he had better not ask them any more questions because he was being paid to keep the three in the hospital.

About three weeks after admission, the oldest sister had a massive cerebro-vascular accident and died within hours of the attack. The two younger sisters at first became severely depressed, but then, as often happens with separation from the dominant person in such *folies,* several weeks after the death, they began talking about going back to their home and spoke of "letting bygones be bygones."

Schizophrenics usually respond well to chlorpromazine and other phenothiazine drugs, but medications do not usually produce a permanent cure for the disorder. Some schizophrenics are in or in-and-out of mental hospitals for a large portion of their lives, growing old in institutions (see Report 5-2). Generally these chronic cases are meek, mild individuals who have adapted to institutional life and would probably be unable to cope with life outside an institution. If they are not being actively treated for the disorder, a nursing home or some other less expensive facility is preferable to a mental hospital.

*From Kleinmuntz (1974), p. 248.

*Report 5–2   Hebephrenic Schizophrenia**

Wilma F. is a 53 year old woman who was first admitted to a mental hospital 30 years ago when she became excited, tore off her clothing, and struck her mother. She talked to herself, believed other people were in the room with her, assumed bizarre poses, giggled constantly, and acted in a silly manner. She was given a diagnosis of schizophrenia, hebephrenic type, and was discharged as improved after 15 months. After leaving the hospital, the patient remained at home and helped with the housework. She had her first illegitimate child when she was 34, and a second by a different man four years later. While both babies were placed in foster homes by a charitable organization, one of the children has since been admitted to the same psychiatric hospital, although neither the mother nor the daughter knows of the presence of the other.

When the patient was 40 years old, she again became mentally disturbed with a recurrence of her silly behavior and episodes of violence. When seen at the hospital she smiled excessively and laughed inappropriately. She blamed her difficulties on "getting mixed up with the wrong man." There was some indication of delusional thinking, although hallucinations could not be elicited. The most outstanding symptom was her inappropriate laughter, giggling, and meaningless smiling. The patient's condition remained unchanged, and she was still in the hospital after a period of 12 years.

AFFECTIVE PSYCHOSES

Not uncommon in old age are affective disorders, which involve disturbances in mood—either extreme elation (mania) or depression or a periodic fluctuation between the two extremes. In addition to extremes of emotion, there is a loss of contact with reality. The major types of affective psychoses are manic-depressive psychosis and involutional melancholia. The symptom picture in the circular type of manic-depressive psychosis, which is seen in about 25 per cent of patients diagnosed as manic or depressive psychotics, consists of severe mood swings from depression to elation, remission, and then recurrence. With aging, the times of occurrence of the manic and depressive phases of the cycle become more regular and hence predictable. During the manic state the patient is overtalkative, elated, or irritable, manifesting increases in motoric activity and bizarre ideas. During the depressive phase of the cycle he or she is deeply depressed in mood and activity, becoming agitated in some instances and stuporous in others.

The *Diagnostic and Statistical Manual of Mental Disorders* (1968) differentiates between the manic and the depressed types of manic-depressive psychosis. The symptoms of the manic type, which is fairly common in those who are diagnosed as psychotic, include overtalkativeness, elation, or irritability, increased motor activity, and the rapid production of bizarre ideas. Hostile, paranoid

---

*From Kisker (1972), p. 326.

behavior of an accusatory nature may also be shown. The depressed type is characterized by feelings of deep depression, together with motor inhibition and either mental slowness or agitation (see Report 5–3).

Report 5-3   Manic-Depressive Psychosis—Depressed Type*

   Pauline B. is a 57 year old widow who graduated from high school, attended business school, and had training as a nurse. She has had three commitments to mental hospitals for her depressions. When seen at the hospital on her most recent admission, the patient presented the typical picture of depression. She appeared sad, talked in a somewhat whining voice, and showed psychomotor retardation. She had numerous self-condemnatory ideas and was preoccupied with thoughts of suicide. Her general attitude was one of hopelessness. She said that life is not worth living and that she would be better off dead. She had no interest in anything, and there was nothing left to live for. Between her depressive episodes, the patient is regarded as a happy person although subject to rather wide swings in mood.

   There is evidence indicating that manic-depressives are more rounded in body build than schizophrenics, but the average age at first admission to mental hospitals is also greater in the former diagnostic group. Since older people in general have a more rounded body shape, the interpretation of the difference in body build between the two diagnostic groups is not clear. For many years electroshock therapy (EST) was the recommended treatment for severe psychotic depression, but antidepressant drugs (amitriptyline, imipramine) have replaced EST to some extent. At one time there was no truly effective treatment for manic excitement, but in recent years good results have been obtained with lithium carbonate.

   Textbook descriptions of the so-called "change of life" disorder, involutional melancholia, list the following symptoms: extreme depression, agitation, self-deprecation, feelings of guilt and failure. This disorder, which is termed "involutional" because of its onset after age 40, is more common in women than in men. Many authorities seriously question the need for such a diagnostic category, since depressive conditions can occur at any period of life and do not show a sudden rise in frequency after age 40 (Winokur, 1973).

ORGANIC DISORDERS

   Organic brain disorders are one of the most common causes of death in old age, but many people who are diagnosed as having an

---

*From Kisker (1972), p. 348.

organic disorder live for years, manifesting gradual, insidious changes in personality. There are two major classes of mental disorders associated with organic brain disease: cerebral arteriosclerosis and senile brain disease. These irreversible conditions account for approximately one half of the cases of major mental disorders in old age.

Cerebral Arteriosclerosis

Cerebral arteriosclerosis (hardening of the arteries of the brain) usually has its onset in the mid-60s, and the victim dies of a heart attack or stroke within three to four years. In old age the walls of the arteries of the brain become thickened, and the diameter of the vessels is reduced owing to fatty deposits. These accumulations of fatty tissue and calcified material, known as *senile plaques,* clog the channels of the arteries and interfere with blood circulation. As a result the vessels are unable to carry enough nutrients, vitamins, and oxygen in the blood to the brain, and the probability of a blockage or rupture increases.

The blockage (thrombosis) or rupture (hemorrhage) of a cerebral blood vessel, referred to as a cerebrovascular accident (CVA), or stroke, can result in heart failure. Blockage of a small blood vessel is technically known as a "small stroke," and blockage of a large vessel as a "major stroke," or CVA. Cerebral arteriosclerosis affects over 3 million people in the United States, with

---

Report 5–4   Cerebral Arteriosclerosis*

Elizabeth R. was admitted to a hospital at age 73. The present attack began about 5 years before her admission, when the patient developed the idea that she was being hypnotized by her relatives. She heard voices, with members of her family cursing her and telling her that she was no good. Other voices hinted that someone wanted to kill her. The patient's husband is blind, and just before her admission to the hospital she tried to pour scalding water over him. She thought he hypnotized her and wanted to kill her. For five months, the patient refused to sit at the same table with her husband. She argued constantly with her family and with neighbors, cursing constantly anyone who came near her. She was afraid that she would be killed and thought that she must kill other people for her protection. She boiled water all day long to break the "spell" and kept the lights on at all times in different places in the house to scare away the evil spirits. She believed that when the train whistled near her home, it ordered her to do different things. She grew increasingly destructive and dangerous toward her blind husband, who attempted to quiet her by hitting her with his cane. At the hospital, the patient said' "The electric light catches me every time I walk from room to room. My husband makes money behind my back. He hypnotizes me. My grandfather sent you doctors to see me."

---

*From Kisker (1972), p. 391.

CVAs killing more than 200,000 annually (Terry and Wisniewski, 1974). A typical patient is in his early 70s and manifests the organic brain syndrome symptoms of confusion, disorientation, incoherence, restlessness, and occasionally hallucinations. Complaints of headaches, dizziness, and fatigue also occur, with some patients becoming paralyzed on one side (hemiplegia) and having seizures. Superimposed on these symptoms are the anxiety and depression resulting from the severe stress of a CVA. As with any stress situation, maladaptive personality traits that existed before the trauma are accentuated by a CVA.

Senile Brain Disease

Senile brain disease is the result of atrophy (shrinking) and related degenerative changes in the brain during old age. The shrinkage, which can reduce the brain to 15 to 30 per cent of its normal weight, occurs primarily in the frontal cortex, the temporal cortex, and the associated white matter. The disorder becomes apparent after age 65, peaks in frequency at about age 70, and then begins to decline. During the past 30 years, the incidence of this disorder in the general population has doubled. Over one third of the people who live past 80 have senile brain disease, and it is ranked number five among all killer diseases. It is estimated that 50 per cent of the people who enter nursing homes for the aged are suffering from senile brain disease, and one fourth of all people admitted to mental hospitals have this disorder. Undoubtedly owing to their longer life span, slightly more women than men develop the condition.

Among the psychological symptoms of senile brain disease—a syndrome referred to as senile dementia—are self-centeredness, difficulty assimilating new experiences, and childish emotionality. The changes in personality are gradual, beginning with simple memory failure (e.g., difficulty remembering names). As the disorder progresses, memory, confusion, and disorientation in time and place become progressively worse. For example, the patient may be unable to remember when he ate last, whether or not he took his medicine, and whether the stove was turned off. He may lose the ability to perform certain routine tasks, showing little interest in external events, untidiness, and a preoccupation with eating, eliminating, and other bodily functions. Memory, speech, and personal habits deteriorate even further as time progresses.

Most older people never become so severely disturbed as to

Report 5–5   Senile Brain Disease*

Alice A. is a 78 year old widow who was admitted to a psychiatric hospital from a home for the elderly where she had become unmanageable. She was very confused, did not recognize her relatives, and thought her son was her father. Frequently she was excited and noisy and used profane language. At the hospital she had to be led to the examining room, and while she was somewhat agitated, she tried to be cooperative. In spite of her agitation, her facial expression changed little during the interview. Once a question was put to her, she continued to talk but was seldom able to answer intelligently. She rambled on and on, frequently mentioning her "daddy." She said her daddy had been at the hospital only a short time before, that he had talked to her, and that he would return soon to take her home. From time to time she interjected a word or phrase in French. She knew her name but was otherwise completely disoriented. Her memory for both remote and recent events was defective, and rational conversation was impossible. There was a total lack of insight.

be labeled "senile," and the extent of pathological behavior in those who do is influenced by the patient's environment and premorbid personality. The importance of psychological factors is seen in the fact that postmortem examinations of the brains of senile patients reveal little or no relationship between the degree of brain damage and the magnitude of deterioration in behavior (Gal, 1959). Recognizing the variety of behavioral symptoms in senile brain disease, Coleman (1976) categorizes the symptom picture into several reaction tendencies or types: simple deterioration, paranoid reaction, presbyophrenic type, depressed and agitated types, delirious and confused types.

Although true senile brain disease is considered irreversible, many patients who manifest symptoms of senility can be treated. A special x-ray technique known as computerized tomography can help determine the degree of brain atrophy, and if little or no atrophy is present it may be that the patient is suffering from a disorder other than senile brain disease, such as thyroid deficiency, anemia, diabetic coma, or even a heart attack. Butler (1975) reports that physicians often fail to distinguish between reversible and irreversible brain disorders. He points out that malnutrition, anemia, heart failure, drugs (overdoses of tranquilizers and barbiturates in particular), alcohol, CVAs, and reactions to dehydration have all been misdiagnosed as irreversible brain disease. Severe depression, the clinical picture of which includes forgetfulness, difficulty concentrating, and helplessness, has also been mislabeled as senile brain disease.

Among the symptoms of reversible brain disorder listed by Butler (1975), of which medical diagnosticians should be aware, are:

---

*From Kisker (1972), p. 387.

a fluctuating level of awareness (from mild confusion to stupor to delirium), disorientation, misidentification of people, and impairment of intellectual functions. Hallucinations, unusual aggressiveness, and a dazed expression may also be present. Many of these same symptoms, of course, occur in irreversible senile brain disease, but they may go untreated if the physician does not recognize the presence of a treatable, reversible disorder.

Other than custodial care and medication for the control of emotions, little is done to treat patients who are accurately diagnosed as having senile brain disease. Severely senile patients simply while away the time in institutions, remaining there and receiving minimal care for the rest of their lives. Since senile patients tend to accumulate in mental hospitals, which are supposed to be treatment centers, relatives are advised to move these patients to less expensive facilities that are expressly custodial in nature.

Presenile Dementia

The clinical picture in presenile dementia is similar to that of senile brain disease, except that it occurs in a younger age group. Alzheimer's disease and Pick's disease are the major disorders in this category, but Jakob-Creutzfeldt disease and even parkinsonism and Huntington's chorea are sometimes classified as presenile dementia. All of these disorders are named after men who discovered or conducted research on the respective condition.

The degree of brain atrophy in Alzheimer's disease, a type of atrophy known as neurofibrillary degeneration, is greater than that usually found in senile dementia. The average age of onset of the disorder is 56, with deterioration progressing rapidly and death occurring in an average of four years after onset. Alzheimer's patients are usually overactive, agitated, and under emotional stress and frequently show disturbances in language and movement. Pick's disease, which is 1½ times more common in women than in men but less common than Alzheimer's disease, has an average age of onset in the late 40s. The progress of Pick's disease is slow and insidious, involving first the frontal and temporal lobes and causing difficulty with thinking, fatigability, and lowered inhibitions. As the disorder progresses the patient becomes disoriented and apathetic, and intellectual functions are affected. Both Alzheimer's and Pick's diseases are relatively rare, and both are considered to have a genetic basis. There is no specific treatment for either disorder other than routine hospital or custodial care.

COMMITMENT AND COMPETENCE

The elderly can avail themselves of a wide range of community, state, and federal treatment facilities. Unfortunately, these facilities, and community mental health clinics in particular, are not sufficiently used by old people. Among the reasons cited by Butler (1975) for this state of affairs are pessimism and lack of interest by the general practitioners and clergymen who serve as referral sources and by mental health practitioners themselves. Lack of enthusiasm for treatment of the elderly and for gerontological research is also revealed by the fact that less than 5 per cent of the budget of the National Institute of Mental Health is typically allocated to studies of mental disorders in old people. Other reasons why elderly people fail to make adequate use of treatment facilities are inexperienced or poorly educated mental health workers, lack of knowledge of resources on the part of the elderly, and a scarcity of transportation to the clinic or other mental health facility.

Voluntary and Involuntary Admission

In spite of this bleak picture, older patients who realize that they need help or are encouraged by others to obtain it frequently seek assistance at a community mental health facility or voluntarily admit themselves to a mental hospital for examination and treatment. A patient who voluntarily admits himself to a mental hospital can sign out at any time unless, in cases where the patient is considered dangerous to himself or others, the head of the hospital is granted a legal postponement of release. Involuntary admission or commitment,[2] the laws and procedures for which vary from state to state, may be obtained after a petition by the patient's family or another person who is responsible for him. Following the petition is a legal hearing at which it is determined whether the patient is harmful to himself or others, and if so a decision is then made as to where he should be admitted for treatment. The length of initial commitment varies according to the judgment of hospital officials and other authorities, but it is usually 30 to 90 days and may be extended indefinitely by subsequent legal action.

The question of protecting the civil rights of patients who are involuntarily admitted to mental hospitals has been hotly debated in recent years and has led to laws that require more attention to the patient's rights. Since these laws state that the patient must be either treated or released, mental hospitals can no longer serve as ''dumping grounds'' for elderly people who are unwanted by their families. In every case, however, an attempt must be made to balance the rights of the individual against the welfare of the larger society. While some people argue that the practice of involuntary commitment should be abolished totally, others maintain that society has a right to protect itself against potentially dangerous mental patients, both young and old. With sufficient legal safeguards of a patient's civil rights and periodic reviews of his therapeutic progress, most experts now agree that families should not feel guilty about having an older person admitted to an institution with good treatment facilities.

Competence and Testamentary Capacity

The question of *competence* to handle one's life and property arises when one or more relatives make a legal declaration that because of physical or mental infirmity resulting from old age the person is unable to take care of his property, and they formally request that the court appoint someone to handle it for him. Obviously, legal action of this sort should be considered only after other possibilities have been examined carefully. Being forced to become entirely dependent on someone else can be the last straw for an elderly person who is barely managing to hold his own.

Testamentary capacity is a less general concept than mental competence, in that the former refers only to competency to make a will. In order to possess testamentary capacity, which is also legally determined, the patient must know the nature and extent of his property, that he is making a will, and who his natural beneficiaries are (Freedman, Kaplan, and Sadock, 1972).

TREATMENT

It might seem that older people, by virtue of the fact that they have lived until old age, have a proven track record of coping with the stresses of life. But as we have seen, old age brings its own special crises—physical deterioration, retirement, widowhood—and a continuing need for helpful understanding and emotional assistance.

The prognosis with older patients who are seriously mentally ill is not always good, and the goals of treatment may be more limited than with younger patients. Decreasing the patient's suffering so that his complaints and the complaints of others about him are minimized is important. A combination of physical and psychological procedures is almost always needed in order for treatment to be effective. Among the physical treatment measures, several of which have already been mentioned, are drugs, special diets, electroshock, and brain surgery. In this section we shall focus on the psychological treatment measures—counseling for milder mental disorders and psychotherapy for more severe ones.

Whether the adjustment problem is large or small, mental health in old age is improved by maintaining a sense of interest, curiosity, and wonder. Problems and crises do occur, but the conquest of disillusionment and cynicism stemming from unresolved conflicts and frustrations begins with the recognition of one's feelings through the assistance of a warm, supportive counselor. One must learn to cope with old age and its special problems in the same manner as any skill is learned. Only by maintaining a continued focus on learning and growth in the face of seeming hopelessness can one use his or her last days valuably and serve as an example for and influence the lives of others.

Counseling

Lombana (1976) describes a variety of situations in which remedial counseling or psychotherapy is needed by the elderly. Serious mental health concerns, especially depression, may require in-depth personal counseling. People with debilitating physical problems, which are aggravated by emotional reactions, require supportive counseling—sensitive listening, reassurance, and efforts to motivate the person, elevate his spirits, and reinforce the will to recover and live. This is especially necessary when the person receives little or no emotional support from family or friends. Elderly people who reside in nursing homes or similar institutions also need counseling to help them redevelop feelings of worth and independence that will sustain them in the institution and help them to cope with life outside its walls. Avocational counseling and retraining are frequently needed to help retirees cope with feelings of resentment and apathy that accompany forced retirement.

Perhaps even more valuable to mental health than remedial counseling, at least in the long run, is preventive counseling. Some of the preventive approaches discussed by Lombana (1976) are preretirement counseling and continued health education, as well as information about and provisions for avocational activities, educational opportunities, and recreation. Nursing homes usually provide a variety of avocational and recreational activities (arts, crafts, music therapy, exercise classes, field trips) to stimulate and interest older people and emphasize the fact that they are still among the living.

Direct counseling services to the elderly should be accompanied by education of the general public about the stereotypes and myths pertaining to old age, counseling the families of the elderly as a unit during critical times for the latter, and arranging for adequate training of both professional and paraprofessional counselors. Most experts agree that training for workers in residential centers for the elderly should deal not only with the routines of physical care but also with techniques for protecting the dignity and rights of patients and trying to get them to accept life and live it to the fullest extent possible. The "Empathic Model," which was discussed in Chapters 2 and 4, has also been used in the training of nurses and technicians in nursing homes. In some instances, employees are provided with an "Instant Aging Kit" containing a white wig, wire-rimmed spectacles, and theatrical make-up. Health personnel who don these get-ups frequently acquire greater empathy with the elderly.

Psychotherapy

The term *psychotherapy* refers to a variety of techniques for treating emotional and mental disorders by increasing the patient's self-understanding and providing him with realistic techniques for coping with stress and anxiety. As noted above, the term psychotherapy, which is often and incorrectly used interchangeably with "counseling," has traditionally referred to psychological treatment in greater depth or for more severe mental disturbances. Many psychotherapists, including Sigmund Freud, have felt that because of the purported inflexibility or lesser learning and problem-solving abilities of the elderly, psychotherapy is not as useful with older as with younger patients. There is, however, little evidence that older people are any more difficult to treat or that they gain less from psychotherapy than younger people.

Most psychotherapists or counselors are psychiatrists, psychologists, clergymen (pastoral counselors), or social workers. Unfortunately, in many states almost anyone can call himself a psychotherapist or counselor and "treat" people for a fee. Consequently, elderly people who need psychological treatment should be aware of the credentials of the persons to whom they are referred. A list of competent professional psychotherapists can usually be obtained from a family physician, clergymen, or community mental health agency. Most mental health organizations publish directories of professional people who are qualified to offer psychological assistance to the elderly. But unless the therapist has also been trained in geriatric problems he may make mistakes of the kind described in Report 5–6.

A variety of psychotherapeutic approaches—psychoanalysis, behavior therapy, humanistic-existential therapy, etc.—are practiced. In working with the elderly patient, the central focus of all these psychotherapies is to attempt to motivate the patient to take an interest in things and to use his abilities in personally and socially acceptable ways. It is also important that the patient be helped to feel wanted and needed by his family and community. Many psychotherapeutic techniques have been found somewhat effective in achieving these goals. For example, group psychotherapy,

---

Report 5–6   A Success for Psychotherapy*

Anna was nearly 80 and living with a married daughter. For the past 5 years Anna had experienced a progressive loss of memory. At first, she just forgot a few insignificant things, such as where she had placed her reading glasses. Gradually, the problem got more serious until she sometimes could not maintain a conversation: she forgot what she had just been told and asked the same question again. At times she would get lost or would even lose her way inside her daughter's house. Anna became more and more of a burden. The advice of Anna's doctor was to have her placed in a home for the aged.

Anna's experience is all too common. Many older persons suffer from some sort of short-term memory impairment: they forget what just happened but can tell you the details of an incident that occurred half a century ago. All sorts of medical theories have been proposed to explain this phenomenon of senility. The one taught in most medical schools is that such mental deterioration is caused by physical changes in the brain . . . and is irreversible. Therefore, most physicians and medically trained psychiatrists tend to give up too easily on an older person with a failing memory.

Fortunately for Anna, her daughter did not take the advice of the first doctor. They saw another physician, who referred Anna to a psychotherapist specializing in geriatric practice. In less than two months, Anna's deteriorating mental condition was reversed. This psychotherapy was not cheap. However, it was less expensive than psychoanalysis and certainly a bargain compared to the cost of keeping Anna in a home for the aged.

---

*After Brink (1976), p. 24.

which is less expensive than individual therapy, is especially valuable in helping to overcome loneliness and in sharing worries with others (Butler, 1975). In a new technique referred to as "scribotherapy," patients write down their feelings about certain topics and then, after group discussion and individual interviews, develop them into a news format.

Butler (1974) advocates *life review therapy* and *life cycle group therapy* as being especially helpful to older patients. The former consists of obtaining an extensive biography of the patient from the patient himself and from family members. Tape recordings, diaries, family albums, and other memorabilia can assist in the life review process. Some goals of this type of therapy are atonement for feelings of guilt, getting rid of childhood identifications that are continuing to cause trouble, and resolution of intra- and interpersonal conflicts. Life review therapy can also be either individual or group. Extended to a group setting consisting of 8 to 10 members of different ages, life review becomes life cycle therapy. The groups are oriented toward individuals who are experiencing life crises, ranging from adjustment difficulties in adolescence to fear of impending death. By interacting with people of different generations in a group setting, the elderly individual comes to see his problem in the perspective of the life cycle and continuing development.

Environmental (Milieu) Therapy

The modern viewpoint toward mental health recognizes the importance of physical and social surroundings in the progress and treatment of mental disorders. It has been found, for example, that introduction of some simple changes—a record player, decorated bulletin board, games, dressing patients in white shirts and ties, serving beer and crackers every day at two o'clock—can markedly alter the behavior of patients on a senile ward (Volpe and Kastenbaum, 1967). These changes were found to produce decreased incontinence and a lessened need for restraint and medication; the mental and social functioning of patients also improved markedly. Such improvements may be interpreted as being produced by more positive patient attitudes, accompanied by an increase in the expectations on the part of the staff and the patients themselves of what the latter are capable of doing. In a very real sense, mental patients—like people in general—become what they are seen and labeled as being, and they do what they are expected to do.

A similar explanation can be used to account for the findings of Kahana and Kahana (1970). Aged male psychiatric patients were assigned at random to one of two types of hospital wards. In the age-segregated wards, the patients on each ward were all within a fairly narrow age range. On the age-integrated wards, the patients comprised the entire adult age range. When re-examined after three weeks, it was found that improvements in responsiveness and performance on mental status examinations by patients on the age-integrated wards were significantly greater than observed in patients on the age-segregated wards. Apparently, simply being around younger people, who act as more youthful behavior models, can alter an older person's negative attitude toward himself and his situation and consequently improve his behavior.

SUMMARY

Owing to a combination of organic changes and psychological stress, the mental health of the aged tends to be poorer than that of younger adults. Among older people the incidence of mental disorder is related to sex, socioeconomic status, urban vs. rural residence, and other demographic variables.

Although many authorities decry the practice of labeling mental disorders, the American Psychiatric Association's classification of mental disorders into organic vs. functional and psychotic vs. nonpsychotic categories is still employed in mental hospitals and other clinical contexts. Organic disorders have a known biological basis, whereas functional disorders are considered to be caused by psychological stress and possible unknown biological factors.

Psychoneuroses, psychophysiological reactions, and personality disorders are functional conditions that occur at all stages of life. Psychotic disorders, which are characterized by pronounced distortions of reality and may also involve disturbances in perception, language, memory, and mood, are less common and more serious than the other functional disorders. The two major types of psychoses are schizophrenia and affective psychoses. Among the latter are manic-depressive psychosis and involutional melancholia.

The organic disorders that are fairly common in old age are cerebral arteriosclerosis and senile brain disease. Confusion, disorientation, incoherence, restlessness, and occasionally hallucinations occur in cerebral arteriosclerosis. Self-centeredness, difficulty in assimilating new experiences, and childish emotionality are symptoms of senile brain disease. The symptoms of irreversible senile brain disease are similar to those of many other, reversible conditions such as those produced by overdoses of certain drugs, malnutrition, and dehydration. Therefore, the physician must be wary of misdiagnosing one of these reversible conditions as senile brain disease. Alzheimer's disease, Pick's disease, and Jakob-Creutzfeldt disease are irreversible presenile disorders involving the destruction of brain tissue and a psychological symptom picture similar to that of senile brain disease.

Legal aspects of mental disorders in old age are concerned with the concepts of incompetence, testamentary capacity, voluntary and involuntary admission, and commitment. Professional and public concern with the legal rights of mental patients has increased in recent years. One stimulus for this increasing concern has been the practice of committing elderly people to mental institutions, where they receive little or no treatment, merely to get them out of the way of the family and society.

A combination of physical (electroshock, drugs, brain surgery, etc.), psychological (individual and group counseling or psychotherapy), and sociological (milieu, occupational, and recreational therapy) therapeutic techniques is used in treating mentally disturbed old people. Various types of remedial and preventive counseling and psychotherapy have been used in helping both young and old people who have psychological problems. Butler reports good success with life review therapy and life cycle group therapy in treating guilt feelings, childhood identifications, and interpersonal conflicts in the aged. The importance of the living environment in affecting the attitudes and functioning of older patients is documented by the milieu research of Volpe, Kastenbaum, and others.

suggested readings

Brink, T. L. Psychotherapy after forty. *MH*, 1976, *60*(2), 22–26.

Butler, R. N., and Lewis, M. I. *Aging and mental health.* New York: C. V. Mosby, 1973.

Calhoun, J. F. *Abnormal psychology: Current perspectives* (2nd ed.). New York: Random House, 1977, Chap. 17.

Coleman, J. C. *Abnormal psychology and modern life* (5th ed.). Glenview, Ill.: Scott, Foresman & Co., 1976. Chap. 13.

Committee on Aging of the Group for the Advancement of Psychiatry. *Toward a public policy on mental health care of the elderly.* New York: Author, 1970.

Folsom, J. C., and Folsom, G. S. The real world. *MH*, 1974, *58*(3), 29–33.

notes

[1]Even the distinction between "organic" and "functional" is not complete, since a person can simultaneously have both an organic and a functional disorder.

[2]Mental health professionals and legal experts object to the term "commitment" with its implications of imprisonment, and have recommended that it be replaced by "hospitalization," "admission" or some other less offensive term.

Chapter 6

Employment and Retirement

For those who have a choice, sooner or later the question of if or when to retire from one's occupation arises. Some people look forward to retirement and the opportunity it offers to pursue secondary interests and goals. Others, especially those who enjoy their work and perceive it as more than simply a way of making a living, prefer to continue working even after they are eligible for retirement. Such people view the job as a central part of themselves, and becoming permanently detached from it has a marked effect on their self-concepts. This is more likely to be true of those who are higher up on the occupational ladder than of laborers, who are more apt to view their work as mere drudgery.

WORK VERSUS RETIREMENT

Whether to retire or continue working is a decision that is not entirely in the hands of most employees. Management, frequently after consultation with labor unions, makes policies concerning retirement. For most occupations, the marker retirement age is in the 60s, usually 65. It was an accident of history (specifically, social legislation concerning Social Security and other pension funds) that age 65 was set as the beginning of the retirement years. As a consequence, this age has come to be viewed as the end of middle age and the beginning of old age. There are, however, extensive individual differences in the rate of aging, and many people can easily continue working well beyond this arbitrary retirement point. The typical 65 year old of today is not "over the hill," being still quite capable of achieving and contributing to society.

As indicated repeatedly throughout this book, the 65-and-over group is growing more rapidly than the general American population. As of 1977 it accounted for approximately 11 per cent of the population, or 23 million people. But by the year 2030 it is estimated that the population of the United States will include 52 million elderly, 15 to 20 per cent of the total ("The Graying of America," 1977). If the present employment situation continues, the great majority of these people—even those who are willing and able to work—will be unemployed.

Employment Statistics

Omitting wartime statistics, the percentage of elderly people in the work forces of industrialized nations has declined steadily throughout the present century. Nearly 70 per cent of American men aged 65 and over were employed in 1900, a figure that dropped to 46 per cent in 1950 and to less than 20 per cent in 1975 (Schultz, 1976: "The Graying of America," 1977). It is possible that the percentage will decrease even further by the year 2000. Among the probable causes of this decrease are advanced technology, declines in agricultural work and self-employment, and more attractive incentives to retire. In addition, increased education and educational requirements for most jobs have favored younger workers.

In contrast to the pronounced decline in the percentage of employed elderly men, the proportion of employed elderly women has remained fairly constant during the past few years, fluctuating between 8 per cent and 11 per cent and expected to drop to 7.5 per cent by 1990. That many of the nonworking elderly—both men and women—prefer to be employed was demonstrated by the results of a 1974 Harris poll (National Council on the Aging, 1975), in which 37 per cent of the sample of retired Americans stated that they would still be working if they could.

The Worker and the Job

Some time during middle age, at the height of their careers as well as their economic needs and responsibilities, most people begin to assess their accomplishments in terms of the time they have left.

If their goals are found to be unrealistic, an adjustment may be in order (Neugarten, 1967):

> Men perceive a close relationship between life-line and career-line. Middle age is the time to take stock. Any disparity noted between career-expectations and career achievements—that is, whether one is "on time" or "late" in reaching career goals—adds to the heightened awareness of age. One 47-year-old lawyer said, "I moved at age forty-five from a large corporation to a law firm. I got out at the last possible moment, because after forty-five it is too difficult to find the job you want. If you haven't made it by then, you had better make it fast, or you are stuck."

To the middle-ager, faced with Erikson's crisis of generativity vs. self-absorption, the job is a central part of the self. Sexual, avocational, cultural, and even family interests may be perceived as less important than the job. People are identified by the kind of work they do, and their status, social relationships, identity, and reason for living are all involved with their work. This is especially true of men, who have traditionally been perceived as the family breadwinner. But with the women's movement and the associated extension of the social identities of women beyond those of housewife and mother, it is also becoming true of more and more women.

Because a person's job is such an important part of his or her life space, satisfactions derived from working are affected by and affect physical and mental health. It has been found that severe job stress, produced by heavy responsibilities and dissatisfaction with the achievement of one's goals, is related to heart attacks (Romo, Siltanen, Theorell, and Rahe, 1974). Job dissatisfaction is also associated with peptic ulcers, which, incidentally, affect blue-collar and white-collar workers alike (Kahn, 1969). The results of other studies have shown that the rate of suicide is greater among the unemployed than the employed (Rosenfeld, 1976b) and that work satisfaction is positively correlated with longevity (Palmore, 1969; Rose, 1964). Most people who live a long time continue to work at something throughout their lives.

The relationship between work satisfaction and health is, of course, reciprocal. Satisfying work contributes to both physical and psychological health (see Report 6–1), but the state of one's health also affects the ability to work and one's feelings about the job. Furthermore, people who are higher on the socioeconomic scale tend to like their work more and to be healthier than those of lower socioeconomic status.

*Report 6–1. The Psychological Significance of Work**

Mr. Winter single-handedly ran an operation that nobody else in his company fully understood, nor in fact cared to understand. As Mr. Winter reached his 64th birthday, a bright and talented younger man was assigned as an apprentice to learn the complex set of activities so that at the end of the year, he could take over the operation and the old master could benefit from a well-deserved retirement. Mr. Winter objected, claiming that he did not want to retire, but the company had rules.

Not long after retirement a substantial change in Mr. Winter took place. He began to withdraw from people and to lose his zest for life. Within a year after his retirement this once lively and productive businessman was hospitalized, diagnosed as having a senile psychosis. Friends from work and even family soon stopped coming to visit, as they could evoke no response. Mr. Winter was a vegetable.

About two years after the apprentice had stepped up to his new position of responsibility he suddenly died. The company found itself in a serious predicament. The function that was vacated was essential to company operations but was one which no one else in the company could effectively perform. A decision was made to approach Mr. Winter and see if he could pull himself together enough to carry on the job and train somebody to take over. Four of his closest co-workers were sent to the hospital. After hours of trying, one of the men finally broke through. The idea of going back to work brought the first sparkle in Mr. Winter's eyes in two years. Within a few days, this "vegetable" was operating at full steam, interacting with people as he had years before.

The Older Worker

Irrespective of age, a person who likes his work and finds it meaningful tends to want to remain on the job (Offir, 1974). Older workers are usually more committed to their jobs than younger people, and they typically experience greater job satisfaction. Older workers also resent the assumption, which is contradicted by research, that they are incapable of doing a good day's work. Despite the fact that they often perform poorly on laboratory-type tasks, under actual working conditions older workers usually do as well as or better than younger ones (Riley and Foner, 1968). Older workers are also quite capable of learning new job skills, especially when the methods of training take their capabilities into account.

Two population experts of the French National Institute of Demographic Studies, Alfred Saury and Paul Paillat, have expressed a fear that the world of the future, which may be dominated by elderly persons, will be sluggish, conservative, and lacking in vitality. These demographers see technological innovation as slowing down in a society controlled by a "population of old people ruminating over old ideas in old houses," (see Paillat and Bunch, 1970). But as was pointed out in Chapter 3 and echoed by other experts, elderly people are not necessarily less creative nor less dynamic than younger ones. Many original ideas have been initiated and developed by people in their 80s and 90s.

---

* After Margolis and Kroes (1972).

The Elderly Unemployed

Despite the fact that their job performance is not generally inferior to that of younger workers, the rate of unemployment is higher for the elderly. In addition, once out of a job older people tend to remain unemployed up to 70 per cent longer than their younger counterparts (Entine, 1976). Even the official unemployment figures for the elderly, although high, are underestimates of the actual state of affairs. One reason is that, after a time, many older people simply give up and stop looking for jobs, thereby no longer being counted among the unemployed.

The referral rate of older workers to jobs by the U.S. Employment Service is only about half that of younger workers, even though once he is referred to a job an older worker is just as likely to be placed as a younger one (Quirk, 1976). The consequence of the lower referral rate of the elderly is that the older would-be worker is often forced into early retirement, a retirement that should be based on individual needs and capacities rather than chronological age.

The problem of obtaining employment is even worse when the elderly job-seeker is black. In fact, it has been said that as far as employment is concerned, being young and black is functionally equivalent to being old and white in our society (Kastenbaum, 1971). This does not mean that unemployment is necessarily psychologically harder on blacks than on whites. Psychological reactions to being unemployed depend, to some degree, on what a person is accustomed to or prepared for. Margaret Mead (Hechinger, 1977) has suggested, for example, that one reason women live longer than men is that older men are cut off abruptly from their jobs, having a full life one day and nothing to do the next. On the other hand, the typical woman does not retire from her housework but continues doing in old age what she has been doing throughout her married life.

More Jobs for the Elderly

Many of the unemployed elderly, at least half of whom are physically capable of doing a day's work, are wasting their and society's resources by not working. This may seem like a harsh statement, but many of the elderly would agree. The majority of the elderly want to see the system changed to make employment available to those older people who need or desire to continue working

Figure 6-1. In many other societies, the elderly have an honored place and perform valued work. Surely it is time for America to utilize the talents of its older citizens. (Drawing by Val; Copyright 1969 by Saturday Review/World, Inc.)

(see National Council on the Aging, 1975). This has been proposed by many authorities and is being done in several European countries. Faced with zero population growth and potentially fewer people in the work force, many industrialized nations perceive older workers as a valuable resource and attempt to delay their retirement by the use of various incentives. The effectiveness of these plans in countries such as Sweden, the Soviet Union, and Japan is seen in statistics that point to a large percentage of those eligible for retirement electing to remain on the job.

A particularly valuable resource are elderly doctors, lawyers, and businessmen, who possess professional knowledge and skills that have taken years to develop. For example, retired lawyers can offer legal services to the aged, retired teachers can give courses, and retired doctors and nurses can supply home medical care (Butler, 1975). A few business firms have started "skill banks" of retirees, which permit former employees of a firm to be hired for specific projects and programs.

An interesting new social phenomenon is the "young-old" retiree aged 55 and over who, having retired from a first career but still in relatively good health, begins looking around for more varied life options (Neugarten, 1975). This well-educated, demanding individual frequently begins a second career and finds new avocational, educational, and even political pursuits. It has been suggested that, with breakthroughs in prolongevity up to 100 years, people may look forward to as many as three different careers in a single lifetime. Legislators and/or chief executives might continue to work for several generations. Members of Congress could be elected for as many as 40 consecutive terms, and junior executives may have to wait 50 years for their bosses to retire before they are promoted! (Anderson, 1974.)

Whatever the future may hold in terms of superlongevity, the governments of most modern nations are faced with the immediate problem of using the abilities of elderly citizens who want to work. A number of federal employment programs that benefit older Americans are described in Table 6–1. Perhaps the best-known of these is the Foster Grandparent Program, which was designed primarily to give elderly people the opportunity to provide love and care for institutionalized and handicapped children. Another noteworthy public service program, the "Project Green Thumb" sponsored by the National Farmers Union, paid old people for part-time work in beautification, conservation, and improvement projects in rural areas. Many other federally aided volunteer programs (e.g., RSVP, SCORE, and VISTA) that make use of the services of the elderly have been enacted over the past several years (Table 6–1).

As the population grows even larger, the service-providing sector will need to expand. New job opportunities will open up for the elderly in education, social services, and health areas. Elderly people could staff day-care centers and kindergartens, work on historical projects and crafts, and even become small-scale food producers by operating abandoned farms. Projects at Miami-Dade Community College, New York City Community College, and other educational institutions have been concerned with constructing lists of potential employers of the aged on a full- or part-time basis. Cooperating employers in these programs recognize that the primary qualification for employment should be ability to perform the job rather than chronological age. Legislation is now pending in the U.S. Congress to include age, along with sex and race, under the Civil Rights Act. If passed, the bill would eliminate 65 as the cutoff age in the Age Discrimination in Employment Act and prevent employers from asking an applicant's age as a condition of employment.

Table 6–1. MAJOR FEDERAL EMPLOYMENT
PROGRAMS BENEFITING THE ELDERLY*

Program	Agency	Description
Age Discrimination in Employment	Office of Fair Labor Standards, Department of Labor	Investigation of charges of discrimination by certain employers against persons between the ages of 40 and 65.
Employment Programs for Special Groups	Employment and Training Administration, Department of Labor	Secretary of Labor may establish and operate manpower programs for special groups, including older workers.
Foster Grandparent Program	ACTION	Federal grants to public and private nonprofit agencies for creating volunteer services opportunities for low-income persons age 60 and over as companions to children and to older individuals. Volunteers receive at least the federal minimum wage.
Older Americans Community Service Employment Program	Employment and Training Administration, Department of Labor	Secretary of Labor may contract with public and private nonprofit agencies to develop and administer part-time work in public service activities for low income, unemployed persons aged 55 or older; to be paid at least federal minimum wage.
Retired Senior Volunteer Program (RSVP)	ACTION	Federal grants to public or private nonprofit agencies to establish or expand volunteer activities for the elderly; providing compensation for out-of-pocket expenses incidental to their services.
Service Corps of Retired Executives (SCORE)	Small Business Administration	Volunteer services organized through field offices of Small Business Administration; retired professional and businessmen assist persons with business-related problems.
Volunteers in Service to America (VISTA)	ACTION	Provides volunteer service opportunities for persons aged 18 or older in urban and rural poverty areas, on Indian reservations, with migrant families, and in federally assisted institutions for the mentally ill and retarded. Most older VISTA volunteers serve part-time.

*Adapted from Select Committee on Aging. *Federal responsibility to the elderly.* Washington, D.C., U.S. Government Printing Office, 1976, pp. 4–5.

THE PROCESS OF RETIREMENT

The usual retirement ages of 65 for men and 60 for women were selected by the federal government in the 1930s to serve as a base for paying Old Age and Survivors Insurance, commonly known as Social Security. These age figures were determined in a political move to curb unemployment in younger and therefore presumably more productive workers by replacing older workers with them. Although the expected role for older people today involves retirement rather than work, certain professions have no fixed retirement age. On the other hand, employees of police departments and high-risk jobs in other organizations face early retirement. Still other organizations have policies of gradually reducing employee work loads during the years just prior to retirement. In any event, 65 has become a kind of magic age in the United States, a benchmark between middle and late life.

There are, of course, pros and cons for retirement at or before age 65, depending to some extent on which side of the 65 fence one is on. As noted above, it can be argued that the jobs vacated by retirees are made available to younger workers and hence help combat the high unemployment rate in the latter group. An argument against this point is that many new jobs become available each year, presumably enough to provide employment for younger workers without requiring early retirement by older workers.[1] Another argument in favor of forced retirement is that it enables employers to get rid of incompetent workers by means of the natural attrition process of retirement without having to prove incompetence to perform the job. For both humane and political reasons, supervisors are frequently reluctant to tell an employee that he is incompetent, particularly when competence is not easily judged.

On the side against involuntary retirement is the fact that competent elderly workers can be kept on the job and continue to pay in rather than withdrawing money from Social Security and other retirement plans. Not only do such workers contribute their skills and productivity, but also more and more people are maintaining that simple justice and humanity demand that we recognize the value of older lives and the right of older people to continue performing those activities which contribute to their sense of well-being.

Retirement Statistics

Owing to the relatively rapid growth rate of the older population, the proportion of retirees in the general population has steadily

Report 6–2. Congressional Age Profile*

Senior citizens of this nation have a powerful lobby in the U.S. Senate. Although those Americans over 65 constitute a little more than 10 per cent of the country's population, their members make up 24 per cent of the Senate.

A study of the 94th Congress, which adjourned last month, reveals that less than 12 per cent of the House members are senior citizens, which reflects approximately the national proportion.

Herewith an age breakdown of the 94th Congress:

Age	House	Senate
25–34	24	1
35–44	90	11
45–54	157	33
55–64	110	31
65–74	43	18
75–84	7	6

In the 94th Congress, the median age in the Senate was 56, in the House, 50.

increased in recent years. If the present trend continues, it is estimated that by the year 2000 there will be approximately 33 million retired Americans. One reason for the increased number of retirees is seen in the fact that more people are beginning to choose early retirement. Thus, at the turn of the century the average retirement age is expected to be 55 years rather than the 62 years that it is now. Not only is the number of retirees increasing, but also the length of the retirement period will soon be such that people will be spending up to one third of their lives as retirees. The average American now lives 14 years after retiring, but projections indicate that by the year 2000 Americans will be spending on the average 25+ years in retirement (Entine, 1976). The situation is similar in other industrialized nations.

Another way of looking at the situation is in terms of the ratio of retirees to active workers, since it is the actively employed who are being asked to increase their financial contributions to support retired workers. It is estimated that this ratio, which is now 1:4.6 in the United States, will have increased to 1:3.5 or perhaps even 1:2.5 by 1990 ("Retirees May . . .", 1976). One important cause of the decreasing average age at retirement and the increasing ratio of retirees to workers is that many people are being forced to retire before they need or want to do so.

From the standpoint of many potential retirees, however, retirement is not necessarily a dreadful event. Even though some people prefer to keep on working, others look forward to the leisure

---

*From *Parade Magazine*, Nov. 7, 1976.

Report 6–3. No Vote on Forced Retirement–Louis Harris*

The American people are having second thoughts about desirability of early retirement. As a result, they now come down hard for ending all mandatory retirement practices in the future. By 86–12 percent, an overwhelming majority agrees that "nobody should be forced to retire because of age, if he or she wants to continue working and is still able to do a good job." By 52–35 percent, a majority also believes that "most older people can continue to perform as well on the job as they did when they were younger." Among those in the 65 and older group, the response here is more emphatic: 55–36 percent.

The turnabout on the retirement issue has been dramatic, according to the findings of a recent Harris Survey of 1,491 adults nationwide: In 1974, a narrow 45–40 percent plurality of the public thought it was a "good thing that the age at which people are required to retire has become younger in recent years." Now, a 51–39 percent majority thinks that lowering the mandatory retirement age is "not a good thing." On specific measures to outlaw mandatory retirement, the public holds these views: A 53–32 percent majority favors "abolishing the mandatory age for people to retire from employment in the federal government." A 60–31 percent majority favors passage of a new law by Congress that would "not allow any private employer to force an employee to retire before the age of 70." Such a law is before Congress now and is given a reasonably good chance for passage. A smaller 49–39 percent plurality favors an even tougher new law that would "not allow any employer to force an employee to retire at any age."

Among the adult population, 15 percent are now in the category of "retired from work." Here are the key experiences of work people 65 and older say they miss: Eighty percent report they miss "the money the job brought in." Seventy-seven percent miss "the people at work." whom they used to see every day at their place of employment. Sixty-seven percent miss "the feeling of being useful." Sixty-three percent miss "the work itself." Fifty-six percent miss "the respect of others" at work. Fifty-five percent miss "things happening around me." Forty-eight percent miss "having a fixed schedule every day."

When people who are now still working were asked if they thought they would miss these experiences if they stopped, they gave approximately the same replies as those who are retired did. In other words, it is not difficult at all for people still working to empathize with the strong frustration of those who are retired. Given this basic agreement between the generations on the retirement question, it is little wonder that the public would like to pass laws that will allow the work life of people to extend well past the normally expected times of retirement.

time afforded by retirement. Those who decide to retire early are influenced by such factors as the anticipation of a comfortable income, the relatively high rate of technological obsolescence of workers in their 50s and 60s, increasing relocation of major firms, cyclical unemployment, and stagnation of certain sectors of the economy (Binstock, 1977). A sizable majority of these early retirees claim to be satisfied with their lives since retirement (Neugarten, 1971).

Of course, many people are not happy at all with early retirement, and between those who are highly satisfied and those who are highly dissatisfied are many individual differences in reactions. In a study of 1486 men and 483 women, it was found that people

---

with larger incomes, more education, and occupations of higher social status preferred to keep working longer than those lower on the economic, educational, and occupational scales (Streib and Schneider, 1971). Working women as a group were more reluctant to retire than men, but single and married women tended to retire earlier than divorced women and widows.

Another important fact affecting the decision to retire is the state of one's health. Maddox (1968b) found that nearly 50 per cent of retired people chose to do so because of poor health. Finally, for certain people there may be no formal retirement at all, mandatory or voluntary. Vontress (1976) points out that for the lower-class black man, whose entire life consists of a series of starts and stops, there is no precise stage that can be labeled as "retirement."

Challenges to Mandatory Retirement

Whether they choose to retire or not, an overwhelming majority of the elderly (86 per cent in one poll) agree that mandatory retirement policies should be abolished (National Council on the Aging, 1975). Those who support a mandatory retirement policy claim that not only does it help reduce the rate of unemployment among younger people but it enables employers to weed out personnel without engaging in the difficult and highly subjective task of evaluating work performance. But those who oppose mandatory retirement policies are more vocal and persuasive. They point out that life expectancy has increased since the 1930s, that forced retirement pushes experienced and talented workers aside, and that older people have a right to determine their own futures.

Report 6–4 is illustrative of the legal challenges that have been directed toward mandatory retirement policies. The American Medical Association, submitting a "friend-of-the-court" brief in connection with the first case, maintained that there is no evidence that older workers are any less efficient than younger workers. Combined with the smaller work force anticipated in the last quarter of the current century, legal suits such as those described in Report 6–4 will undoubtedly result in the raising—if not the complete elimination—of mandatory retirement ages. Even now, U.S. Steel has no mandatory retirement age for its nonoffice employees as long as they can do their jobs and pass annual medical examinations. Many recent union contracts with other companies

*Report 6-4. Legal Challenges to Forced Retirement**

An impending decision from the U.S. Supreme Court could strike down many state laws mandating a fixed retirement age for certain employees. The case initially was brought by Robert D. Murgia, a 53-year-old former Massachusetts state police officer. Murgia, who then had the rank of colonel, was retired three years ago at 50, the compulsory age for retiring state police in Massachusetts.

A lower court ruled the state law unconstitutional. The state appealed the decision to the Supreme Court.

"There are elaborate medical screening processes the state police use on personnel every two years until age 40. After that the exam is annual," said Robert City, Murgia's attorney. "Murgia passed all tests and met all standards, which meant he was fit."

Murgia, of Andover, Mass., now works as a security manager for a computer firm. "I'm not against mandatory retirement per se, but I am at age 50," he said. "I don't think the law was right and that's why I did it. Win, lose or draw, I still don't think it's right."

Thelma Davis, the Griffin, Ga., schoolteacher, also is involved in a court proceeding. The mandatory retirement age for teachers in Georgia is 70, but the school board passed a ruling to retire certain teachers over 65. She sued. A district court judge ruled the board's recommendation was unconstitutional.

"I love what I do, and I'm damn good at it," she said. "If they couldn't find out what kind of teacher I was during the 24 years I taught here, then something's wrong with them." Miss Davis is a former president of the National Educational Association Classroom Teachers.

have also increased the retirement age from 65 to 67 years. These contracts provide for additional years of optional employment, depending on a joint decision between worker and employer. On the federal level, U.S. Representative Claude Pepper introduced legislation to do away with the policy of requiring U.S. Government employees to retire at age 70. The Pepper bill, which was passed overwhelmingly by the House and Senate in 1977, would, if signed into law, ban mandatory retirement at any age in the federal government while raising the retirement age from 65 to 70 for most employees in the private sector.

Preretirement Planning

Many older employees look forward to retirement with optimism and eagerness for release from work and routine. Others, however, are concerned about money or anxious about how they will use their time. The anxiety felt by these people about retiring tends to increase as they reach retirement age, but once they have retired and become adjusted to a new way of life, their level of anxiety decreases (Reichard, Livson, and Petersen, 1962). At least some of this anxiety and "postretirement shock" could be eased by

---

*From Barclay, D. System ignores talents and abilities. Associated Press, June 9, 1976.

planning and preparing for retirement: This is the goal of preretirement counseling. As stated in the proposed Federal Employees Preretirement Assistance Act of 1975 (Mondale, 1975, p. S.19393):

A person's retirement years are perhaps the most challenging and potentially devastating period of his or her life. It can be satisfying and rewarding, a culmination of a successful life. Or it can be a cruel, gradual, or sudden breakdown in the person's life style. "Retirement shock" is a common phenomenon. A combination of confusion and anxiety accompanying retirement is added to declining health and reduced income to produce not only general unhappiness but often physical symptoms as well.

Planning for retirement can help workers make the transition from years of active employment to their leisure-time years. Our society is work oriented and youth oriented: retirement can produce a real identity crisis, and often a loss of interest in living. Yet, with adequate advance preparation, retirement from a job does not need to mean retirement from life. By learning to avoid the pitfalls of retirement, and how to get the most from the new opportunities being opened up, preretirement planning can facilitate the vital and necessary continuation of personal growth.

According to Porter (1977), at least 10 questions should be asked by anyone considering retirement:

1. When will I retire?
2. Will I lead a life of leisure or continue to work?
3. How much am I worth today?
4. Where will I retire?
5. What can I save by retiring?
6. How much money do I need in retirement?
7. When can I start drawing Social Security and my other pension benefits?
8. What precisely is my benefit deal under my corporation's pension plan?
9. Will I have enough health insurance?
10. What kind of investments can help me obtain additional retirement income?

Finding answers to these 10 questions should be among the immediate objectives of preretirement planning.

In a recent Harris survey (National Council on the Aging, 1975), a sample of older Americans was asked what they had done to prepare for retirement. Although many of the respondents reported having made some preparations, the plans of the group as a whole were considered inadequate in terms of savings, preparing a will, arranging for employment (full- or part-time), and enrolling in retirement counseling programs. Furthermore, only a small proportion (19 per cent) had taken a preretirement planning course or planned to do so. These findings underscore the fact that although industrial and governmental organizations have increased the number of preretirement counseling programs in recent years, only a small minority of workers actually participate in such programs (Ullmann, 1976).

Depending on the ambitions of the program planners, a preretirement program may involve literature handouts, lectures on rights and benefits, and in-depth seminars and workshops held during duty hours. Preretirement counseling workshops cover such topics as the provision of adequate retirement income, social relationships, avocational and new vocational interests, as well as physical and mental health needs. Other topics of discussion are legal rights and procedures, sexual behavior, adjusting to changing morals and values, and even such mundane matters as planning and cooking meals. The use of leisure time for hobbies, entertainment, and further education is also an important subject for consideration in these workshops, especially with those older people whose work-value systems have heretofore permitted little indulgence in leisure activities.

Two of the organizations having preretirement counseling programs are the American Management Association and the American Association of Retired Persons (AARP). The eight topics in the AARP Retirement Planning Seminar series[2] are: Challenge of Retirement, Health and Safety, Housing and Location, Legal Affairs, Attitude and Role Adjustments, Meaningful Use of Time, Sources and Amounts of Income, and Financial Planning. Each of the two-hour sessions devoted to each topic includes a series of organizing questions, brief readings, and filmstrips to use as discussion aids. As the list of topics suggests, these programs emphasize the practical aspects of retirement rather than more subtle psychosocial matters. Among the latter are stresses within the family and the loss of a sense of being important to others (Ullmann, 1976). These are circumstances that the preretiree may be unable to anticipate, a fact that points out the need for postretirement as well as preretirement counseling (Sheldon, McEwan, and Ryser, 1975).

Individual Differences in Reactions to Retirement

The activity orientation and work ethic of Western culture do little to prepare the aging individual for a lengthy period of retirement. When people are almost religiously devoted to their work, the experience of suddenly being unemployed and presumably unproductive can be very damaging to one's sense of self-esteem. Retirement in these cases is often accompanied by feelings of diminished usefulness, significance, and independence, and perhaps a sense that life is over. A rather bleak picture is presented by Perlman (1968, p. 152):

> After his first weeks or even months of freedom from work, relished as his just deserts, the old man without a regular job begins to feel lost, somehow, missing the affiliation and regularization of his daily life that was present in his work role. He may find these in part in some forms of leisure activity or in various kinds of volunteer good works. He may attach himself to other old men for shared opinions and fragmental chit-chat and for the comfortableness of being in the company of his peers, the "retired." But with a few exceptions, the sense of being-to-a-purpose has gone out of his life, and it is hard to know whether his unconscious need for withdrawal and for husbanding his energies makes his investment in relationships and activity superficial or whether some increasing emotional withdrawal and lack of social purposefulness and value results from his loss of role. The old woman holds on to her householding duties long after her role as mother and spouse has ended. But when she has tidied up the house and washed her cup and saucer and talked to her grandchild on the telephone—what, then, is she to be or do? And when she is no longer able—sight dim, hearing dulled, legs a-totter—to manage for herself and is taken into her child's home or put to live in a "home for senior citizens," when all tasks are dispatched by the swifter, stronger, more efficient others, what is she?

The loss of meaning and significance in one's life, which has been referred to as the "retirement syndrome," can accelerate the processes of physical and mental deterioration with age.[3] But the retirement syndrome is far from universal, and in the great majority of cases retirement per se does not produce negative reactions. Research has shown that, for the most part, satisfaction with life, self-acceptance, and overall adjustment do not decrease after retiring (Neugarten, 1971). Rather than looking upon retirement as a process of "being put on the shelf," most old people see it as providing an opportunity to satisfy previously neglected needs. When immediate postretirement depression and anxiety do occur, they are usually mild and shortlived. Severe, acute depression at this time of life is usually attributable to physical disabilities or illness rather than retirement (Lowenthal, 1964; Spence, 1966). Also, those surveys that have reported poorer adjustment in retirees than nonretirees have not adequately controlled for the fact that less healthy people retire earlier while more healthy workers—both physically and mentally—are actively employed for a longer period of time.

In addition to overall health and attitude toward work, one's economic status affects reactions to retirement. Relief from monetary worries can cushion the psychological shock of being unemployed. Streib and Schneider (1971) report, however, that although there is a sharp reduction in income for most people on retirement, there is no corresponding increase in concern about money. Two other factors that affect adjustment to retirement are personality characteristics and the ability to develop new roles for onself.

Personality and Retirement

In terms of good versus poor adjustment to retirement, Reichard, Livson, and Peterson (1968) described three types of personalities associated with good adjustment and two with poor adjustment. The largest category in the "well-adjusted" group consists of "mature men," who accept retirement easily, without regrets over the past, and are able to find new tasks and cultivate new relationships to occupy their time. A second category of well-adjusted retirees, the "rocking chair men," welcome retirement as a time to sit back, relax, and passively enjoy their old age. The final category of well-adjusted retirees, labeled as "armored men," develop an active, highly organized life style to defend themselves against the anxiety of growing old.

The two categories of poorly adjusted retirees were labeled the "angry men" and the "self-haters." The former, unable to face the prospect of growing old, bitterly blame others for their failure to achieve their life goals. In contrast to the "angry men," the "self-haters" blame themselves for their misfortunes. Instead of reacting with anger, this group is quite depressed.

Rather than attempting to describe reactions to retirement in terms of overall personality types, other researchers have concentrated on a single psychosocial variable. Concerning the variable of social status, for example, Barrett (1972) found evidence for four types of retirees: (1) those who achieved adequate status as adults and are happy with the residue, (2) those who have been unable to achieve any position of esteem and have accepted it, (3) those whose need for status is satisfied through affiliating with other people, and (4) unhappy people who are still seeking status. With respect to the satisfaction of psychosocial needs, Sheldon, McEwan, and Ryser (1975) have also identified four ways of reacting to retirement: (1) by trying to satisfy the same old needs in the same way as before retirement, (2) by discontinuing many old interests and expressions of needs while developing few new ones, (3) by attempting to satisfy the same needs by new activities, and (4) by changing one's needs or attempting to satisfy secondary needs that have remained unsatisfied during the years of active employment.

Roles and Retirement

Viewed from a sociological perspective, retirement is a time when people exit from certain roles and must find other roles to replace those that have been terminated (Blau, 1973). Society's attitude toward the older person's social status as one of "role obsolescence" may also cause that person to withdraw into a feeling of outlived usefulness. This feeling appears to be especially pronounced in our century of rapidly changing life styles and the consequent isolation of generations. The segregation of old people from the rest of society is unfortunate, but those who have at least one or two close friends (confidants) are much better able to deal with the use of time and changing roles.

Since there are few formal roles for retirees in our society, they have to more or less work out their own social roles. This may be less troublesome for the older woman, especially the housewife, than for her retired husband who now finds himself spending almost all of his time in his wife's domain. The role of "mother-without-children" whose retired husband is always around represents a change that can create new marital tensions. Nevertheless, adjustment to retirement would appear to be easier for a woman, except perhaps when she becomes a widow.

On the whole, retirees adjust rather well to their changed occupational, familial, and other social roles. Some find the sick role or eccentric role easier to tolerate than the role of failure, and so they become hypochondriacs or neurotics (Busse and Pfeiffer, 1969). But for most, and especially those who engaged in some preretirement planning of postretirement roles, activities, and interests, retirement itself is a challenge and an opportunity.

Retirement may signal a decrease in interpersonal interactions and activities, but this is not necessarily bad. The *theory of disengagement* (Cumming, Dean, Newell, and McCaffrey, 1960; Cumming and Henry, 1961) characterizes old age as a time of declining involvement of the individual with society and society with the individual. According to this theory, aging brings about a change in self-perception such that the individual is less interested in being actively involved in things but is content to reflect on his past life and accomplishments. To the disengaged person, adjustment comes through gradual withdrawal from responsibility and participation rather than continued activity.

Disengagement does occur, beginning as early as the 40s, but in many instances it is forced on older people as a consequence of society's failure to provide ways for them to continue being productive (Havighurst, Neugarten, and Tobin, 1973). Contrasting with the position that disengagement is voluntary is the *activity theory* that continued productivity and social interaction are essential to satisfaction and a sense of well-being (Maddox, 1968a, 1970). An extreme form of this concept sees the individual as "dying with his boots on," but the usual form of the theory incorporates the facts of reduced activity and partial retirement due to decreased energy. Depending on interests, temperament, health, and environmental circumstances, some retirees find satisfaction in a greater degree of activity than others. It is noteworthy that 79 per cent of the retirees in Maddox's (1970) sample showed a high activity life style pattern, which was accompanied by high satisfaction. On the other hand, only 14 per cent showed the disengagement pattern and high satisfaction. Regardless of how active an individual retiree elects to remain, society should obviously make adequate provisions for those who want to stay involved.

INCOME OF THE ELDERLY

Individual variations in the incomes of older people are large, with about 50 per cent of the elderly being covered by a pension plan other than Social Security and some being quite wealthy. Many older people have accumulated substantial material assets over a lifetime of working and saving. On the average, however, the income of retired men is only about half that of younger working men, and the average income of elderly women is approximately half that of elderly men. In 1974, the median income of American families headed by individuals 65 and older was $7300, compared to an overall national average of $12,800 (Schultz, 1976). If present trends continue, income differences among the elderly will increase, with the society of the future including a large number of elderly people living on pensions but supported by a decreasing number of working people.

Social Security

In most agrarian societies, the aged have been kept within the shelter of their own extended families, contributing whatever they could and being respected for their age and experience. The giving of alms and the construction of institutions for the elderly have been fostered by religious organizations for thousands of years. During the nineteenth century, state support of the aged became law in many European countries. These legislative acts served as a stimulus and model for the "old age pension laws" of individual states in the U.S. during the first three decades of the current century.

The major federal programs that presently assist the elderly to maintain a subsistence income are listed in Table 6–2. The most important and costly of these programs are the Old Age and Survivors Insurance Program ("Social Security") and the Supplemental Security Income Program, both administered by the Social Security Administration. The Social Security program, which was initiated in 1935, provides for federally administered old-age, survivors', and disability insurance payments. The Social Security system is supported by employee paycheck deductions combined with employer contributions but receives no funds from federal sources. Retired workers are eligible for 80 per cent of full monthly old-age benefits at age 62 and for full benefits at 65. The amount of a family's benefits is higher if the wife is 62 or older and/or there is a disabled child under 18 or a child aged 18 to 21 in school. People between 65 and 72 can earn up to $3000 a year and still receive these benefits. Supplemental Security Income (SSI) payments, a welfare program supplied by most states, were made in 1977 to 4.3 million aged, blind, or disabled persons whose financial needs were not completely met by Social Security ("Social Security Checks . . .", 1977).

The magnitude of the Social Security program is demonstrated by the fact that in 1973 benefits were received by approximately 30 million people, of whom 15 million were retired workers and 3.6 million aged widows (Myers, 1974). By 1976–77, the number of beneficiaries of Social Security had risen to over 33 million. The total benefits paid in fiscal 1976–77 was $76 billion, one fifth of the entire federal budget (Kohlmeier, 1977).

Several changes were enacted in the Social Security system in 1973. The amount of the deceased spouse's benefits received by widows and dependent widowers was raised from 82½ to 100 per cent. Also, the amounts that employers and employees contribute

Table 6–2. MAJOR FEDERAL PROGRAMS IN INCOME
MAINTENANCE BENEFITING THE ELDERLY*

Program	Agency	Description
Civil Service Retirement	U.S. Civil Service Commission	Principal retirement system for federal civilian employees; financed by employee contributions matched by employing agency plus congressional appropriations. Provides monthly retirement benefits based on past earnings and length of service to eligible retirees and their survivors.
Old-Age, Survivors Insurance Program	Social Security Administration, HEW	Financed through the payroll tax on employees, employers, and self-employed persons. Social Security pays monthly cash benefits to retired workers (their dependents or survivors). Entitlement and level of benefits is based in part on covered earnings. Eligibility at age 65 or may opt for permanently reduced benefits at 62.
Railroad Retirement Program	Railroad Retirement Board	Financed through a payroll tax on employees and employers. Monthly benefits are paid to retired workers (their wives and survivors) after 10 years' employment. Coverage for individuals with less than 10 years' service is transferred to the Social Security system.
Supplemental Security Income Program	Social Security Administration, HEW	Aged, blind, and disabled persons, with no other income or with limited resources, are guaranteed monthly income. States may, and in some cases, must, supplement federal payments.
Veterans Pension Program	Veterans Administration	Provides monthly cash benefits to veterans aged 65 or older with at least 90 days military service, including 1 day wartime service, and who meet income limitation requirements. Benefits are also paid to designated survivor. Benefits vary according to veteran's annual income.

*Adapted from Select Committee on Aging. *Federal responsibility to the elderly.*
Washington, D.C., U.S. Government Printing Office, 1976, pp. 12–13.

was changed to 5.85 per cent of a portion of the latter's salary. Currently, the equivalent of over 12 per cent of an employee's salary is being paid into Social Security. The taxable income base was also raised in 1977 and again in 1978. This maximum "wage base" of taxable income was $16,500 in 1977 and $17,700 in 1978, and inflation is expected to raise it to $22,900 in 1979 and $25,900 in 1980. It is even possible that Congress will pass legislation requiring the employer to pay Social Security on the full earnings of every employee.

Realizing that annual increases in the cost of living were greater than rises in Social Security payments, the U.S. Congress passed legislation that attempts to link payments to the cost of living. During the early 1970s this amounted to a 10 to 20 per cent increase in benefits each year. In 1976, all those on Social Security received a 6.4 per cent cost-of-living increase, and in 1977 a 5.9 per cent increase. By July, 1977, the average Social Security benefit for an elderly widow or retired worker living alone was approximately $233 a month.

Although the Social Security system was designed to be self-supporting, the ratio of wage-earners to recipients decreased from a comfortable margin of 35 to 1 in 1945 to 3.2 to 1 thirty years later ("The Graying of America," 1977). In 1977–78 the system will pay out $5 billion more than it takes in, and if the current rates of contributions to the system are not increased substantially the system's reserve fund will be exhausted in a few years (Kohlmeier, 1977). Another suggested solution to the problem of financing the Social Security system is to accept the fact that the system can no longer be self-supporting and requires contributions from federal income tax revenues. Without such support the system may well be bankrupt within the next five years. Many members of Congress, however, have voiced a concern that if the U.S. treasury is thus "opened" to retirees, organizations of the elderly will exert considerable pressure for increased old-age benefits without commensurate tax increases, thus worsening the fiscal situation of the U.S. government. Whatever the level of financial support of the Social Security system by the government may become, as the cost of living and the number of elderly people increase still further, future generations of younger people will find themselves contributing more and more to the economic welfare of their elders.

In spite of difficulties in sustaining the present level of support, many public officials and social scientists maintain that old-age assistance programs in the U.S. are inadequate (Eisdorfer,

1975). They point to the more comprehensive programs of England, France, Germany, Israel, the Low Countries, Scandinavia, and certain Eastern countries as well. By their governmental programs and cultural attitudes that old-age benefits are a right and not charity, these nations reportedly do a better job of assisting their elderly populations (Rosow, 1968).

Other Pension Plans

The first federal pensions in the United States were the military pensions granted in 1792 to the veterans of the American Revolution. The present-day counterpart of those pensions is the Veterans Pension Program. Other federal pension programs are the Civil Service Retirement and the Railroad Retirement Program (see Table 6–2). In addition to government pensions, many business, industrial, and professional organizations have their own retirement plans. These pension programs, which cover less than 20 per cent of retirees, are experiencing many of the same problems as the Social Security system. The costs of all retirement programs have soared during recent years, and the ratio of the number of workers who contribute to the plans to the number of retirees has decreased by over 50 per cent in the past decade.

It is estimated that employees of the 100 largest American corporations have a $38 billion mortgage on the future of these corporations for pensions the workers have earned. This figure represents the estimated total for pensions promised by these corporations but for which there is currently no money in the bank (see "Pensions . . .", 1977). A company's pension liability is higher not only when it has more workers and a larger number of older workers but also when employees are represented by a strong union and the accounting policies of the company do not require full funding of pensions.

The Aged Poor

There is a great deal of truth in the saying that being sick but rich is better than being healthy but poor. Denials of the poets notwithstanding, money is related to happiness in old age, because it determines to some extent what people do with their time—whether they sit idly at home and brood, or get out, see people, and become interested in external affairs.

Approximately 16 per cent of the more than 20 million older Americans in the early 1970s were below the official poverty level (U.S. Bureau of the Census, 1973), and 2 million more were too poor to pay their medical expenses.[4] Owing to federal assistance programs, however, the number of older people below the poverty level decreased from 1 in 3 in 1967 to 1 in 6 in 1974.

Race, of course, is related to economic status, with almost three times as many blacks as whites being below the poverty level. Low income is also characteristic of American Indians, Mexican-Americans, and Puerto Ricans, but blacks constitute the largest minority group afflicted with poverty. Perry (1974), in comparing the economic condition of black and white elderly in 1969–70, cited the following statistics:

1. 50% of the black elderly and 23 per cent of white elderly were poor.
2. Most elderly black men had annual incomes of less than $3000, compared to $6000 for whites.
3. The median combined income of an elderly black couple was $3222, compared to $4884 for an elderly white couple.

Those elderly couples whose annual income is less than $3000, the majority of whom live in large cities, wage a daily battle against rising costs of food, clothing, housing, and medical care. This group includes many people who have not been accustomed to poverty but whose savings have long been depleted and who are now attempting to live on small Social Security payments. Unlike the traditional order of importance—food, clothing, and shelter—the elderly poor spend the greatest amount for rent and utilities, with clothing second, and food last. The difficulties that the aged poor encounter in attempting to live on fixed incomes is dramatically illustrated by a newspaper story of an elderly New York couple freezing to death after the heat in their apartment was turned off when they were unable to pay the fuel bill.

The Affluent Retiree

Currently over a half-million retirees in the United States are

Figure 6–2. Shuffleboard game with visiting granddaughter at Miami's Park West Community. (© 1978 Paul Barton.)

living in retirement villages or adult communities. These communities provide lifetime facilities for people who are able to invest $30,000 to $65,000 plus a maintenance charge in an apartment or house and who have a sizable annual income. Among the best-known of the "gerontopolises," which have blossomed throughout the nation but especially in the Southwest and Florida, are Sun City near Phoenix; Rossmoor Leisure Worlds of California, New Jersey, and Maryland: Park West in Miami; and The Sequoias in San Francisco. Two of the major developers are Del E. Webb, who founded Sun City with the slogan "happiness equals activity plus friendliness," and Ross W. Cortese, the entrepreneur of Leisure Worlds and Rossmoor (Walnut Creek, California).

Retirement communities have certain restrictions, and some are more luxurious than others. For example, no one under 50 can buy property in Sun City (pop. 35,000), and Park West bars dogs and has a time limit of three weeks for visits by children. The cost of a condominium apartment in a large metropolitan area or suburb or a house in a retirement village is usually beyond the financial resources of most retirees, especially the expensive facilities of Leisure World (Fig. 6–3). In spite of the cost, Leisure World, a cluster of Spanish-style dwellings in Laguna Hills, California, housing 14,000 retirees aged 52 and up, has no scarcity of applicants. Among its features are four heated swimming pools, tennis courts, a 27-hole golf course, bowling greens, restaurants, libraries, classrooms, a medical clinic, closed-circuit TV, and free bus rides to Los Angeles. Life at Leisure World, which is protected by six-foot walls and security guards who patrol around the clock, consists of a diversity of activities in physically safe surroundings (Fig. 6–3). About the only activity that it doesn't offer is employment, but some of its residents hold full- or part-time jobs.

There are, of course, disadvantages to retirement communities, even in the plush atmosphere of Leisure World. One retiree declared that Leisure World is a "pain in the neck" if you don't play golf or pool. Living exclusively with one's own age and socioeconomic group can also be boring and, one might argue, unrealistic. Some of the most successful and talented people in our society—which badly needs their problem-solving "know-how"—may become segregated from real life and stultified in a community dominated by play and relaxation.

SUMMARY

The percentage of employed elderly men has decreased steadily during this century, whereas the percentage of employed women has remained fairly constant. The unemployment rate among elderly men has been raised by those who are forced to retire before they are ready to do so. These men, who, like their younger counterparts, view their jobs as psychologically important parts of themselves, want to continue working as long as they are able.

Lack of satisfying work can affect both mental and physical health. This is especially true of older workers, who are even more committed to their jobs than younger people. Certainly the former group typically performs as well on the job as the latter. Despite this fact, unemployment is higher among elderly than younger men, especially in the case of minority groups. Many Western countries, faced with zero population growth, are raising retirement ages; certain U.S. industries have done the same.

The usual retirement ages of 60 for women and 65 for men were established by Social Security legislation in the 1930s and have

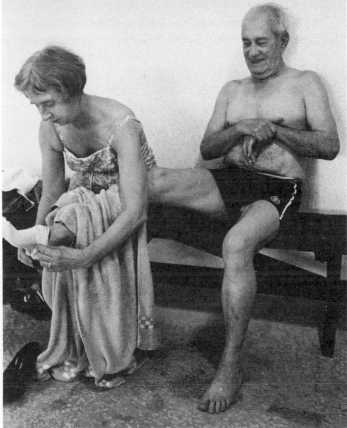

Figure 6-3. "Leisure World" and similar retirement centers offer the good life—to those older persons who can afford to pay the price. (Burk Uzzle/Magnum Photos, Inc.)

no real medical or psychological foundation. When, where, how, and with what to retire are decisions that workers should face but which are not always in their hands. Retirement is not necessarily a dreadful event; many people look forward to retiring and pursuing other goals. In any event, when to retire is a decision that should, insofar as possible, be made by the retiree. Recent challenges to mandatory retirement have emphasized this point and the injustice of pushing aside experienced and talented older workers. Preretirement planning can help the individual face and prepare for retirement. Clearly, not all of the stresses of retirement can be anticipated, but this fact can also be pointed out in preretirement counseling.

Reactions to retirement vary with personality, socioeconomic status, and whether or not the individual has meaningful roles to play. Reichard, Barrett, and others have described a number of personality types and their reactions to retirement. Blau emphasizes the tendency of modern society to view the social status of older people as one of "role obsolescence." The lack of meaningful roles to play is less true of older women, who continue to take care of the home, than of unemployed older men. The theory of disengagement views old age as a time of reduced involvement with society, whereas the activity theory emphasizes the importance of continued productivity and social interaction to personality adjustment in old age.

The income of retired elderly people is, on the average, no more than half that of the actively employed. The most common source of income is Social Security payments, although private pension funds and other government sources also contribute. Because of rapid increases in the ratio of retirees to workers, almost all of these pension plans, including Social Security, are presently on an unsound financial basis. In spite of the low average income of the elderly, the income range is quite wide, varying from that of the three million or more older Americans who subsist below the official poverty level to the affluent retirees of Leisure World and other retirement communities.

suggested readings

Atchley, R. C. *The social forces in later life* (2nd ed.). Belmont, Calif.: Wadsworth, 1977. Chaps. 7, 8, 9.

Fischer, D. H. *Growing old in America.* New York: Oxford University Press, 1977.

Kart, C. S., and Manard, B. (eds.). *Aging in America: Readings in social gerontology.* Part IV. Work, retirement and leisure. Port Washington, N.Y.: Alfred Publishing Co., 1976.

Plonk, M. A., and Pulley, M. A. Financial management practices of retired couples. *The Gerontologist,* 1977, *17*(3), 256–261.

Schultz, J. H. *The economics of aging.* Belmont, Calif.: Wadsworth, 1976.

notes

[1] The accuracy of this argument can certainly be questioned in light of the current employment situation.

[2] Available from the American Association of Retired Persons/1909 K St., N.W./Washington, D.C. 20006.

[3] In studies of the long-lived Abkhasians, it was found that almost all were still respected, productive members of their communities (Benet, 1974).

[4] The official poverty level in 1977 was $2572 per year for one person and $3232 for a family of two (Van Wey, 1977).

Chapter 7

Health Care, Living Environments, and Activities

According to authorities, income, housing, health, nutrition, and transportation are serious problems for the elderly. The first of these—income—is a source of difficulty for the majority of older Americans. Inadequate housing is a problem for a slightly lower percentage, but over 75 per cent of older Americans are afflicted with poor health. The problems are, of course, not independent of one another. Insufficient income, for example, is both a cause and an effect of other problems, with expenditures for housing, medical care, food, and transportation accounting for most of the income of the aged. Among the other problems encountered by older people are social roles, use of leisure time, safety, and the tendency to become segregated from the rest of society. Elderly people also admit to needing assistance with a host of mundane matters, ranging from the filling out of income tax forms to home repairs.

Since families are usually unable to take care of the expenses and other needs of their elderly members, the latter must either rely on their own resources or turn to governmental agencies and other organizations for help. This in itself can lead to the further problem of having to become familiar with a complex network of bureaucratic procedures. The bureaucratic maze is one in which no one seems to be acquainted with all of the rules or willing to explain them to the older people, who must place themselves in the hands of strangers. Lacking sufficient knowledge of organizations that were ostensibly established to help them, the elderly find themselves trapped not only by physical disability and lack of transportation but also by inadequate information and bureaucratic "know-how."

HEALTH CARE AND NUTRITION

Medical and dental bills are particularly destructive to the savings and income of the elderly, and the resources of the older person's family to help meet rising medical costs are generally limited. Per capita medical expenses for the elderly are estimated as averaging twice as much as for persons under 65. Consequently, the elderly must turn to federal and state governmental agencies for assistance in paying medical bills.

Health Care Insurance

The major federal health care programs that benefit the elderly are described in Table 7-1. Medicare and Medicaid, which are administered by the Social Security Administration, are the best-known and most widely applicable of these programs. Medicare, covering all people who are eligible for Social Security benefits, is divided into two parts. Part A (Health Insurance for the Aged— Hospital Insurance) pays for a large portion of hospital care and health care needed after leaving the hospital. Coverage under Part A is automatic, but individuals must apply for Part B (Supplemental Medical Insurance) and pay for it by a deduction from their Social Security checks. Part B pays for outpatient physician services, certain types of therapy, home health services, and other services and supplies. A premium of $7.70 per month was paid for Supplemental Medical Insurance by 24.8 million elderly and disabled persons in 1977. These premiums, however, took care of less than 30 per cent of the costs of the program; the federal government paid the remainder.

The Medicare program, initiated in 1965, pays only about half of the medical expenses of the elderly. The remaining amount must come from personal savings, private medical insurance, and other sources. One of these sources is the Medicaid program, which was designed for older people whose incomes are so low that they cannot afford Part B of Medicare or private health insurance. Medicaid (Medical Assistance Program) benefits come from federal grants to the states and cover 50 to 80 per cent of medical care. In order to be

Table 7–1. MAJOR FEDERAL HEALTH CARE
PROGRAMS BENEFITING THE ELDERLY*

Program	Executive Agency	Description
Health Resources Development Construction and Modernization of Facilities (Hill-Burton Program)	Health Service Administration of HEW	Federal formula grants and loans to public and private agencies, and to state governments for construction, expansion, or modernization of long-term care institutions and other outpatient and inpatient facilities. Federal share of project cost determined by designated state agency.
Construction of Nursing Homes and Intermediate Care Facilities	Federal Housing Administration (Housing and Urban Development)	Federal government insures loans to nonprofit agencies or individual sponsors to finance the construction, rehabilitation, or equipment supply of certified nursing homes or intermediate care facilities.
Grants to States for Medical Assistance Programs (Medicaid)	Social and Rehabilitation Service of HEW	Federal grants to states to cover 50–80% of costs of medical care for eligible low-income families and individuals. Within federal guidelines, states establish eligibility and scope of benefits.
Program of Health Insurance for the Aged and Disabled (Medicare)	Social Security Administration of HEW	Coverage of specified health care services for persons aged 65 or older and eligible disabled persons covered by Social Security.

*Adapted from Select Committee on Aging. *Federal responsibility to the elderly.*
Washington, D.C.: U.S. Government Printing Office (1976), pp. 6–7.

eligible for Medicaid benefits, the person must demonstrate a financial need ("means test"). In general, people who are eligible for old age assistance or welfare are also eligible for Medicaid.

There have been many criticisms of the federal health care programs, from both the elderly themselves and health-care professionals. Many older people object to the requirement that they pay the first $60 and 20 per cent of the remaining portion of their medical expenses in each calendar year. Poor people who cannot pay for Part B of Medicare may also be humiliated by the Medicaid means test. Health-care professionals may object to the paperwork involved in filing health insurance claims, to government "control" of medical services, and to the apparent unfairness of certain Medicare

Table 7-1. MAJOR FEDERAL HEALTH CARE
PROGRAMS BENEFITING THE ELDERLY
(*Continued*)

Program	Executive Agency	Description
		Part A (Hospital Insurance) covers hospital and post-hospital skilled nursing home care and home health services. Part B (Supplemental Medical Insurance), subject to premiums, covers physicians and other specified outpatient services.
Veterans Domiciliary Care Program	Veterans Administration	Federal funds for federal facilities, and project grants to states to construct and rehabilitate domiciliary care facilities for veterans, provides medical and personal care in residential type setting to aged and disabled veterans not requiring hospitalization; provides payments to facilities for provision of such services.
Veterans Nursing Home Care Program	Veterans Administration	Federal funds for federal facilities, and grants to states for construction of homes providing nursing home care to veterans, and for covering medical care services for veterans receiving such care.

provisions. As an illustration, when an elderly American who has been hospitalized with an acute medical condition (e.g., a broken leg) is transferred to a nursing home for convalescence, Medicare will pay most of the bill. But when he or she is sent directly home or judged unlikely to recover, Medicare will pay none of the post-hospital bill. Furthermore, Medicare does not cover the cost of spectacles, dental work, hearing aids, foot care, or drugs prescribed outside the hospital.

Added to the ever-increasing cost of medical bills, such criticisms and shortcomings as those noted above make it likely that current programs will be extended to some form of national health insurance during the next decade. More emphasis will also be placed on preventive medicine and perhaps less on spectacular medical achievements such as organ transplants that make headlines but cost a great deal and benefit a relatively small number of people. Beyond national health insurance, Butler (1975) envisages that it may even be necessary for medicine to become a public utility.

Nursing Homes

The "typical" older person is more likely to be found on a sunny park bench than in a nursing home, but there are approximately 30,000 of these homes in the United States, housing over a million people in all. Approximately 70 per cent of nursing-home residents are women, the majority of whom suffer from chronic brain disorders, heart disease, or cancer. They have been placed in these homes because they became disoriented and confused, wandered away from home, were incontinent, and/or showed the need for extensive nursing care (Butler, 1975). Some experts argue that 10 to 15 per cent of the elderly population should be in nursing institutions, whereas others feel that only about 2 per cent of the aged require nursing care.

The reputation that nursing homes have of being "houses of death" comes from the high mortality rate in these institutions. Up to 20 per cent of all deaths of the elderly occur in nursing homes (Kastenbaum and Candy, 1973), frequently during the first weeks or months of residency. One factor related to survival in a nursing institution is the attitude of the patient. A depressed attitude suggests a poor prognosis, and an angry or hostile attitude a good prognosis for living more than a few months after being admitted to a nursing home (Ferrare, 1962). A related variable is the degree of control that the patient feels over the situation: patients who feel that they have some influence over their environment tend to have more positive attitudes and hence to survive longer.

Illustrative of the relationship between degree of control and the attitudes of patients are the results of an experiment by Langer and Rodin (1976). The subjects, nursing-home patients between the ages of 65 and 90, were divided into two groups. One group was told by the home administrator that they still had a great deal of control over their own lives and should therefore decide how to spend their time. For example, they were encouraged to decide whether or not they wanted to see a movie that was being shown, and they were made responsible for taking care of a plant. The second (comparison) group of patients was assured that the nursing home staff was concerned with their well-being, but they were not encouraged to assume greater control over their own lives. They were told that the staff would inform them when they were to see the movie, and although they were also given a plant, they were told that the nurses would take care of it. Subsequent ratings of the happiness, alertness, and activity of the residents were obtained from the nurses and the residents themselves. The results showed significant increases in the happiness, alertness, and activity of the group urged to assume greater control over their lives, whereas the ratings of the comparison group on these variables declined.

The federal government began paying for nursing-home care through Medicaid in 1966, and the result has been very profitable for many businessmen. Money invested in a private nursing home may yield 40 per cent or more interest on one's investment in a single year. Unfortunately, the quality of the home typically fails to keep pace with the investors' profits. Ideally, a nursing home should provide excellent medical and convalescent care in a homelike atmosphere. It should be run by a trained hospital administrator who recognizes the need for both liveliness and quietness, depending on the patient and the situation, and makes provisions for them. This picture is reportedly truer of homes in England, Holland, and Scandinavia than in the U.S. and many other Western countries, where institutions for the aged too often merit the title of "deathbed dormitories" (de Beauvoir, 1972) (see Reports 7–1 and 7–2).

The quality of nursing homes varies widely, depending to some degree on whether the home is a skilled nursing facility, an

---

Report 7–1   A Profile of America's One Million Nursing Home Patients*

They are old:	Average age 82; 70 per cent are over 70.
Most are female:	Women outnumber men three to one.
Most are widowed:	Only 10 per cent have a living spouse. Widowed, 63 per cent; never married, 22 per cent; divorced, 5 per cent.
They are alone:	More than 50 per cent have no close relatives.
They are white:	Whites, 96 per cent; blacks, 2 per cent; others, 2 per cent.
They come from home:	Some 31 per cent come from hospitals, 13 per cent from other nursing homes, the remainder from their own homes.
Length of stay:	An average of 2.4 years.
Few can walk:	Less than 50 per cent are ambulatory.
They are disabled:	At least 55 per cent are mentally impaired; 33 per cent are incontinent.
They take many drugs:	Average, 4.2 drugs a day.
Few have visitors:	More than 60 per cent have no visitors at all.
Few will leave:	Only 20 per cent will return home. Some will be transferred to hospitals, but the vast majority will die in the nursing home.

---

* From *Parade*, July 17, 1977, p. 10.

Report 7-2   A Granddaughter's First Visit to a Nursing Home*

The smell of the place was so strong that I stepped back, trying to fight it off.... We stood for a moment looking at the recreation room. . . . A few of the residents chatted together. Several of them looked up hungrily at us, and one old lady in a wheelchair beckoned to me with a clawlike hand. Two bored attendants exchanged laconic comments, and a nurse in a starched white cap wiped the face of a sweating, palsied old man. A few old people had visitors and, jealously guarding them in inescapable clusters of chairs, they leaned forward to grab onto every word. The visitors looked guilty and uncomfortable and miserably self-conscious.

After the visit in the car, my mother turned to me. The brittle smile was gone from her face and she looked exhausted. "Well, Deb, what did you think?" I looked out at the street. "It's awful," I said flatly. "It's horrible and ugly and smelly and I can't understand," my voice rose, "how you can let Gram be so miserable!" My mother turned her head slightly so I couldn't look directly into her eyes. My father glanced away from the icy street long enough to give Mom a look of compassion.

"We know, Deb," he said mildly. "We know. But there's really nothing else to do."

intermediate care facility, or a nonskilled institutional or private-home facility. Los Angeles' Keiro ("Home for Respected Elders"), for example, is a nursing home in which members of the Japanese-American community have no misgivings about placing their parents. On the other hand, the nursing care in many private homes is so poor that a number of experts have advocated replacing all existing nursing homes with government-owned and professional-staffed facilities. People who entrust their parents to a nursing home should be much more concerned about such matters as nurse/patient ratio, the availability of creative facilities and physical therapy equipment, and the frequency of physicians' visits (Jacoby, 1974). Furthermore, federal standards for these institutions, which were actually lowered in 1974, should be raised and enforced.

Among the alternatives to institutionalization that have been proposed is the multigenerational household. One investigator (Sussman, 1977) reported that members of 60 per cent of the 365 households that he interviewed indicated that they would be willing to care for elderly relatives in their homes, particularly if the family were financially reimbursed by a monthly check of $200 to $400. Only about 20 per cent of the respondents stated that they would not accept an older person in their home under any circumstances, the primary reason for refusal being a bad experience with an aged relative.

Nutrition

Eating alone or out of loneliness and skipping meals because food is too expensive or because of loss of interest in cooking or

---

*After Saul, 1974, pp. 63, 68. Reproduced with permission.

eating can cause serious nutritional problems for the elderly. Realizing that a large percentage of the elderly either fail to select or cannot afford a nutritionally balanced diet, the federal government has provided funds for several tax-supported nutrition programs. The Nutrition Program for the Elderly (Title VII of the Older Americans Act of 1965, as amended) provides, through state agencies, low-cost group meals and home-delivered meals for persons 60 years old and older. A part of this program known as "Meals on Wheels" provides for the delivery of hot food to the homes of the aged, whereas another section of the program arranges for transportation for the elderly to nutrition sites in the community.

Another nutrition program, even more extensive than the Nutrition Program for the Elderly because it involves all age groups, is the Food Stamp Program. Under this program, individuals or families with low incomes may purchase food stamps that are worth more than the purchase price. The exact value of the stamps depends on the purchaser's income. Also under this program, homebound or handicapped people over 60 can exchange food stamps for meals delivered to their homes.

LIVING ENVIRONMENTS

The living environment of a person includes not only the house, apartment, or room in which he or she lives but also the immediate community and even the wider world if it has an effect on his or her behavior. Older people live in a variety of settings, mostly in rural areas, small towns, and the poorer sections of large cities. As described in the preceding section, 5 per cent of them live in nursing homes. And as noted in Chapter 6, only a small percentage can afford the plush accommodations of a Leisure World retirement community. Residences of people who are 60 years old or older are clustered in special buildings in large cities, in certain neighborhoods within suburbs, and even in specific regions of the nation. On the lower end of the socioeconomic scale are thousands of older people who survive in $15-a-week rooms in the shabbiest sections of large cities. When they are not in their rooms, many of these urban elderly congregate in large outdoor parks near old hotels (e.g., MacArthur Park in Los Angeles) or at bus terminals and other sheltered public places. Whatever their living accommodations may be, more than 70 per cent remain in their home communities and in the same homes. One reason that the elderly do not relocate even when it is advantageous to do so is that they are greatly affected by the psychological shocks and losses that result from severing ties with their home communities.

Seventy per cent of the elderly live in their own homes, and only about 20 per cent live with their children. Over 25 per cent of old people, a large majority of whom are widows, live alone. Most elderly men, but a minority of elderly women, live with their spouses. The elderly value their independence, and most prefer to live in their own homes rather than with family members, taking occasional walks about the neighborhood and visiting family and friends. Arguing for a more flexible type of extended family, Curtin (1972) noted that the separation of grandparents from other family members favors nuclear rather than extended families and places an even greater stress on housing facilities. Because they live in their own households and require more services, the expense of maintaining older people is greater than that for other age groups. It is generally true that only when they cannot fend for themselves do older individuals express a willingness to live with a family.

Housing

In spite of low incomes, as a result of a lifetime of work and house payments, two thirds of the elderly own their own homes. Many of these homes, however, are fairly humble dwellings, having been built during an earlier era. They are frequently unsafe and in need of repairs, but the costs of home repairs, property taxes, and utilities have risen greatly in recent years. These accelerated costs make it difficult for people living on fixed incomes to maintain independent households. Many states give a property tax break to senior citizens, but housing and attendant costs are still more than the average retirement income can handle. Those elderly people who live in rental housing are no better off, usually paying a disproportionate amount of their income for rent. The best that many of them can afford is an apartment in a center-city neighborhood where the crime rate is high.

Because of the rapid increase in the number of people in this age group, coupled with inflation, the need for better housing has received a high priority among the many federal programs for the elderly. U.S. government statistics indicate that 20 to 30 per cent of the housing units for the elderly are substandard, unsafe, in disrepair; they lack private bathrooms, hot water, and other conveniences. Table 7–2 describes the major federal housing programs designed to benefit the elderly. These programs are particularly concerned with subsidizing the construction and repair of housing for older people who are living on low or moderate incomes. Another federal service, a directory of housing constructed especially for older people, is provided by the National Council on the Aging. Information on low- to moderate-income housing, tax relief, and grants for rent payments can be obtained from local housing authorities, tax collection agencies, and Senior Citizens Centers in the community.

Social designers and space managers have not shown enough concern for the needs of the elderly in the planning of living environments. More attention obviously needs to be given to the kinds of housing that are adequate now and will be appropriate for older people in the foreseeable future. This requires the combined efforts of architects, home economists, builders, and developers in designing living spaces that are suitable during later life. In 1977 there were only about three million housing units in the United States designed specifically for the aged, including everything from apartments to intermediate and advanced medical-care facilities ("Housing the Aged," 1977). These facilities may be classified according to the age groups for which they are intended: (1) fully independent, including apartments for "go-go" people in the 65 to 75 year age range; (2) partially dependent, comprising something in between apartments and nursing homes for "slow-go" people in the 75 to 85 year age range; (3) totally dependent, including nursing homes for the "no-go" people over age 85.

Promises made during the 1976 presidential campaign included better housing for the elderly, but so far little has been done by way of keeping those promises. A primary reason for this failure is undoubtedly a shortage of money, but many of the adjustments needed to make housing more suited to the needs of the elderly are neither difficult nor terribly expensive (Table 7–3). Furthermore, lack of government funding should not keep us from thinking and proposing solutions: We need to determine whether, for example, there should be more planned towns, one-level apartments, and single-person family dwellings.

In spite of their well-intentioned efforts, designers of retirement homes, geriatric clinics, and other living environments for the aged do make mistakes. For example, the designers may emphasize the provision of more space for social interaction, only to have the increased space result in decreased social interaction. Perhaps the most serious error in designing a living environment for the elderly is

Table 7–2. MAJOR FEDERAL HOUSING PROGRAMS
BENEFITING THE ELDERLY*

Program	Executive Agency	Description
Housing for the Elderly	Housing Production and Mortgage Credit of HUD	Federal loans for construction or rehabilitation of multifamily rental housing for elderly (aged 62 and over). Tenants may qualify for rent supplements under the Section B program.
Low and Moderate Income Housing	Housing Production and Mortgage Credit of HUD	Provides housing assistance payments for low-income persons and families who cannot afford "decent and sanitary housing in the private sector." Rent supplements cover the difference between the community's fair market rent down to 15–25% of the tenants' adjusted income.
Mortgage Insurance on Rental Housing for the Elderly	Housing Production and Mortgage Credit of HUD	Federal government insures against loss on mortgages for the construction and rehabilitation of multifamily rental housing for the elderly (aged 62 or over) or disabled whose income is higher than the low or moderate income level.
Rural Rental Housing Loans	Farmers Home Administration of Dept. of Agriculture	Federal government makes direct and guaranteed loans to construct, improve, or repair rental or cooperative housing in rural areas for low-income persons including senior citizens aged 62 or over.

*Adapted from Select Committee on Aging. *Federal responsibility to the elderly.* Washington, D.C.: U.S. Government Printing Office, 1976, pp. 8–9.

to assume that because of their age all older people have basically the same needs and desires. Nothing could be further from the truth. A special age-segregated environment may help some old people to maintain a sense of dignity in the face of advancing years, whereas for others it results only in detachment and loneliness.

Living in a society always involves relationships with other people, even if the relationship is one of total disregard. Recognizing this fact, we are faced with the questions of whether greater efforts should be made to reinstitute the extended family and/or to integrate

Table 7–2. MAJOR FEDERAL HOUSING PROGRAMS
BENEFITING THE ELDERLY (*Continued*)

Program	Executive Agency	Description
Community Development	Community Planning and Development of HUD	Formula grants to urban communities, based on poverty population and other economic and population factors, for variety of community development activities, including construction of senior citizens' centers.
Rental and Co-operative Housing for Lower and Moderate Income Families	Housing Production and Mortgage Credit of HUD	The federal government subsidizes down to 1% of the interest on mortgages for private developers of multifamily housing for low and moderate income families, persons aged 62 and over, and handicapped individuals.
Low Rent Public Housing	Housing Production and Mortgage Credit of HUD	Local housing authorities receive federal loans to aid in the purchase, rehabilitation, leasing, or construction of multifamily housing for low income families, individuals aged 62 and over, and handicapped individuals. Housing designed for the elderly may have congregate dining rooms and other special features. Rents may not be more than 25% of the family's income.

older people into the total community. One interesting and apparently successful experiment in Philadelphia involves the Quaker idea of ''life centers'' in communal living, where people of all ages live in a large house, sharing costs, housework, meals, and, perhaps most important, conversation and feelings.

Transportation

The ability to extend one's environment and to participate in the wider community depends greatly on communication and transportation facilities. Among the services supported by Title II of the

Table 7–3. RECOMMENDED ADJUSTMENTS IN
HOUSING FOR THE ELDERLY*

Entrances	For persons with limited mobility, single-story or ground floor residences are best. At least one incline should have a ramp, properly mounted handrails being placed on either side of the ramp. An open space adjacent to the door should be provided.
General Structural Features	Carefully designed doors for disabled persons lacking in strength, grasping power, coordination, or visual acuity. Eliminate raised thresholds if possible; if not, paint them with a contrasting color. Cover floors with nonslip but easy-to-maneuver surfaces. Make walls smooth.
Kitchen	Storage facilities should allow for easy retrievability of items. Open storage shelves, revolving and pull-out shelves, peg-boards, and magnetic catches are recommended. Kitchen counters should be low and have recesses. Dishwasher, washer, dryer, oven, and other large appliances should be front-opening.
Bathrooms	Should be larger than is customary in new homes, to allow for wheelchair or walker. Install grab-bars near tub, shower, sink, and toilet. Install seat in tub or shower; nonslip floors, shower floor flush with outside floor and sloping slightly toward drain. A wall-hung toilet which is higher than usual is an advantage in transferring from a wheelchair. Other fixtures should be low enough to permit easy use by those with limited mobility. Help buttons, nonscald controls on mixing faucets, warm air dryers, counters on either side of lavatory, sinks positioned for ease of access—all are recommended features.
Bedrooms	Should be large enough to permit elderly to move around with ease. Mattresses should be level with wheelchair seat height. Closets should have sliding or swing-out doors and at least one rod. Light switches, telephone, and alarm units must be near the head of the bed.
Lighting	Light switches must be approximately 90 cm. (3 ft.) from the floor, wall outlets 45–60 cm. (18–24 in.) high. Lights must be placed near bed, bath, and medicine cabinet.
Other Considerations	Large elevators should be provided in multiple-family dwellings. Easy accessibility to public transportation; climate, air quality, and noise control are also recommended.

*After Agan, Casto, Day, and Schwab (1977).

Older Americans Act of 1965 (as amended) are telephone reassurance and information, as well as transportation and outside assistance with household chores. Title III of the same act supports Model Projects to provide transportation to older persons.

Transportation is often a problem for the elderly, not only in rural areas that have little public transportation but also in many suburban and urban areas. Whenever food stores, doctors' offices, banks, and other shops and facilities are not near their residences, transportation problems arise for older people. Those who are impaired by disease or disability have special difficulty in getting from place to place, particularly when they do not drive and public transportation is scarce and costly. Even taxicabs frequently pass old people by, because of the perception of the elderly by many cab drivers as passengers who take more time and tip less.

Because of their dependence on others to take them from place to place, lack of transportation restricts the life space and life style of the elderly in many cities. This is especially true in the case of the poor, who become isolated and lonely. Transportation is less of a problem for the elderly in places where transit companies offer reduced fares to senior citizens and in those states that provide free statewide public transportation to the elderly. Title II of the Older Americans Act of 1965 provided some transportation facilities, but sections of the Urban Mass Transportation Act and the Federal Highway Act of 1973 (both administered by the U.S. Department of Transportation) are broader in scope. The first of these acts provides capital assistance grants for use by public and nonprofit private groups to support mass transportation and reduced fares for the elderly and handicapped during non-peak hours. The Rural Highway Public Transportation Demonstration Project of the Federal Highway Act has awarded project grants to public and nonprofit private agencies for projects aimed at developing and improving the use of public mass transportation in rural areas.

CRIME AND THE ELDERLY

Living in a neighborhood with a high crime rate can be dangerous for anyone, but especially for old people who are alone or in poor health. In fact, the elderly view crime, and the fear of it, as their number-one problem ("Step-up in Fight . . .," 1977). The newspapers are full of stories of defenseless elderly people who have been the repeated victims of burglary, robbery, purse-snatching, assault, and even rape. These are the most common violent crimes against the elderly, although nonviolent fraud occurs even more frequently.

Checkday is especially dangerous for older people; nearly 20,000 Social Security checks and thousands of relief checks are stolen each year in purse-snatchings, burglaries, and muggings. Because of their inability to resist, aged widows and others who live alone are the favorite targets of teenage and young-adult hoodlums. Unable to sleep at night through fear of being robbed or mugged, elderly people in large cities must frequently sleep during the day.

Some are so afraid that in spite of the need to get out and enjoy exercise and social interaction, they literally become prisoners in their own homes. Occasionally, an elderly victim of continued muggings and thefts is murdered or simply gives up out of weariness and despair and decides to die by his or her own hand.

Coping with Crime

Regardless of where they live, it is a good policy for old people (and all people, in fact) not to keep large sums of money on their person or in the home, not to open the door to strangers, not to go out alone (especially at night!) unless absolutely necessary, and not to fight back if attacked. Meanwhile, top priority is being given in many American cities to the prevention of crime against the elderly and to assisting its victims. Representative of these efforts are specially trained police units that perform surveillance and escort services for the elderly at times when the latter are most vulnerable (at night, while shopping, going to the bank, etc.). The officers in these units also inform the elderly about recent trends in crime, how to detect criminal behavior, and how to serve as witnesses in criminal cases. The officers of the Bronx Senior Citizens Robbery Unit are trained not only in the prevention of crimes against the elderly but also in helping older victims cope with the shock and loss resulting from a crime and in being of assistance in finding and prosecuting the criminal(s).

Other programs that have been instituted in many cities include "Neighborhood Watch," which teaches people how to spot ongoing crimes and to protect themselves against burglaries and other felonies. Special buses and drivers, especially on checkday, and "ride along" escorts and security aids to walk the streets in high crime areas are other new features of the crime-prevention programs in certain cities. Furthermore, not all of the programs cost the taxpayers money. New York City's service of 1000 teenage escorts for the elderly, for example, is completely voluntary.

Exploitation of the Aged

Assaults on old people who are walking or traveling by bus to the supermarket or bank, or robbery in their homes, are not the only ways in which they are relieved of their checks. Con men, door-to-door salesmen, and medical quacks also exploit the elderly by falsely promising them renewed health, physical attractiveness, a comfortable estate in the Southwest, or a way to get rich quick on a small monetary investment. For example, old people are the victims of 90 per cent of the swindles in California, the amount of money that they lose from con games in Los Angeles being greater than the total amount netted in bank robberies in that city ("Step-up in Fight . . .," 1977). Fraud need not be flagrant or obvious. Cosmetic, pharmaceutical, and real estate firms all promise the moon and frequently give nothing but false hopes and empty pocketbooks to the aged. Even funeral directors are suspect; some of them capitalize on the guilt and grief of widows and widowers at a time when the survivors need psychological support and other forms of assistance, not separation from their pension checks and meager savings.

The Criminal Aged

Like people of all ages, old people themselves may be perpetrators as well as victims of misdemeanors and felonies. One elderly woman, for example, devised an effective technique for shoplifting in department stores by pretending to be senile. She would "accidentally and awkwardly" knock piles of items off the shelves and slip them under her clothes during the resulting confusion.

Barrett (1972) argues that the typical crimes committed by the elderly—drunkenness, liquor law violations, vandalism, gambling—are "companionship delinquencies" because they result primarily from a search for companions. In any event, aged criminals usually commit relatively harmless illegal acts rather than crimes involving violence against persons. Whatever the type of crime, criminal behavior on the whole declines consistently after adolescence and is much less common among the elderly than in other age groups. A possible exception to this age decline in crime is suicide, which, especially in white males, increases with age (see Chap. 5). Many authorities, however, criticize the classification of suicide as a crime. In the seriously ill, for example, it may be viewed rather as self-euthanasia.

ACTIVITIES OF THE AGED

Engaging in illegal activities is hardly one of the major pastimes of the elderly, but when it occurs it may be caused by boredom or the desire for something interesting to do rather than mere acquisitiveness. Men who are facing retirement often worry about how they will use their time, and, to be sure, the complaint of "too much time on my hands" is often heard from the recently retired. Those who fail to develop hobbies or other interests can easily become worried and anxious when faced with a succession of empty days. For this reason, preretirement counselors stress that it is just as important for the retiree to develop a program of activities as it is to make financial plans.

Planning for the use of leisure time should certainly not be confined to later life. As people put in fewer and fewer hours each day on the job and retire earlier, the question of how the increased leisure time can be used to help them grow and fulfill their potentialities becomes crucial for all age groups. Just as people are taught to have the traditional, culturally prescribed "right" attitude toward work, so too must they learn the newer "right" attitude toward leisure (Neulinger and Raps, 1972).

Workers who think of their occupations as dull or taxing, and those (e.g., teachers) who have become accustomed to long vacations are less likely to experience problems in occupying themselves after retirement. But many other retirees have to learn by themselves or be taught how to cope with leisure time. The retired urban office worker whose situation does not permit part-time work and who has failed to plan for post-retirement activities may find himself or herself at a loss for something to do. By way of contrast, the retired farmer or carpenter can continue to till or tinker within the limits of his or her strength and ability.

Using Leisure Time

The ways in which older people fill their time are greatly influenced by the leisure activities in which they engaged during middle age. The activities of retired men need not be limited to the traditional old-age pastimes of fishing, gardening, shuffleboard, pool, and golf. Only 15 per cent of retirees who are not in institutions are seriously restricted in their activities (Van Wey, 1977b). Consequently, many older people take up tennis, jogging, and other vigorous activities which they may never have attempted in earlier years. But for most elderly individuals, daily walks constitute the best kind of physical exercise.

The importance of regular physical exercise at any stage of

Report 7–3   Sex vs. Athletics*

Dear Dr. Solomon: Is it actually a fact that cutting out sex during training can help make for better athletic performance?—Chuck W.

Dear Chuck: That used to be the theory, and athletes were kept on a pretty short tether just before major events. But now it has gone by the board—with one or two exceptions. There was a report from Athens not so long ago about Dimitri Iordanidis, 98, who had run 42 miles in seven hours, forty minutes in the annual marathon for all comers. He explained that in order to be up to this at his age you had to give up sex—which he had done at 85.

life cannot be overemphasized. Many people who do not realize that immobility can cause serious physical disorders are stricken by illness at a time of life when they are not even thinking about old age. Enforced limitations on one's activities can increase the rate of both physical and mental deterioration. For example, in studies con-ducted by N. D. Mankovsky of the Soviet Institute of Gerontology it was found that a 50 to 60 year old person who is put to bed for three weeks and prevented from moving will show many of the same symptoms as a heart attack patient ("Soviets Say . . . ", 1977). From these experiments and interview data collected on very old people, Mankovsky concluded that work is an invaluable remedy against premature aging.

As discussed in Chapter 6, people who continue to work at something, at least part-time, appear to adjust better to old age than those who act as if retirement were synonymous with idleness. Un-fortunately, retirees are not always able to do what they desire. Many cannot afford to pursue the crafts and hobbies or the intellectual and artistic pursuits in which they are interested. Furthermore, arbitrary age limits sometimes inhibit the minority who try to become proficient in a new craft or vocation. A case in point is that of a retired furniture salesman who finally had the time to become what he had always wanted to·be—a carpenter. Offering to work free as an apprentice to learn the trade, he was told that unions would object or that insurance would not cover the risk. Since he was too old to join a trade-school carpentry class, he was directed to a hobby shop where he was forced to settle for wood-burning rather than the furniture-making that he had wanted to learn all his life (Curtin, 1972).

Many older people read a great deal, principally newspapers and magazines, but also books. The facilities of libraries are used extensively by the aged for recreational purposes and for obtaining information about health, financial, and vocational matters. Special

---

* From *Albuquerque Journal,* August 27, 1977, p. B–12.

book lists, books with large print, and places where older people can meet for discussions are also made available by libraries. The Older Reader Services program, financed by the U.S. Office of Education, makes grants available to public libraries for the purchase of special materials and the development of other programs and services for the aged.

Some of the organizations that sponsor activities for the elderly (e.g., Senior Citizens Centers and Golden Age Clubs) have been mentioned previously. These organizations make available discount tickets for entertainment programs, travel, and other forms of recreation, along with many other services. Golden Age Passports, which are issued to permanent U.S. residents aged 62 years and older, provide free admission to national parks, monuments, and recreation areas, and a 50 per cent discount on fees for the use of federally controlled facilities and services (camping, boat launching, parking, etc.) in these areas. Older people also take part in volunteer work, clubs, and lodges, and visit with their friends and relatives frequently. Additional activities include going to church and other meeting places, taking walks, watching television, and listening to the radio. Closed-circuit radio and television programs designed especially for the elderly, whether in households or institutions, are broadcast in many cities.

The leisure-time activities of the older generation differ in many respects from those of younger people, but this is certainly caused as much by generational (cohort) differences as by chronological age. Consequently, rather than playing checkers or shuffleboard, and doing gardening, the next generation of older people may spend more of their leisure time swimming, playing musical instruments, visiting museums, and engaging in other interests of today's young and middle-aged adults. And in spite of the differences, there is at least one similarity between the interests of young and old Americans of today: at times they both enjoy shopping and bargain-hunting.

The Aged Consumer

The buying power of the American elderly population is currently over $75 billion a year, representing a sizable market for goods and services that older people need or desire. Vitamins, laxatives, and other health and beauty aids are not the only items purchased by the elderly. Sales of clothing, books, games, art supplies, and vacation trips also thrive in the over-65 population.

Although the elderly are not nearly as homogeneous in their purchasing behavior as teenagers, the disproportionate growth of the elderly population and the likelihood that this trend will continue during the foreseeable future is affecting the plans of manufacturers of consumer products. Among the items that are predicted to sell well in the near future are various games (backgammon, mah-jongg, electronic games of all kinds), smaller automobiles, motor homes, and campers.

Whatever the future may hold for the marketers, as was pointed out earlier in the chapter many elderly people are being cheated by salesmen right now. "Bargains," "free gifts," "prizes," and other commercial "come-ons" find susceptible victims in elderly people who are searching for more interesting and satisfying lives. Such is also the case with fraudulent nostrums and other ineffective health items. There are organizations that attempt to provide information and protection for the elderly consumer, but too many old people continue to pay exorbitant prices or throw away their money on empty promises.

Politics and the Elderly

Responding to the challenge to fight back against their public image and exploitation as well as the need for companionship with a purpose, the elderly are becoming more organized today than at any time since the Townsend movement of the 1930s. Older people are showing a greater interest in demanding self-respect and protesting such discriminatory practices as fixed retirement ages and segregation by age.

Approximately six million older Americans, compared to only 250,000 ten years ago, now belong to local, state, and national organizations. Chief among these organizations, which are not mere social clubs but political action groups, are: American Association of Retired Persons (AARP), National Council of Senior Citizens (NCSC), Gray Panthers, International Senior Citizens Association (ISCA), National Alliance of Senior Citizens (NASC), and the National Caucus on the Black Aged (NCBA) (see Appendix for addresses). The two largest of these organizations—AARP and NCSC—boast memberships of several million.

That the elderly can wield a great deal of political power when

Figure 7-1. Politically-oriented organizations of the elderly are becoming a powerful voice for the rights of the American aged. (*Mental Health,* 1974.)

they are organized behind a common cause is shown by the fact that 90 per cent are registered to vote, representing some 15 per cent of the electorate, and they vote quite regularly. Sixty-four per cent of this "crutch, cane, and Cadillac" vote, as it was dubbed by one pundit, cast ballots in the 1972 presidential election, and 70 per cent voted in the 1974 congressional elections (Flieger, 1976). By way of comparison, only 41 per cent of young people between the ages of 18 and 24 voted in the elections of 1974.

What political issues are of concern to the elderly? To begin with, as a group the elderly are admittedly more conservative in their political attitudes than younger people. Kastenbaum (1971) believes that the conservative streak of older people is a reaction to what society has taken away from them in terms of status and opportunity. He suggests that the elderly might feel less threatened and not so obsessed with clinging to what they possess if they were given more positive social roles to play and equality with younger adults in employment.

Older people as a group are concerned with self-maintenance, but this does not necessarily imply retaining the status quo. Members of the Gray Panthers, a 6000-member political lobby founded by Margaret ("Maggie") E. Kuhn, are quite "liberal" or "progressive" in their efforts to improve tax laws, health laws, bus service, and other rights and benefits for the elderly ("Gray Panther Power," 1975). In addition, considering the high level of education in the current generation of young and middle-aged adults and the experiences they have lived through (thermonuclear bomb threats, Vietnam War, Watergate), it is likely that the next two generations of older people will be more liberal than the current one. Not only should these future generations possess a greater understanding of the problems of their own age group and those of the wider society, but also it can be hoped that they will be more willing and able to do something about those problems.

Most politicians recognize that the 1980s will be a time to

Figure 7–2. Elderly demonstrators in Chicago: "Don't agonize—organize." (Used by permission of *Newsweek*. Photo by Julie Jensen.)

focus on the rights of the aged and that the organized over-65 vote will carry a great deal of political clout. Political action by organized groups of older people has already been successful in shutting down inadequate nursing homes in Illinois, stopping Medicaid cuts in New York, arranging for the placement of traffic lights at busy intersections in Michigan, and obtaining bus fare discounts in several dozen cities. A "Rosie the Riveter" convention to encourage older working women to keep working was held in Oakland, California, in 1977.

The elderly populations of several large American cities (New York, Boston, Chicago), each with several hundred senior-citizens clubs, are quite active politically. Some of the aims of their efforts are to obtain property- and income-tax reforms, more extensive health-care benefits, better housing, and better transportation for the elderly. Other issues, on which congressional legislation is pending, are reforms in Social Security and private pensions. It is even possible that the city of Washington, D.C., may one day soon be treated to a retirees' march down Pennsylvania Avenue!

SUMMARY

Income, housing, health, nutrition, and transportation are serious, interrelated problems for the elderly. In spite of Medicare and Medicaid, medical and dental bills can be destructive of the savings and income sources of the elderly. The ever-increasing cost of medical bills necessitates changes in current government health programs, probably to some form of national health insurance, within the next few years.

The quality of nursing and rest homes for the elderly is a source of continuing concern, although old-age care facilities vary greatly in quality. Various alternatives to institutionalization of the elderly have been proposed, including the multigenerational household. At the very least, closer supervision of the facilities, staff, and practices of nursing homes needs to be maintained by official agencies.

Nutrition programs for the elderly, including "Meals on Wheels," have been prompted by the recognition that many elderly people are unable to select or afford a nutritionally balanced diet. Greater public concern regarding the living environments, especially housing, of the elderly is also being witnessed. The expertise of social designers, architects, home economists, physicians, and other professionals is, at least to a limited degree, being brought to bear in the design of safe and comfortable living environments for the elderly. Many of the recommended changes in current housing are not particularly expensive, but entire communities designed for the elderly may run into millions of dollars. Also recognized in federal legislation, as well as state and local action, is the need for more convenient and safer transportation facilities for the elderly.

Both nonviolent and violent crimes against the elderly have increased in recent years. Especially common are purse-snatchings, burglaries, and muggings. Law enforcement agencies in many large cities have special programs designed to inform the elderly about crime and protect them against it. The elderly are also exploited and swindled as repeated victims of commercial fraud. Finally, although the incidence of crime declines in later life, certain elderly people commit misdemeanors and felonies. The most common crimes of the elderly are drunkenness, liquor law violations, vandalism, and suicide.

Effective use of leisure time is one factor emphasized by preretirement counseling. In addition to the traditional activities of fishing, gardening, and the like, many old people engage in jogging, tennis, and other vigorous activities. Both physical and mental exercise appear to be contributing factors to a long and interesting life. Participation in the arts and crafts, in addition to reading and travel, can be enjoyable and not necessarily costly pursuits.

Because of increasing numbers of old people, coupled with the civil-rights spirit of the times, the elderly have taken a much more active interest in politics during recent years. Organizations for the elderly, many of which are politically quite active, abound. Of primary concern to the members of these organizations are the issues and problems that have been discussed in Chapters 6 and 7: employment, retirement, Social Security, health care, housing, transportation, and crime.

suggested readings

Antunes, G. E., Cook, F. L., Cook, T. D., and Skogan, W. G. Patterns of personal crime against the elderly. *The Gerontologist,* 1977, *17*(4), 321–327.

Housing the aging. *Architectural Record,* 1977, *161*(5), 123–144.

Jacoby, S. Waiting for the end: On nursing homes. *The New York Times Sunday Magazine,* March 31, 1974, pp. 13–15ff.

Kart, C. S., and Manard, B. (eds.). *Aging in America: Readings in social gerontology.* Part VI. Institutionalization. Port Washington, N.Y.: Alfred Publishing Co., 1976.

Tobin, S. S., and Lieberman, M. A. *Last home for the aged: Critical implications of institutionalization.* San Francisco: Jossey-Bass, 1976.

Chapter **8**

Death and Bereavement

The realization that people are mortal and the fear of death begin very early in life, but it is often difficult for a person to conceive of and accept the inevitability of his own death. People in modern societies, which keep the dying and deceased away from public view, usually go through life without thinking much about death and the fact that "life is as fragile as a dream." Consequently, they are surprised when someone whom they know—especially a person of their own generation—dies. However, the physical deterioration that accompanies aging, coupled with the aging and dying of family members and friends, forces people to face the event in life that they look forward to the least. Erikson (1968) feels that it is the realization that time is short and death is imminent that precipitates the integrity vs. despair crisis of the terminal period of life. Attempting to deal with death is, however, not something that waits for the final developmental period. Conquest of the fear of death usually begins in young adulthood or middle age, and by the time one reaches old age it is the process of dying rather than death itself that is feared.

DEATH: BIOLOGICAL, PHILOSOPHICAL, AND LEGAL CONSIDERATIONS

Until recent years, *thanatology,* the study of death (Greek *thanatos* = death), was something of a taboo topic for research and study. This situation has changed rapidly, and there are now many research investigations and writings on the biological, psychological, philosophical, and legal aspects of dying.

174

The Biology of Dying

Quite a bit has been discovered about the biological processes involved in dying, although there is still ample room for debate. The death of a human being does not occur in a single instant. Certain body structures—the thymus gland, for example—deteriorate before the person is fully mature. In fact, even before an individual is born body cells are constantly dying and being replaced by new cells. The building up and breaking down of body cells and structures, known as anabolism and catabolism, respectively, are complementary metabolic processes. As the individual grows older, the rate of breaking down begins to exceed the rate of building up, a point that is reached earlier with some body structures than with others.

The traditional definition of death as the cessation of heartbeat and brain activity has been a popular topic of discussion. "Brain death," in which all electrical activity of the brain has ceased for a certain period of time and which is indicated by no response on the electroencephalogram, is the usually accepted medical definition. When the individual is said to be "dying," the cells of the higher brain centers, which are very susceptible to oxygen deprivation, die first (5 to 10 minutes after their oxygen supply is cut off). Next, the lower brain centers die, including the medulla oblongata, which regulates respiration, heartbeat, and other vital reflexes.

When the heart stops beating but its pumping action is restored by electric shock ("countershock") before the vital centers of the brain are affected, a person who is technically dead has been restored to life. Unfortunately, if the higher brain centers have been affected, the person will probably not regain all of the sensory-motor or mental skills. The cells of certain glands and muscles die only after the medulla has stopped functioning, but skin and bone cells can live for several hours longer. The cells of certain tissues—the intestines, for example—continue to function for an even longer period of time, and when placed in a special physiological solution have been kept "alive" for years (Selkurt, 1975).

It is an article of faith of the Cryonics Society (Greek *kruos* = cold) that bodies deep-frozen in liquid nitrogen at the time of death and kept in aluminum capsules may be thawed out and restored to life at some time in the future when a cure for the disease of which the person died is discovered. Whether it will be possible to restore to life those few bodies that have been preserved in this way is debatable, but most authorities are doubtful.

The "Giving Up" Syndrome

A wealth of data, some anecdotal and some experimental, support the notion that a feeling of helplessness or simply "giving up" and refusing to resist any longer can lead to death under certain conditions. This "giving up" syndrome has been observed in animals, primitive tribesmen, and highly civilized people (see Seligman, 1975). For example, instances of death due to "giving up" have been observed frequently among prisoners of war and convicts. An occurrence of sudden death in an institutional setting was reported by Lefcourt (1973):

This writer witnessed one such case of death due to a loss of will within a psychiatric hospital. A female patient who had remained in a mute state for nearly 10 years was shifted to a different floor of her building along with her floor mates, while her unit was being redecorated. The third floor of this psychiatric unit where the patient in question had been living was known among the patients as the chronic, hopeless floor. In contrast, the first floor was most commonly occupied by patients who held privileges, including the freedom to come and go on the hospital grounds and to the surrounding streets. In short, the first floor was an exit ward from which patients could anticipate discharge fairly rapidly. All patients who were temporarily moved from the third floor were given medical examinations prior to the move, and the patient in question was judged to be in excellent medical health though still mute and withdrawn. Shortly after moving to the first floor, this chronic psychiatric patient surprised the ward staff by becoming socially responsive such that within a two-week period she ceased being mute and was actually becoming gregarious. As fate would have it, the redecoration of the third-floor unit was soon completed and all previous residents were returned to it. Within a week after she had been returned to the "hopeless" unit, this patient, who like the legendary Snow White had been aroused from a living torpor, collapsed and died. The subsequent autopsy revealed no pathology of note, and it was whimsically suggested at the time that the patient had died of despair. (p. 242)

A similar type of reaction was produced in wild rats in a series of experiments by Richter (1957). It was found that rats, placed in a vat of warm water, would swim for approximately 60 hours before drowning. But if they were restrained by a human hand until they stopped struggling and then placed in the water, they swam for only a few minutes before sinking to the bottom. Death due to drowning occurred even sooner when the animals were both restrained and their sensitive whiskers cut prior to placing them in the water. The rats that stopped swimming long before they were exhausted apparently "gave up" because they had learned during the restraint period that escape was impossible.

One physiological explanation of the deaths of Richter's rats and similar occurrences in humans is that they were caused by excessive activity of the parasympathetic nervous system, resulting in extreme relaxation, slowing down of heart action, and consequently decreased blood pressure. Parasympathetic death is different from the sympathetic deaths of most mammals. In the latter the heartbeat speeds up rather than slowing down, and the blood pressure increases just before dying. At any rate, the data on death caused by feelings of helplessness underscore the recommendation that nursing home patients and people in related circumstances should be given as much control as possible over decisions affecting their own lives. They should be encouraged to plan their own meals and activities, select their own clothes, and in other ways become involved in choices related to the management of their lives.

Evidence underscoring the importance of individual choice was obtained in Ferrare's (1962) study of nursing home applicants. On the basis of interviews, 55 female applicants (average age, 82 years) to a nursing home were classified into one of two categories: those who perceived that they had no choice but to go to the home, and those who perceived that they had other alternatives. No medical differences between the two groups were observed on admission. Of the 17 women in the "no-choice" group, 8 were dead after four weeks and 16 after ten weeks following admission to the home. However, only one of the 38 women in the "choice" group died during the initial period.

Philosophy and Death

The importance of making decisions or having a choice as to what one's life will mean has been stressed by existentialist philosopher Jean-Paul Sartre (1957). Sartre, Martin Heidegger, and other writers have also maintained that the awareness of our mortality creates a condition of anxiety and concern over whether we are living meaningful lives. As a result, it is said that the true meaning of one's life comes from the awareness that it will end. Faced with the inevitability of a personal ending, the individual is spurred into action to live a life that will have some significance. Fearing not death so much as an absurd, valueless life, existential philosophers see death as losing much of its terror for the person whose life has been filled with meaning.

Unlike Eastern philosophy, in which both life and death are viewed as complementary experiences, most people in Western societies think of death as being outside of life and foreign to the self.

The emphasis of Western culture on individualism, activity, and self-determination makes death—something beyond our control—an insult and an outrage to the living. The mythology and literature of Western culture have tended to depict death (the "Grim Reaper") as a person's greatest enemy. Since time immemorial, the threat of death has been used by rulers and religions to make people obey. Religions also describe death as the door to immortality, an afterlife where people will have to account for their actions on earth and be rewarded or punished for them.

Many dying people draw strength from music, literature, and the visual arts. Strong philosophical or religious convictions can also be a comfort to people on their deathbeds. This was attested to in a statement by thanatologist Ernest Becker while he lay dying of terminal cancer (Keen, 1974, p. 78): "What makes death easier is . . . to know that . . . beyond what is happening to us is the fact of the tremendous creative energies of the cosmos that are using us for some purposes we don't know."

Legal Aspects

The existentialists, emphasizing freedom of action, point out that even in death one has a choice. This choice has been expressed succinctly by Albert Camus in "The Myth of Sisyphus": "Is one to die voluntarily or to hope in spite of everything?" Or, as asked by an old man named Charlie who had been rescued after sticking his head in a gas oven: "But a man has a right to die, don't he? He don't have to sit and wait, sit and wait for death" (Curtin, 1972, p. 167). The decision to end one's life is not limited to the existentialists and the Charlies. The choice of death may be quite rational in a helpless, hopeless person who feels that he or she has no meaningful reason to continue living. These feelings are often quite strong, and the suicide rate is higher than average in patients suffering from malignant neoplasms or other terminal illnesses (Farberow, Shneidman, and Leonard, 1963; Abram, Moore, and Westervelt, 1971).

The active and/or passive "mercy killing" of animals and humans that are too ill or injured to recover is known as *euthanasia* (from the Greek, meaning good death). Most of the legal debate concerning the concept of euthanasia relates to passive euthanasia, that is, letting a patient die naturally rather than using extraordinary, artificial methods (transplants, life-sustaining drugs, etc.) or machines (e.g., heart-lung machines, respirators) to keep him or her alive in a state of constant suffering or unconsciousness. Some pcople, concerned with the physical and financial cost to themselves and their loved ones of a long terminal illness, are beginning to assert their "right to die" in the form of a "living will" (Fig. 8-1). Although such a document is not legally binding, it does represent an attempt to permit the dying individual some choice, even during the last days or months of life.

REACTIONS OF OTHERS TO THE DYING PERSON

Attitudes toward death, although reportedly less negative in the well-educated and those with strong religious beliefs (Riley,

---

*From *Greensboro Daily News,* August 1, 1977, p. A12.

TO MY FAMILY, MY PHYSICIAN, MY LAWYER, MY CLERGYMAN
TO ANY MEDICAL FACILITY IN WHOSE CARE I HAPPEN TO BE
TO ANY INDIVIDUAL WHO MAY BECOME RESPONSIBLE FOR MY HEALTH, WELFARE OR
AFFAIRS

Death is as much a reality as birth, growth, maturity and old age—it is the one certainty of life. If the time comes when I, _____ can no longer take part in decisions for my own future, let this statement stand as an expression of my wishes, while I am still of sound mind.

If the situation should arise in which there is no reasonable expectation of my recovery from physical or mental disability, I request that I be allowed to die and not be kept alive by artificial means or "heroic measures". I do not fear death itself as much as the indignities of deterioration, dependence and hopeless pain. I, therefore, ask that medication be mercifully administered to me to alleviate suffering even though this may hasten the moment of death.

This request is made after careful consideration. I hope you who care for me will feel morally bound to follow its mandate. I recognize that this appears to place a heavy responsibility upon you, but it is with the intention of relieving you of such responsibility and of placing it upon myself in accordance with my strong convictions, that this statement is made.

Signed _____

Date _____

Witness _____

Witness _____

Copies of this request have been given to _____

_____

_____

_____

Figure 8-1. A "Living Will." Prepared by the Euthanasia Educational Council, it expresses the signer's wish to avoid the use of "heroic measures" to preserve his/her life in the event of irreversible disease or injury. (Reprinted with permission of the Euthanasia Council, 250 West 57th Street, New York, N.Y. 10019.)

1968), are sufficiently negative in most people to make them very anxious and inadequate in dealing with the questions and concerns of the dying person. Many older people attempt to cope with death and want to talk about it, but the topic remains taboo for a large portion of society. Unlike preindustrial cultures, in which personal contacts with the spirits of the dead were accepted as fairly commonplace, thoughts of death and the deceased tend to be avoided among more modern societies. These negative reactions toward death generalize to old people, who remind us of death, and act as a factor in the decline of respect for the aged. Unfortunately, a large number of people perceive the elderly as a homogeneous group merely sitting around waiting to die. As an illustration, Curtin (1972) enlisted the services of a Mrs. Duffy to pose as a prospective

Figure 8–2. Mark Jury and his grandfather. (From *Gramp*, by Mark Jury and Dan Jury. Copyright © 1975, 1976 by Mark and Daniel Jury. Reprinted by permission of Grossman Publishers.)

resident of a retirement community. When describing the features of the community to Mrs. Duffy, the salesman boasted: "Here you are free from worry. We have a security patrol 24 hours a day, just looking after your welfare so you can sleep in peace." Not one to be bested, the skeptical Mrs. Duffy replied: "That's exactly what the man said when I bought a plot in the cemetery for me and my husband" (Curtin, 1972, p. 116).

Trained to save lives and to view death as an enemy, even medical workers are frequently uncomfortable with the topic and do not like to be present when their patients die. Whether or not to tell terminal patients that they are going to die is a persisting medical dilemma. According to Butler (1975), less than 20 per cent of attending physicians voluntarily tell their patients that they are going to die. The feeling, obviously sometimes justified, is that patients are unable to handle the prospect of their own demise and that the knowledge may cause their physical condition to become worse. This is true in spite of the fact that most older people view death as inevitable, have made some preparation for it, and are willing to discuss it with others. Too often physicians, as a result of training that emphasizes only the physical and technical side of medical treatment and the saving of lives, overlook the human needs of patients to ask questions of the doctor and to receive emotional support and understanding. In general, the reactions of a typical hospital staff toward the terminally ill patient are technically efficient but impersonal (Buckingham, Lack, Mount, MacLean, and Collins, 1976). Trapped in a "conspiracy of silence" on the part of family, friends, and medical personnel, the dying person is left to face death alone or with impersonal nursing care—a frightened, machine-like object attached to life-giving equipment rather than a valuable human being. This conspiracy of silence was described eloquently by Tolstoy (1886) in "The Death of Ivan Ilych":

> What tormented Ivan Ilych most was the deception, the lie, which for some reason they all accepted, that he was not dying but was simply ill, and that he only need keep quiet and undergo a treatment and then something very good would result. He, however, knew that do what they would nothing would come of it, only still more agonizing suffering and death. This deception tortured him—their not wishing to admit what they all knew and what he knew, but wanting to lie to him concerning his terrible condition, and wishing and forcing him to participate in that lie. Those lies—lies enacted over him on the eve of his death and destined to degrade this awful, solemn act to the level of their visitings, their curtains, their sturgeon for dinner—were a terrible agony for Ivan Ilych. And strangely enough, many times when they were going through their antics over him he had been within a hair-breadth of calling out to them: "Stop lying! You know and I know that I am dying. Then at least stop lying about it!" But he had never had the spirit to do it. The awful, terrible act of his dying was, he could see, reduced by those about him to the level of a casual, unpleasant, and almost indecorous incident (as if someone entered a drawing-room diffusing an unpleasant odor) and this was done by that very decorum which he had served all his life long. He saw that no one felt for him, because no one even wished to grasp his position. Only Gerasim recognized it and pitied him. And so Ivan Ilych felt at ease only with him (pp. 137–138).

Elisabeth Kübler-Ross (1969) finds that most dying patients want to talk about their fears and feelings and to be given the opportunity to make some decisions pertaining to their lives and deaths. They may need to spend this time working through unresolved conflicts with others, expressing meaningful farewells, and generally putting their lives in order. Weisman (1972) advocates giving the dying patient some autonomy, as in deciding how much medication he wants. Most important, however, is that the dying person have a relationship of mutual trust with a compassionate individual to help him or her face fears of the unknown.

There is a growing emphasis in medical schools on teaching doctors to assist dying patients and their families in accepting death as a natural event rather than the frightening consequence of a medical mistake. The aim of these efforts is to enable the dying patient and the family to view death less fearfully and thus to make the passage from life a more dignified experience for all. One procedure designed to train medical personnel for such a service is the *psychological autopsy* (Weisman and Kastenbaum, 1968). This is a post-mortem analysis of the psychosocial aspects of a patient's death, with the goal of helping hospital personnel to become more aware of the importance of psychological factors in dying.

As in the case of physical treatment, there is no set prescription for dealing with the emotional needs of dying patients and those who are close to them. What the physician, clergyman, or social worker tells the patient and the family must be adapted to the particular needs of the individuals who are being counseled. Many counseling methods may be employed, but Carey (1976) recommends that counselors of terminally ill patients and their families be careful not to force their own moral or religious values on the counselees. In general, the counselor should attempt to understand and share the feelings of those involved and help them to find their own ways of handling death, whether these be religious or secular.

REACTIONS OF THE DYING PERSON

Studies indicate that older people do not think a great deal about death (Lieberman and Coplan, 1969) and that they are also less afraid of it than younger people (Kalish and Reynolds, 1976). The conscious awareness of death, however, can become quite strong after a serious accident, a prolonged illness, or the death of someone close to the person. Whether the resulting preoccupation with death produces motivational paralysis on the one hand or a beneficial or destructive change in the individual's life on the other depends on the person.

The Life Review

A psychological reaction of particular interest to thanatologists is the *life review*. Life review can refer to either a prolonged reminiscence or preoccupation with the past or a split-second review of one's life during the actual experience of dying or near-death. To Butler (1968, 1971), the life review is a universal process, occurring at any time of life and providing the opportunity to relive old pleasures and sufferings and to work out persisting conflicts. The fact that this process is going on may be signaled by frequent "mirror gazing" and an enhanced interest in discussing the past.

Ideally, a life review culminates in a sense of continuity with the past, an integrated life, and resulting wisdom and inner peace. To quote Curtin (1972, pp. 76–77): "There seems to be a particular point in the lives of old people when they've reached the top of the mountain, when they seem . . . to see everything with dreadful clarity. All ambition gone, all sense of having a coherent future lost, they have no veils to shield a vision of themselves, their past, the world. Some old people cannot bear this 'amazing grace' because it seems to signal their closeness to death." Reminiscing about the past can also result in feelings of guilt, anger, and depression, and even suicidal impulses. In any event, Cameron (1972), who was unable to confirm the supposition that old people think more about the past than the future, concluded that the life review process is not as common in old age as it is presumed to be.

Individual Differences in Reactions and Attitudes toward Death

Throughout this book we have noted that individual responses to stress situations and crises vary widely and that personality makes its imprint on almost all behavior. This is very true of dying; reactions and attitudes toward dying are quite different in different individuals. Weisman and Kastenbaum (1968) observed two broad response patterns in their dying patients. Some seemed unaware of impending death or accepted it, gradually withdrawing into inactivity; others remained actively involved in hospital life right up until the day they died.

The attitude that a person has toward death usually reveals something about the personality and the kind of life that has been lived. One person views death as a punishment for aggressive impulses, while in another it arouses early fears of separation, and in a third it represents a reunion with departed loved ones. Some older people possess a strong religious faith in the significance of human existence and in an afterlife, and this faith helps them to approach death with greater composure. Others, perhaps those who have lost too much—including the will to keep trying and enduring—embrace death as a solution to their personal problems. Kastenbaum (1971) found, for example, that 25 per cent of the terminally ill patients whom he interviewed wanted to die before their time. For some, however, rather than being a solution to problems, death represents a highly stressful event that is approached with fear and conflict. Afraid of dying, but also afraid of becoming unable to cope with prolonged illness and pain, these people continually vacillate between the desire to live and the desire to be released from pain and suffering. Added to the fear of being unable to cope and becoming a burden on others is the concern about what will happen to surviving friends and relatives who depend on the patient.

Some of the factors that are related to attitudes toward death are emotional adjustment, educational level, financial security, experiences with the deaths of others, family relationships, and religious orientation. In general, the poorer a person's emotional adjustment, the greater will be his or her discomfort in relation to death. Attitude toward death is positively related to educational level, a more accepting attitude being characteristic of the more highly educated. But education is also related to emotional adjustment, and all three variables—education, emotional adjustment, and attitude toward death—are associated with financial security. With respect to the other variables listed above, as they approach the end of life, few people emphasize the religious side of death—heaven, hell, the last judgment, etc. And rather than being merely affiliated with some religious organization, it is the quality of the affiliation that is associated with a person's attitude toward dying (Carey, 1976). Finally, experiences with the deaths of others and strong interpersonal ties to family and friends can help provide strength to face the inevitable and a sense of the continuity of life.

Psychological Stages in the Dying Process

As a result of interviews with over 200 dying patients, Elisabeth Kübler-Ross (1969) postulated five psychological stages through which people pass as they become aware of impending death. Kübler-Ross maintains that most people, whether they die slowly or quickly, pass through these successive stages in their attempts to deal with death. Throughout all of the stages, which do not invariably occur in the order described below, the patient continues to hope for recovery or a cure.

During the first stage, *denial,* the patient refuses to accept the

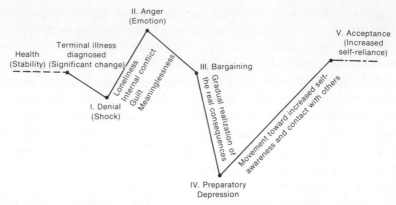

Figure 8–3. Psychological stages in the dying process. (After Kübler-Ross, 1975, p. 161.)

doctor's diagnosis and consults other medical and nonmedical people. It is always important for a seriously ill patient to ask for a second opinion on medical matters, but in an attempt to defend himself against the realization that he is dying, the patient may spend a great deal of money on faith healers and medical quacks. According to psychoanalysts, most people at the unconscious level do not really believe that they are going to die, and by refusing to accept the fact of death they protect themselves against the anxiety that would be caused by the realization that their time is short.

As the patient's health continues to deteriorate, it becomes increasingly difficult to deny the imminence of death. Thus, denial gradually fades into a partial acceptance of the inevitable. During this second stage, which Kübler-Ross refers to as *anger,* the patient feels angry and even enraged at the unfairness of having to die before his or her work has been completed and while other people continue to live. It is important for the family and hospital staff to be alert to this stage, because they may be the apparent targets of the patient's anger. The anger, however, is actually directed not so much toward them but toward the unfairness of death. This emotion is expressed in lines from a poem by Dylan Thomas:

> Do not go gentle into that good night.
> Old age should burn and rave at close of day;
> Rage, rage against the dying of the light.
>
> And you, my father, there on the sad height,
> Curse, bless, me now with your fierce tears, I pray.
> Do not go gentle into that good night.
> Rage, rage against the dying of the light.

Patience and understanding on the part of the hospital staff and family are very important during the second stage. In any event, the anger slowly abates, to be replaced by desperate efforts on the part of the patient to buy time by *bargaining*—with fate, God, the doctors, or anyone who offers the possibility of hope. The patient promises to take his medicine and go to church regularly, prays for forgiveness, and even engages in rituals or magical acts to ward off the demon Death. The bargaining stage is not obvious in all patients, but when it occurs it appears to represent a healthier, more controlled approach than denial and anger.

During the fourth stage, *depression,* the patient now fully accepts his impending death, but becomes depressed by all that he has suffered and all that he will be giving up by dying. Depression, at least to some degree, is a necessary part of the acceptance of death and the final peace that comes with acceptance. Consequently, the patient should be allowed to feel depressed for a while, and not be continually pestered by denying, "sweet lemon" Pollyannas. He should be permitted to share his grief with people who are important to him, and, after he has been sad for a time, then reassured and cheered up.

The last psychological stage of dying, *acceptance,* is characterized by "quiet expectation." The patient, who is now very weak and tired, accepts the inevitability of death and desires only freedom from pain. This is a time to be alone with one or two loved ones, erasing old hurts and saying last goodbyes. The calm acceptance of death has been expressed by William Cullen Bryant ("Thanatopsis"), and Robert Louis Stevenson ("Requiem").

> Under the wide and starry sky
> Dig my grave and let me lie.
> Glad did I live and gladly die,
> And I laid me down with a will.
>
> This be the verse that you grave for me:
> Here he lies where he longed to be,
> Home is the sailor, home from the sea,
> And the hunter home from the hill.
>
> (Robert Louis Stevenson)

Just before he died, the noted journalist Stewart Alsop wrote: "A dying man needs to die as a sleepy man needs to sleep, and there comes a time when it is wrong, as well as useless, to resist" (Alsop, 1973, p. 299).

The Terminal Drop

It has been noted repeatedly throughout this book that intellectual abilities do not invariably decline in old age and that wisdom and experience can compensate for those ability deficits. However, there is an apparent exception to this principle, a psychological phenomenon referred to as the *terminal drop*. The terminal drop is a decline in intellectual functions (IQ, memory, cognitive organization), sensory-motor abilities (e.g., reaction time), and personality (assertiveness, etc.) during the last few months or so of life. The research that revealed the terminal drop phenomenon was prompted by a nurse in a home for the aged who claimed that she could predict which patients were going to die soon just from her observations that they "seem to act differently" (Lieberman, 1965). Subsequent research (Lieberman and Coplan, 1969; Reimanis and Green, 1971) found declines in several areas of cognitive and sensory-motor functioning and in the general ability to cope with environmental demands in those patients who died within a year of the testing. Similar declines were not found in patients who died a year or more after being tested.

BEREAVEMENT AND MOURNING

Historically, the purpose of the funeral rite was to honor the deceased, supply him with things that were thought to be needed in the other world, and to gain favor with the gods. The word "funeral" comes from the Sanskrit word for "smoke," presumably stemming from the early practice in Northern India of burning the dead. Another ancient custom was *suttee,* in which the widow throws herself on the funeral pyre of her deceased husband—to be burned alive. This practice was fairly common in India until it was outlawed by the British in the nineteenth century. Many of our own funeral customs (e.g., wearing black, walking in procession, and raising a mound over the grave) were introduced into Britain by the Romans and subsequently transported by the British to North America (Hambly, 1974).

The Modern Funeral

Mandelbaum (1959) describes several functions of the funeral in our culture, including public acknowledgment of the death of a person and disposal of the body. It also serves as an institutionalized way of reaffirming family ties and, secondarily, the stability of society. Furthermore, by extending the period of mourning over several days, the funeral and other ritualized features of bereavement help the survivors to readjust and reorient themselves to the world of the living. This therapeutic function of the social and religious rites associated with death has been recognized by most societies.

The Stress of Bereavement

Mourning for the deceased and grief at his or her departure do not automatically terminate when the funeral is over. The death of a loved one, and a spouse in particular, is often an extremely stressful experience from which the bereaved has difficulty recovering. Preoccupied with the loss and grief, the bereaved may ignore other people and let things go, having little or no energy left to cope with the external world.

There are various household and business duties which the bereaved must now do alone without the help and guidance of the deceased. Medical bills and funeral expenses must be taken care of, a difficult chore even when life insurance and/or savings cover the costs and a severe burden when they do not. The survivors of a deceased person are usually eligible for some kind of death benefit or burial payment. This typically amounts to a lump sum payment of $255 from Social Security for burial expenses, and, to survivors of eligible veterans, up to $250 for burial expenses and $150 for a burial plot. In cases of service-connected disability, survivors may also be entitled to other veterans' benefits and to labor union or fraternal organization funds. Whatever the benefits may be, when there has been a long terminal illness a good portion usually goes for hospital bills and for the funeral. Standard funeral expenses, including a casket and the use of funeral home facilities and a hearse, are around $1500; a cemetery plot costs $75 to $850, and burial or crematory fees are $225 to $1500. The cost of flowers, obituary notices, clergyman's honorarium, and music for the funeral service must also be taken into account in the overall bill ("If Someone Close Dies," 1976).

The deceased served not only as a satisfier of the physical needs of the bereaved but also as a source of emotional gratification and a confidant. As a consequence, over the years the bereaved's

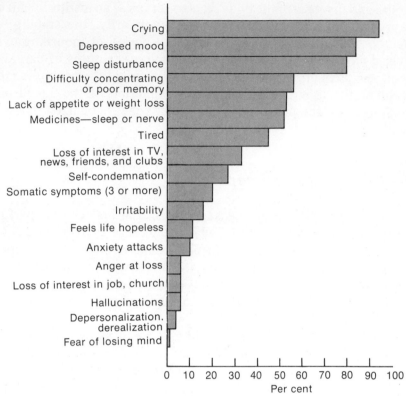

Figure 8–4. Percentages of recently widowed persons expressing various symptoms. (Reprinted from Kimmel, 1974, p. 432. Adapted from Clayton, Halikes, and Maurice, 1971, Table 1.)

sense of identity and the meaning of his or her life became intertwined with the personality of the deceased. The death of a loved one deprives a spouse or other survivor of many kinds of satisfaction, and the latter must somehow learn to cope with these losses.

Among the behavioral reactions observed during the first month of mourning are periodic crying, difficulty sleeping, loss of appetite, and problems in concentrating or remembering (Fig. 8–4) (Clayton, Halikes and Maurice, 1971). In a study of 109 widowed persons, Clayton et al. (1971) also found that the emotional disturbances and insomnia frequently led to a dependence on tranquilizers, sleeping pills, and/or alcohol. The emotional reactions of the surviving spouse, who in 75 per cent of the cases is the wife, may be so intense that severe physical illness, a serious accident, and even death—occasionally from suicide—occur. For example, in a study of 4500 British widowers aged 55 and over, it was found that 213 died during the first six months of their bereavement (Parkes, Benjamin, and Fitzgerald, 1969). The rate of death, most instances of which apparently resulted from heart problems, was 40 per cent higher than expected in this age group. Concluding from a series of related investigations that grief and consequent feelings of helplessness make people more vulnerable to pathogens, Seligman (1975) suggested that individuals who have recently lost a spouse would do well to be very careful about their health. He recommends monthly medical checkups during the first year after the loss.

Although anxiety and depression are the most common reactions to bereavement, anger, guilt, and even psychotic symptoms (hallucinations, feelings of depersonalization, etc.) have been observed. Depression is a normal response to any severe loss, but it is augmented by feelings of guilt in cases where interpersonal hostilities and conflicts with the deceased have not been resolved. For various reasons, survivors may experience unacknowledged anger toward the deceased and relief at his or her death—both of which can lead to feelings of guilt.

Stages of Mourning

It has been observed that many bereaved people appear to go through several stages of mourning. Similar to Kübler-Ross's (1969) psychological stages in dying, Bowlby (1960) found evidence for five stages in mourning: (1) concentration on the deceased; (2) anger toward the deceased or others; (3) appeals to others for help; (4) despair, withdrawal, and disorganization; (5) reorganization and direction of love toward a new object. There has been relatively little research on Bowlby's stages, but, as with Kübler-Ross's stages in dying, it is recognized that not all mourners go through them in the order listed above.

Somewhat more condensed than Bowlby's (1960) description is Gorer's (1965) three-stage conception of mourning: (1) initial shock; (2) intense grief; (3) gradual reawakening of interest. The first stage, which lasts only a few days, is characterized by a loss of self-control, reduced energy, and lack of motivation. The individual is bewildered and disoriented, and loses perspective (Insel, 1976). As the initial shock wears off, the second period, characterized by periodic crying and a bewildered inability to comprehend what has actually happened, takes over. This stage can last for several months, but it gradually gives way to a third stage in which the bereaved acknowledges the reality of the loved one's death and all that it means.

Readjustment and Renewal

The problem of adjusting to the death of a person to whom one has been very close is especially painful when the death was unexpected and if there was insufficient time for the survivors, as well as the deceased, to prepare for it. But when the family members and friends are given ample warning that the person is dying, there is an opportunity to talk through problems with the dying person and each other.

In any event, the ability to go on living and developing new social relationships depends on the kind of gratification that was gained from the relationship with the deceased. It is difficult to begin anew when there are persisting interpersonal problems and negative emotions. But when the relationship has been built on mutual trust and fulfillment and there are no serious unresolved conflicts, the bereaved can more easily begin the process of readjustment and self-renewal.

SUMMARY

The medical definition of death as being the cessation of the heartbeat and brain activity has been a topic of considerable debate. Not all parts of the body die simultaneously; certain tissues can live for hours and even days after the heart and brain have ceased to function. Furthermore, by using countershock it is possible to "resurrect" a person whose heart has stopped beating.

As witnessed by the "giving up" syndrome in lower animals and humans, psychological factors play an important role in dying. Parasympathetic death, resulting from relaxation of the body, apparently stems from feelings of helplessness.

Music, literature, and the visual arts, as well as philosophical and religious beliefs, can be a comfort in the face of death. Existential philosophers have stressed the fact that the true meaning of one's life comes from the awareness that it will end. Western culture, with its emphasis on individualism and self-determination, has tended to view death as a person's worst enemy and as outside of life. Eastern philosophies, on the other hand, view life and death as complementary experiences.

Perceiving themselves as trained to save lives, even physicians are sometimes uncomfortable in the presence of death and the dying. Whether or not a patient should be informed of impending death and encouraged to talk about it is not always an easy question to answer. Kübler-Ross, however, has found that most dying patients want to discuss their fears and feelings and be permitted to make decisions concerning their lives. There is certainly no routine psychological prescription for assisting the dying person, but hospital personnel should be made aware of the importance of psychological factors in dying.

Butler perceives the life review as a universal therapeutic process in the aged and dying, but Cameron maintains that it is not as common as it is presumed to be. Whether or not a life review takes place depends, as do other reactions and attitudes toward life and death, on the individual. Attitude toward death varies with emotional adjustment, experiences with the deaths of others, family relationships, education, economic security, and religion.

Kübler-Ross noted five successive psychological stages in the reactions of the dying person: denial, partial acceptance (anger), bargaining, depression, and acceptance. These five stages have been the subject of controversy, and they need not follow one another in the order listed. Another psychological phenomenon occurring during the last few months of life is the *terminal drop* in intellectual functions, sensory-motor abilities, and personality.

The rituals of the modern funeral stem from several historical practices and serve a number of therapeutic functions. The death of a relative or close friend can have wide-ranging psychological and physical consequences for the survivors. The reactions of the bereaved include anxiety, depression, guilt, anger, and even psychotic behavior. Bowlby listed five stages and Gorer three stages (initial shock, intense grief, gradual reawakening of interest) in the psychological response pattern known as mourning. Not only does the loss of a loved one and the resulting period of mourning have profound effects on a survivor, but dramatic physical changes and even the premature death of the bereaved can result. The quality and intensity of these reactions, and whether or not the bereaved is able to readjust, depend on the kind of gratification gained from the relationship with the deceased and the resolution of any interpersonal problems or negative emotions concerning the latter.

Death is the most profound
  and significant fact of life:
it lifts the very least of mortals
  above the greyness
and banality of life.
  And only the fact of death
puts the question of life's meaning
  in all its depth.
Life in this world has meaning
  only because there is death:
if there were no death in our world,
  life would be deprived of meaning.
Meaning is linked with ending.
  And if there were no end,
if in our world there was evil
  and endlessness of life,
there would be no meaning to life whatever . . .
  The meaning of man's moral experience
throughout his whole life
  lies in putting him into a position
to comprehend death.

Nikolai Berdyaev

suggested readings

Alsop, S. *Stay of execution.* Philadelphia: Lippincott, 1973.

Becker, E. *The denial of death.* New York: The Free Press, 1973.

Jury, M., and Jury, D. *Gramp.* New York: Grossman Publishers, 1976.

Kastenbaum, R., and Aisenberg, R. *The psychology of death.* New York: Springer, 1976.

Kastenbaum, R., and Costa, P. T. Psychological perspectives on death. In Rosenzweig, M. R., and Porter, L. W. (eds.). *Annual Review of Psychology, 1977, 28,* 225–249.

Kübler-Ross, E. *Death: The final stage of growth.* Englewood Cliffs, N.J.: Prentice-Hall, 1975.

Seligman, M. E. P. *Helplessness: On depression, development, and death.* San Francisco: W. H. Freeman, 1975, Chap. 8.

Appendix

ORGANIZATIONS FOR THE ELDERLY

American Aging Association (AGE)
c/o Denham Harman, M.D.
University of Nebraska College of Medicine
Omaha, NE 68105

American Association of Retired Persons (AARP)
1909 K Street, N.W.
Washington, DC 20006

American Geriatrics Society (AGS)
Ten Columbus Circle
New York, NY 10019

Gerontological Society
One DuPont Circle, Suite 520
Washington, DC 20036

Gray Panthers
3700 Chestnut Street
Philadelphia, PA 19104

International Association of Gerontology (IAG)
Section of Biological Ultrastructure
The Weizmann Institute of Science
P.O.B. 26
Rehovot, Israel

International Senior Citizens Association (ISCA)
11753 Wilshire Boulevard
Los Angeles, CA 90025

National Alliance of Senior Citizens (NASC)
Box 40031
Washington, DC 20016

National Caucus on the Black Aged (NCBA)
1730 M Street, N.W.
Washington, DC 20006

National Council of Senior Citizens (NCSC)
1511 K Street, N.W.
Washington, DC 20005

National Council on the Aging (NCOA)
1828 L Street, N.W.
Washington, DC 20036

National Geriatrics Society (NGS)
212 W. Wisconsin Ave., Third Floor
Milwaukee, WI 53203

U.S. GOVERNMENT AGENCIES

Administration on Aging
Social and Rehabilitation Service
U.S. Department of Health, Education and Welfare
300 C Street, N.W.
Washington, DC 20201

National Institute on Aging
National Institutes of Health
U.S. Department of Health, Education and Welfare
9000 Rockville Pike
Bethesda, MD 20014

Office of Education
U.S. Department of Health, Education and Welfare
400 Maryland Avenue, S.W.
Washington, DC 20202

Office of Long Term Care (OLTC)
Public Health Service
U.S. Department of Health, Education and Welfare
5600 Fishers Lane
Rockville, MD 20852

Glossary

Ability.   The extent to which a person is capable of performing a certain task, such capability being the joint product of hereditary endowment and experience.

Acceptance.   According to Kübler-Ross, the final stage in a person's reactions to impending death. This phase is characterized by "quiet expectation" and acceptance of the inevitability of death. The dying person wants to be alone with one or two loved ones and desires only freedom from pain.

Accommodation.   The automatic change in the shape of the lens of the eye so that an image can be brought into sharper focus on the retina.

Activity theory.   The theory that active, productive people are happiest at any age.

Adjustment.   The ability to get along in society and satisfy most of one's needs.

Affective psychoses.   Functional psychoses characterized by extremes of emotion (elation or depression).

Ageism.   Butler's term for the social stereotyping of or discrimination against older people.

Age norm.   Average score on a test made by people of a given chronological age.

Alzheimer's disease.   A type of presenile dementia characterized by progressive mental deterioration.

Anger.   According to Kübler-Ross, the second stage in a person's reactions to impending death. During this stage the person partially accepts the knowledge the he/she is going to die but becomes angry at the unfairness of having to die while others go on living.

197

Angor animi. A fear of impending death, often accompanying a heart attack.

Angry type. According to Reichard, a maladjusted personality pattern, persisting into old age. The person is bitter and blames other people for his/her failures.

Anxiety neurosis. A type of psychoneurotic disorder in which persistent anxiety is the major symptom.

Apoplexy. See *cerebrovascular accident.*

Aptitude. The ability to profit from further training and experience in an occupation or skill.

Arcus senilis. A cloudy ring that forms around the cornea of the eye in old age.

Armored-defended personality. According to Reichard, a personality pattern, persisting into old age, in which the person defends against anxiety by keeping busy.

Arteriosclerosis. Abnormal hardening and thickening of the walls of the arteries in old age.

Atherosclerosis. A type of arteriosclerosis resulting from an accumulation of fat deposits on artery walls.

Audiometer. A frequency generator for measuring a person's sensitivity to various frequencies in the audible range of human hearing. Used to determine degree of deafness.

Autoimmune hypothesis. Theory that the immunological defenses of a person decrease with age, causing the body to "turn on itself," and consequently increasing the likelihood of autoimmune diseases such as arthritis.

Bargaining. According to Kübler-Ross, the third stage in a person's reactions to impending death. This stage is characterized by the person's attempts to buy time by bargaining with the doctors, God, or with anyone or anything that the person believes can protect him from death.

Bereavement. The loss of a loved one by death.

Centenarian. A person who is 100 years old or older.

Cerebral arteriosclerosis. Chronic hardening and thickening of the arteries of the brain in old age.

Cerebrovascular accident (CVA). A sudden rupture (hemorrhage) or blockage (thrombosis) of a large cerebral blood vessel, leading to impairment of brain functioning (stroke, apoplexy).

Chronic brain disorder. Mental illness caused by long-standing injury to the brain.

Climacterium. Period of life during which menopause occurs in women and related glandular changes take place in men.

Cohort. A group of people of the same age, class membership, culture, etc.

Collagen. Fibrous protein found in connective tissue, bones, and skin of vertebrates. It becomes gelatinous on heating.

Competency. Legal determination that a person's judgment is sound and that he or she is able to manage his or her own property, enter into contracts, etc.

Concurrent validity. See *Validity.*

Conduction deafness. Deafness resulting from failure of the mechanical vibrations corresponding to sound waves to be transmitted adequately through the three small bones in the middle ear into the cochlea of the inner ear.

Construct validity. See *Validity.*

Content validity. See *Validity.*

Correlation. The degree of relationship between two variables, signified by an index ranging from -1.00 to $+1.00$ (correlation coefficient).

Cross-linkage. Inadvertent coupling of large intracellular and extracellular molecules, causing connective tissue to stiffen.

Cross-sectional study. Comparisons of the biological or psychological characteristics of people in different age groups.

CVA. See *Cerebrovascular accident.*

Death rattle. A rattling or gurgling sound produced by air passing through mucus in the lungs and air passages of a dying person.

Delusion. A false belief, characteristic of paranoid disorders.

Delusions of grandeur, persecution, and reference are common in these psychotic conditions.

Denial. According to Kübler-Ross, the first stage in a person's reactions to impending death. During this stage the person refuses to accept the fact of death and seeks assurance from other medical and nonmedical people.

Dependent variable. The variable in an experiment that changes as a function of changes in the independent variable. Variations in magnitude of the dependent variable, plotted on the Y axis of a graph, can be viewed as the experimental effect.

Depression. According to Kübler-Ross, the fourth stage in a person's reactions to impending death. The patient fully accepts the fact of death but becomes depressed by all that has been suffered and all that will have to be given up.

Disengagement theory. Cumming's theory that aging brings a change in self-perception, and adjustment occurs through withdrawal from responsibility and participation.

Embolism. Obstruction of a blood vessel by an air bubble or other abnormal particle (thrombosis).

Euthanasia. Either active or passive contribution to the death of a human being or animal suffering from a terminal illness or injury ("mercy killing").

Fraternal twins. Twins resulting from coincident pregnancies in the same person. Originating from two separately fertilized eggs, fraternal twins are genetically no more alike than non-twin siblings.

Free radicals. Broken-off parts of molecules, or molecules with an electron stripped off, that connect to and damage other molecules.

Full scale IQ. See *Wechsler Adult Intelligence Scale*.

Functional psychosis. A psychotic disorder having no clearly defined structural (organic) basis.

Geriatrics. The branch of medicine that deals with the problems of the aged.

Geronto. An old person (Greek *gerōn* = old man).

Gerontocracy. Government by the aged; a social organization in which a group or council of old people govern.

Gerontology. A branch of knowledge (science) concerned with the characteristics and problems of the aged.

Gerontophobia. Unreasonable fear and/or hatred of old people.

Gray Panthers. A politically active group concerned with legislation and programs for the aged.

Hallucination. Perception of an object or situation in the absence of an external stimulus.

Hemorrhage. Heavy discharge of blood from a blood vessel; uncontrollable bleeding. (See also *Cerebrovascular accident.*)

Huntington's chorea. A progressive disorder of the central nervous system, presumably hereditary, characterized by jerking movements and mental deterioration.

Hutchinson-Gilford syndrome. See *Progeria.*

Hyperoxygenation. Breathing of 100% oxygen under high atmospheric pressure, a process that in certain investigations has improved learning and retention of information in the elderly.

Identical twins. Twins produced by a single fertilized egg. Since they are genetically identical, they are often used in studies of the effects of heredity on structure and behavior. Also called monozygotic twins.

Imipramine. A tricyclic drug used in the treatment of depression (Tofranil).

Incompetency. Legal decision that a person is suffering from a mental disorder causing a defect of judgment so that the person is unable to manage his/her own property, enter into contracts, etc.

Independent variable. The variable whose effects are being assessed in an experiment. On a graph depicting the results of an experiment, changes in the independent variable (the "cause") are plotted on the horizontal axis.

Insanity. An imprecise legal term for severe mental disorders involving lack of responsibility for one's actions. According to the M'Naghten Rule, an insane person is one who cannot distinguish right from wrong. However, other precedents such as the Durham decision are used in some states to determine insanity.

Intelligence. Many definitions of this term have been offered, such as "the ability to judge well, understand well, and reason well" (Binet) and "the capacity for abstract thinking" (Terman). Most intelligence tests measure the ability to succeed in academic-type tasks.

Involuntary commitment. Legal process by which a person is committed to a mental hospital against his/her will.

Involutional period. Decline in body energy during middle age or early old age, signaled by the menopause in women.

Involutional psychosis. A disorder characterized by deep depression or paranoia, presumably precipitated by the "change of life" in middle-aged women and somewhat older men.

Life review. Reminiscence or a split-second review of one's life prior to death.

Longevity. Length of life; long duration of life.

Longitudinal study. Investigation of the development of the same individual or group as a function of chronological age.

Major stroke. Heart failure resulting from blockage of a large cerebral blood vessel. (See also *Cerebrovascular accident.*)

Manic-depressive psychosis. An affective disorder characterized by severe mood swings and excitability.

Manic disorder. Excessive agitation and excitability, which may or may not alternate with depression. (See also *Manic-depressive psychosis.*)

Mature type. According to Reichard, a personality pattern that persists into old age, in which the person is relatively free of neurotic conflicts and can accept himself and grow old with few past regrets.

Menopause.   Cessation of menstruation, usually occurring some time between ages 45 and 50.

Mercy killing.   See *Euthanasia.*

Monozygotic twins.   See *Identical twins.*

Nerve deafness.   A form of deafness caused by damage to the inner ear or auditory nerve; usually involves a loss of sensitivity to sounds of high frequency. Also called presbycusis.

Octogenarian.   A person who is 80 to 90 years old.

Organic brain damage.   Damage to brain tissue caused by disease or injury; may result in mental disorder.

Organic psychosis.   Severe mental disorder caused by organic brain damage resulting from alcoholism, encephalitis, cerebral arteriosclerosis, and other diseases, drugs, and injuries.

Osteoporosis.   A gradual, long-term loss of bone mass, occurring especially in elderly women.

Paranoid disorder.   A general term for a broad class of mental illnesses of varying severity characterized by suspiciousness, projection, excessive feelings of self-importance, and frequently complex delusions of grandeur, persecution, and ideas of reference.

Parkinsonism.   A progressive brain disorder resulting from damage to the basal ganglia and occurring most often in later life. The symptoms are muscular tremors; spastic, rigid movements; propulsive gait; and a masklike, expressionless face. Also called Parkinson's disease.

Performance IQ.   See *Wechsler Adult Intelligence Scale.*

Personality.   The sum total of all those qualities, traits, and behaviors that characterize a person's individuality and by which, together with his physical attributes, the person is recognized as a unique human being.

Pick's disease.   A type of presenile, degenerative brain disorder.

Predictive validity. See *Validity*.

Presbycusis. See *Nerve deafness*.

Presbyopia. Literally, "old-sightedness," a condition of farsightedness resulting from a loss of elasticity of the lens of the eye due to aging.

Progeria. A very rare disorder that mimics premature aging. A progeric child typically begins to look old as early as age four. Also called *Hutchinson-Gilford syndrome*.

Psychological autopsy. Postmortem analysis of the psychosocial aspects of a person's death.

Psychosis. Severe mental disorder characterized by faulty perception of reality, deficits of language and memory, disturbances in the emotional sphere, and other bizarre symptoms. Psychoses are classified as organic or functional, depending on whether they are associated with a known organic change.

Psychotherapy. Treatment of mental disorders by psychological methods.

Reliability. The extent to which a psychological test or other measuring instrument is consistent. A reliable test is relatively free from errors of measurement and can therefore be depended upon.

Retirement. Withdrawal from one's occupation or from active work.

Rigidity. Inflexibility or unwillingness to change one's way of thinking or behaving; allegedly a characteristic of older people.

Rocking chair type. According to Reichard, a personality pattern that persists into old age, in which the person views old age in terms of freedom from responsibility and as an opportunity to indulge passive needs.

Role. A social behavior pattern that an individual is expected to display under certain conditions or in certain situations.

Role exit theory. Blau's sociological theory of old age as a time for abandoning certain roles and assuming others.

Schizophrenia. A broad category of psychotic disorders

characterized by distortions of reality and disturbances of thought, behavior, and emotional expression.

Self-hater type.   According to Reichard, a maladjusted personality pattern, persisting into old age, in which the person is depressed and blames himself for his disappointments and misfortunes.

Senescence.   The state of being old or the process of growing old.

Senile dementia.   An organic brain disorder occurring in older people. The symptoms are childishness, self-centeredness, and difficulty in reacting to new experiences.

Senile plaque.   Accumulations of fatty tissue and calcified material in the cerebral blood vessels of old people, resulting in clogged arteries and interference with blood circulation.

Senility.   Exhibiting characteristics associated with old age, especially declining mental capacities and physical deterioration.

Senium praecox.   Premature senility. (See also *progeria* and *Werner's syndrome*.)

Septuagenarian.   A person who is 70 to 80 years old.

Serial anticipation (method of).   System for investigation of learning, in which the learner attempts to anticipate successive items in a list.

Short term memory (STM).   Process of retaining items of information from one second to several minutes at most.

Small stroke.   Blockage of a small blood vessel in the brain.

Stimulus persistence theory.   Theory that aging causes recovery from the short-term effects of stimulation to be slowed down.

Superannuation.   Retirement and pensioning because of age or infirmity.

Suttee.   Old Hindu custom in which a devoted wife is voluntarily cremated on the funeral pyre of her husband.

Terminal drop.   Decline in intelligence and personality during the last few months or so of life.

Testamentary capacity.   The legally determined competency of a person to make a will.

Thanaphobia.   An unreasonable fear or dread of dying and death.

Thanatology. A branch of knowledge concerned with the study of dying and death.

Three-component method (model). Schaie's model (including cross-sectional, longitudinal, and time-lag comparisons) for determining the differential effects of age, cohort, and time of measurement on developmental characteristics.

Thrombosis. See *Embolism*.

Time-lag study. Schaie's procedure for examining several cohorts, each in a different time period; part of the three-component model.

Tofranil. See *Imipramine*.

Tranquilizer. Psychotherapeutic drug such as Valium or Mellaril having anti-anxiety or antipsychotic effects.

Validity. The extent to which a test measures what it was designed to measure. Validity can be assessed in several ways: by analysis of a test's content (*content validity*), by relating scores on the test to a criterion of interest (*predictive* and *concurrent validity*), by a thorough study of the extent to which a test is a measure of a certain psychological construct (*construct validity*).

Verbal IQ. See *Wechsler Adult Intelligence Scale*.

Voluntary commitment. Unforced submission of oneself to a mental hospital for examination and treatment. (See also *Involuntary commitment.*)

Wechsler Adult Intelligence Scale (WAIS). An individual intelligence test designed for adults aged 16 years and over. It consists of 11 subtests grouped into Verbal and Performance scales, and yields three intelligence quotients: Verbal IQ, Performance IQ, and Full Scale IQ.

Werner's Syndrome. A condition of arrested growth occurring between the ages of 15 and 20; thought to be a later-developing progeria *(see)*.

References

Abram, H. S., Moore, G. L., & Westervelt, F. B., Jr. Suicidal behavior in chronic dialysis patients. *American Journal of Psychiatry*, 1971, *127*, 119–121.

Agan, T., Casto, M. D., Day, S. S., & Schwab, L. O. Adjusting the environment for the elderly and the handicapped. *Journal of Home Economics*, 1977, *69*(3), 18–20.

Aging: Primitives handle it better. *Science Digest*, 1976, *79*(3), 17–18.

Alsop, S. *Stay of execution*. Philadelphia: Lippincott, 1973.

American Psychiatric Association. *Diagnostic and statistical manual of mental disorders*. Washington, D.C.: Author, 1968.

Anderson, K. Science probes ways to prolong life. *Science Digest*, 1974, *76*(3), 36–41.

Arehart-Treichel, J. How you age. *Science News*, 1972, *102*, 412–413.

Archart-Treichel, J. Human reproduction and aging. *Science News*, 1976, *110*, 297.

Arenberg, D. Cognition and aging: Verbal learning, memory, and problem solving. In C. Eisdorfer and M. P. Lawton (eds.). *The psychology of adult development and aging*. Washington, D.C.: American Psychological Association, 1973.

Axelrod, S., Thompson, L. W., & Cohen, L. D. Effect of senescence on the temporal resolution of somesthetic stimuli presented to one hand or both. *Journal of Gerontology*, 1968, *23*, 191–195.

Baller, W. R., Charles, D. C., & Miller, E. L. Mid-life attainment of the mentally retarded: A longitudinal study. *Genetic Psychology Monographs*, 1967, *75*, 235–329.

Baltes, P. B., & Schaie, K. W. The myth of the twilight years. *Psychology Today*, 1974, *7*(10), 35–40.

Baltes, P. B., & Schaie, K. W. On the plasticity of intelligence in adulthood and old age: Where Horn and Donaldson fail. *American Psychologist*, 1976, *31*, 720–725.

Barrett, J. H. *Gerontological psychology*. Springfield, Ill.: Charles C Thomas, 1972.

Bayley, N., & Oden, M. H. The maintenance of intellectual ability in gifted adults. *Journal of Gerontology*, 1955, *10*, 91–107.

Bell, A., & Zubek, J. The effect of age on the intellectual performance of mental defectives. *Journal of Gerontology*, 1960, *15*, 285–295.

Benet, S. *Abkhasians: The long-living people of the Caucasus*. New York: Holt, 1974.

Benet, S. *How to live to be 100: The life-style of the people of the Caucasus*. New York: Dial Press, 1976.

Bennett, R. Attitudes of the young toward the old; A review of research. *Personnel and Guidance Journal*, 1976, *55*, 136–139.

Ben-Yishay, Y., Diller, L., Mandelberg, I., Gordon, W., & Gerstman, L. Similarities and differences in block design performance between older normal and brain-injured persons. *Journal of Abnormal Psychology*, 1971, *78*, 17–25.

Biehler, R. F. *Child development: An introduction*. Boston: Houghton Mifflin, 1976.

Binstock, R. H. Aging and the future of American politics. In R. A. Kalish (ed.). *The later years: Social applications of gerontology*. Monterey, Calif.: Brooks/Cole, 1977.

Birren, J. E. Increments and decrements in the intellectual status of the aged. *Psychiatric Research Reports*, 1968, *23*, 207–214.

Birren, J. E., Butler, R. N., Greenhouse, S. W., Sokoloff, L., & Yarrow, M. R. (eds.). *Human aging: A biological and behavioral study.* Pub. No. (HSM) 71–9051. Washington, D.C.: U.S. Government Printing Office, 1963.

Birren, J. E., and Schaie, K. W. (eds.). Handbook of the psychology of aging. New York: Van Nostrand Reinhold, 1976.

Blau, Z. S. *Old age in a changing society.* New York: New Viewpoints, 1973.

Bloom, K. L. Age and the self concept. *American Journal of Psychiatry,* 1961, *118,* 534–538.

Botwinick, J. *Cognitive processes in maturity and old age.* New York: Springer, 1967.

Botwinick, J. Geropsychology. *Annual Review of Psychology,* 1970, *21,* 239–272.

Botwinick, J. *Aging and behavior.* New York: Springer, 1973.

Botwinick, J., & Thompson, L. Age differences in reaction: An artifact? *Gerontologist,* 1968, *8,* 25–28.

Bower, G. H. A descriptive theory of human memory. In D. P. Kimble (ed.). *Learning, remembering and forgetting* (vol. 2). New York: New York Academy of Science, 1966.

Bowlby, J. Grief and mourning in infancy and early childhood. *Psychoanalytic Study of the Child,* 1960, *15,* 9–52.

Brink, T. L. Psychotherapy after forty. *MH,* 1976, *60*(2), 23–24.

Brown, J. H. U. Physiological parameters of human potential. In H. A. Otto (ed.). *Explorations in human potentialities.* Springfield, Ill.: Charles C Thomas, 1966.

Brown, S. Taking senior citizens off the shelf. *Education Digest,* 1977, *40*(9), 45–47.

Buckingham, R. W., III, Lack, S. A., Mount, B. M., MacLean, L. D., & Collins, J. T. Living with the dying: Use of the technique of participant observation. *Canadian Medical Association Journal,* 1976, *115,* 1211–1215.

Busse, E. W., & Pfeiffer, E. Functional psychiatric disorders in old age. In E. W. Busse and E. Pfeiffer (eds.). *Behavior adaptation in late life.* Boston: Little, Brown and Co., 1969.

Butler, R. N. The life review: An interpretation of reminiscence in the aged. In B. L. Neugarten (ed.). *Middle age and aging.* Chicago: University of Chicago Press, 1968.

Butler, R. N. Age: The life review. *Psychology Today,* 1971, *5*(7), 49–51ff.

Butler, R. N. Successful aging. *MH,* 1974, *58*(3), 7–12.

Butler, R. N. *Why survive? Being old in America.* New York: Harper & Row, 1975.

Butler, R. H., & Lewis, M. I. *Sex after sixty: A guide for men and women in their later years.* New York: Harper & Row, 1976.

Buttenwieser, P. *The relation of age to skill of expert chess players.* Unpublished Ph.D. dissertation, Stanford University, 1935.

Cameron, P. The generation gap: Time orientation. *Gerontologist,* 1972, *12,* 117–119.

Campbell, D. P. A cross-sectional and longitudinal study of scholastic abilities over twenty-five years. *Journal of Counseling Psychology,* 1965, *12,* 55–61.

Can oxygen fight senility? *Business Week,* March 25, 1972 (No. 2221), p. 94.

Carey, R. G. Counseling the terminally ill. *Personnel and Guidance Journal,* 1976, *55,* 124–126.

Charles, D. C., & James, S. T. Stability of average intelligence. *Journal of Genetic Psychology,* 1964, *105,* 105–111.

Clayton, P. J., Halikes, H. A., & Maurice, W. L. The bereavement of the widowed. *Diseases of the Nervous System,* 1971, *32,* 597–604.

Coleman, J. C. *Abnormal psychology and modern life* (5th ed.). Glenview, Ill.: Scott, Foresman & Co., 1976. Chap. 13.

Comfort, A. *The prospects of longevity.* Paper read at the Gerontological Society, San Juan, Puerto Rico, Dec. 1972.

Comfort, A. *A good age.* New York: Crown Publishers, 1976.

Cooper, A. F., Curry, A. R., Kay, D. W. K., Garside, R. F., & Roth, M. Hearing loss in paranoid and affective psychosis of the elderly. *The Lancet,* 1974, *2*(7885), 851–854.

Cumming, E., Dean, L. R., Newell, D. S., & McCaffrey, I. Disengagement—A tentative theory of aging. *Sociometry,* 1960, *22,* 23–35.

Cumming, E., & Henry, W. E. *Growing old: The process of disengagement.* New York: Basic Books, 1961.

Curtin, S. R. *Nobody ever died of old age.* Boston: Little, Brown, 1972.

de Beauvoir, S. *The coming of age* (Trans. P. O'Brien.). New York: Putnam's, 1972.

Dennis, W. Creative productivity between the ages of twenty and eighty years. *Journal of Gerontology,* 1966, *21,* 1–8.

Doppelt, J. E., & Wallace, W. L. Standardization of the Wechsler Adult Intelligence Scale for older persons. *Journal of Abnormal and Social Psychology,* 1955, *51,* 312–330.

Eisdorfer, C. The WAIS performance of the aged: A retest evaluation. *Journal of Gerontology,* 1963, *18,* 169–172.

Eisdorfer, C. Resources for the aged reflect strongly held social myths. *The Center Magazine,* 1975, *8*(2), 12–18.

Eisdorfer, C., Nowlin, J., & Wilkie, F. Improvement in learning in the aged by modification of autonomic nervous system activity. *Science,* 1970, *170,* 1327–1329.

Entine, A. D. Mid-life counseling: Prognosis and potential. *Personnel and Guidance Journal,* 1976, *55,* 112–114.

Erikson, E. H. *Childhood and society* (2nd ed.). New York: Norton, 1963.

Erikson, E. H. *Identity, youth, and crisis.* New York: Norton, 1968.

Fantino, E., & Reynolds, G. S. *Introduction to contemporary psychology.* San Francisco: W. H. Freeman, 1975.

Farberow, N. L., Shneidman, E. S., & Leonard, C. Suicide among general medical and surgical hospital patients with malignant neoplasms. Veterans Administration, Dept. of Medicine and Surgery, *Medical Bulletin* MB-9, Feb. 25, 1963, 1–11.

Ferrare, N. A. *Institutionalization and attitude change in an aged population: A field study and dissidence theory.* Unpublished doctoral dissertation, Western Reserve University, 1962.

Flieger, H. We're showing our age. *U.S. News & World Report,* 1976, *80*(8), 80.

Ford, A. B. Casualties of our time. *Science,* 1970, *167,* 256–263.

Freedman, A. M., Kaplan, H. I., & Sadock, B. J. *Modern synopsis of psychiatry.* Baltimore: Williams & Wilkins, 1972.

Gal, P. Mental disorders of advanced years. *Geriatrics,* 1959, *14,* 224–228.

Gergen, K. J., & Back, K. W. Cognitive constriction in aging and attitudes toward international issues. In I. H. Simpson and J. C. McKinsey (eds.). *Social aspects of aging.* Durham, N. C.: Duke University Press, 1966.

Goldhamer, H., & Marshall, A. W. *Psychosis and civilization.* Glencoe, Ill.: Free Press, 1953.

Gorer, G. *Death, grief and mourning in contemporary Britain.* London: Cresset, 1965.

Gots, D. E. The long life diet. *Family Circle,* 1977, *90*(9), 14, 20, 166, 168, 170.

Gove, W. Sex, marital status, and mortality. *American Journal of Sociology,* 1973, *79*(1), 45–67.

Gray Panther power. An interview with Maggie Kuhn. *The Center Magazine,* 1975, *8*(2), 21–25.

Gutmann, D. An exploration of ego configurations in middle and later life. In B. L. Neugarten (ed.). *Personality in middle and late life: Empirical studies.* New York: Atherton Press, 1964.

Gutmann, D. Aging among the Highland Maya: A comparative study. *Journal of Personality and Social Psychology,* 1967, *7,* 28–35.

Hambly, W. D. Funeral customs. *The world book encyclopedia* (vol. 9). Chicago: Field Educational Enterprises, 1974.

Harman, D. The biologic clock: The mitochondria? *Journal of the American Geriatric Society,* 1972, *20,* 145–147.

Harman, D., Heidrick, M. L., & Eddy, D. E. *Free radical theory of aging: Effect of antioxidants on humoral and cell-mediated response as a function of age.* Paper read at the 6th Annual Meeting of the American Aging Assn., Washington, D.C., Sept. 1976.

Havighurst, R. J., Neugarten, B. L., & Tobin, S. S. *Disengagement and patterns of aging.* Paper presented at the meeting of the International Association of Gerontology, Copenhagen, Aug. 1973.

Hayflick, L. Aging under glass. *Experimental Gerontology,* 1970, *5,* 291–303.

Hechinger, G. Margaret Mead: Growing old in America. *Family Circle,* 1977, *90*(8), 27–32.

Hickey, T., & Kalish, R. A. Young people's perceptions of adults. *Journal of Gerontology,* 1968, *23,* 215–219.

Horn, J. L., & Donaldson, G. On the myth of intellectual decline in adulthood. *American Psychologist,* 1976, *31,* 701–719.

Housing the aging. *Architectural Record,* 1977, *161*(May), 123–138.

How does vitamin E prevent aging? *Science News,* 1977, *111,* 341.

If someone close dies. . . . *Changing Times,* 1976, *30*(11), 33–34.

Inglis, J., Ankus, M. N., & Sykes, D. H. Age-related differences in learning and short-term memory from childhood to the senium. *Human Development,* 1968, *11,* 42–52.

Insel, S. A. On counseling the bereaved. *Personnel and Guidance Journal,* 1976, *55,* 127–129.

Jacobs, E., Winter, P. M., Alvis, H. J., & Small, S. M. Hyperbaric oxygen: Temporary aid for senile minds. *Journal of the American Medical Association,* 1969, *209,* 1435–1438.

Jacoby, S. Waiting for the end: On nursing homes. *New York Times Magazine,* March 31, 1974, pp. 13ff.

Jarvik, L. F., Yen, F. S., & Goldstein, F. Chromosomes and mental status. *Archives of General Psychiatry,* 1974, *30,* 186–190.

Jones, H. E., & Conrad, H. S. The growth and decline of intelligence. *Genetic Psychology Monographs,* 1933, *13,* 223–298.

Jowsey, J., & Holley, K. E. Influence of diphosphonates on progress of experimentally induced osteoporosis. *Journal of Laboratory Clinical Medicine,* 1973, *82,* 567–575.

Kahana, B., and Kahana, E. Changes in mental status of elderly patients in age-integrated and age-segregated hospital milieus. *Journal of Abnormal Psychology,* 1970, *75,* 177–181.

Kahn, R. L. Stress: From 9 to 5. *Psychology Today,* 1969, *3*(4), 34–38.

Kalish, R. A., & Reynolds, D. K. *Death and ethnicity: A psychocultural study.* Los Angeles: University of Southern California Press, 1976.

Kallmann, F. J., & Sander, G. Two studies on senescence. In R. G. Kuhlen & G. G. Thompson (eds.). *Psychological studies of human development.* New York: Appleton-Century-Crofts, 1963.

Kaplan, H. B., & Pokorny, A. D. Self-derogation and psychosocial adjustment. *Journal of Nervous and Mental Disease,* 1969, *149,* 421–434.

Kastenbaum, R. On the meaning of time in later life. *Journal of Genetic Psychology,* 1966, *109,* 9–25.

Kastenbaum, R. Age: Getting there on time. *Psychology Today,* 1971, *5*(7), 52–54, 82–84.

Kastenbaum, R., & Candy, S. The 4% fallacy: A methodological and empirical critique of extended care facility population statistics. *International Journal of Aging and Human Development,* 1973, *4,* 15–21.

Kastenbaum, R., & Durkee, N. Young people view old age. In R. Kastenbaum (ed.). *New thoughts on old age.* New York: Springer, 1964, pp. 237–250.

Keen, S. The heroics of everyday life: A theorist of death confronts his own end. *Psychology Today,* 1974, *7*(11), 71–75ff.

Kimmel, D. C. *Adulthood and aging.* New York: Wiley, 1974.

Kinsey, A. C., Pomeroy, W. B., & Martin, C. C. *Sexual behavior in the human male.* Philadelphia: Saunders, 1948.

Kirchner, W. K. Age differences in short-term retention of rapidly changing information. *Journal of Experimental Psychology,* 1958, *55,* 352–358.

Kisker, G. W. *The disorganized personality* (2nd ed.). New York: McGraw-Hill, 1972.

Kleinmuntz, B. *Essentials of abnormal psychology.* New York: Harper & Row, 1974.

Kobrin, F., & Hendershot, G. Do family ties reduce mortality? Evidence from the United States, 1966–68. *Journal of Marriage and the Family,* 1977, *39,* 737–745.

Kogan, N., & Shelton, F. Beliefs about old people: A comparative study of older and younger samples. *Journal of Genetic Psychology,* 1962, *100,* 93–111.

Kohlmeier, L. M. Social security: The deeper dilemma. *Nashville Tennessean,* August 24, 1977.

Kohn, R. R. Human aging and disease. *Journal of Chronic Disease,* 1963, *16,* 5–21.

Kübler-Ross, E. *On death and dying.* New York: Macmillan, 1969.

Kübler-Ross, E. (ed.). *Death: The final stage of growth.* Englewood Cliffs, N. J.: Prentice-Hall, 1975.

Kuhlen, R. G. Changing personality adjustment during the adult years. In J. E. Anderson (ed.). *Psychological aspects of aging.* Washington: American Psychological Association, 1956.

Landis, J. T. What is the happiest period of life? *School and Society,* 1942, *55,* 643–645.

Langer, E. J., & Rodin, J. The effects of choice and enhanced personal responsibility for the aged: A field experiment in an institutional setting. *Journal of Personality and Social Psychology,* 1976, *34,* 191–198.

Learning for the aged. *Time,* 1972, *100*(3), 48.

Lefcourt, H. M. The function of illusions of control and freedom. *American Psychologist,* 1973, *28,* 417–425.

Lehman, H. C. *Age and achievement.* Princeton, N. J.: Princeton University Press, 1953.

Lieberman, M. A. Psychological correlates of impending death: Some preliminary observations. *Journal of Gerontology,* 1965, *20,* 181–190.

Lieberman, M. A., & Coplan, A. S. Distance from death as a variable in the study of aging. *Developmental Psychology,* 1969, *2,* 71–84.

Lobsenz, N. M. Sex and the senior citizen. *New York Times Magazine,* Jan. 20, 1974, pp. 8–9 ff.

Lombana, J. H. Counseling the elderly: Remediation plus prevention. *Personnel and Guidance Journal,* 1976, *55,* 143–144.

Lowenthal, M. F. Social isolation and mental illness in old age. *American Sociological Review,* 1964, *29*(1), 54–70.

Maddox, G. L. Persistence of life style among the elderly: A longitudinal study of patterns of social activity in relation to life satisfaction. In B. L. Neugarten (ed.). *Middle age and aging.* Chicago: University of Chicago Press, 1968. (a)

Maddox, G. L. Retirement as a social event in the United States. In B. L. Neugarten (ed.). *Middle age and aging.* Chicago: University of Chicago Press, 1968. (b)

Maddox, G. L. Persistence of life style among the elderly. In E. Palmore (ed.). *Normal aging.* Durham, N. C.: Duke University Press, 1970, pp. 329–331.

Mandelbaum, D. G. Social uses of funeral rites. In H. Feifel (ed.). *The meaning of death.* New York: McGraw-Hill, 1959.

Margolis, B., & Kroes, W. Work and the health of man. Paper commissioned by the Special Task Force, *Work in America.* Cambridge, Mass.: MIT Press, 1972.

Masters, W. H., & Johnson, V. E. *Human sexual inadequacy.* Boston: Little, Brown and Co., 1970.

McFarland, R. A., Tune, G. S., & Welford, A. T. On the driving of automobiles by older people. *Journal of Gerontology,* 1964, *19,* 190–197.

Meltzer, H., & Ludwig, D. Age differences in positive mental health of workers. *Journal of Genetic Psychology,* 1971, *119,* 163–173.

Mondale, W. S.2632 Federal Employees Preretirement Assistance Act of 1975. *Congressional Record,* 121(164), pp. S. 19393–4. Nov. 6, 1975.

Moore, P. What we expect and what it's like. *Psychology Today,* 1975, *9*(3), 29–30.

Moorehead, H. B., et al. Causes of blindness in 4965 persons whom it stated were added to their MRA registers in 1966. In *Proceedings of the 1969 Conference of Model Reporting Area for Blindness.* Washington, D.C.: U.S. Public Health Service, 1969.

Morgan, C. M. The attitudes and adjustments of recipients of old age assistance in upstate and metropolitan New York: *Archives of Psychology,* 1937, *30,* No. 214.

Mortimer, E. A., Monson, R. R., & MacMahon, B. Reduced coronary heart disease mortality in men residing at high altitude. *New England Journal of Medicine,* 1977, *296,* 581–585.

Myers, G. C., & Pitts, A. M. *The demographic effects of mortality reduction on the aged population of the U.S.: Some baseline projections.* Paper presented at the meeting of the Gerontological Society, San Juan, Puerto Rico, Dec. 1972.

Myers, R. J. Social security. *The world book encyclopedia* (vol. 18). Chicago: Field Enterprises Educational Corp., 1974.

National Center for Health Statistics. *Vital and health statistics.* Series 20, No. 5. Washington, D.C.: U.S. Government Printing Office, 1967.

National Center for Health Statistics. *Vital statistics of the United States,* 1973. Vol. 2, Part A: Mortality. Rockville, Md.: U.S. Department of Health, Education, and Welfare, 1974.

National Council on the Aging. *The myth and reality of aging in America.* Washington, D.C.: Author, 1975.

Neugarten, B. L. The awareness of middle age. In R. Owen (ed.). *Middle age.* London: British Broadcasting Corp., 1967.

Neugarten, B. L. Adult personality: Toward a psychology of the life cycle. In E. Vinacke (ed.). *Readings in general psychology.* New York: American Book Co., 1968.

Neugarten, B. L. Grow old along with me! The best is yet to be. *Psychology Today,* 1971, *5*(7), 45–48 ff.

Neugarten, B. L. The rise of the young-old. *New York Times,* Jan. 18, 1975, p. 29.

Neugarten, B. L. The psychology of aging: An overview. *Master lectures in developmental psychology*. Washington, D.C.: American Psychological Association, 1976. (Cassette tape.)

Neugarten, B. L., & Gutmann, D. Age-sex roles and personality in middle age: A thematic apperception study. *Psychological Monographs*, 1958, *72* (17, Whole No. 470).

Neugarten, B. L., Havighurst, R. J., & Tobin, S. S. Personality and patterns of aging. In B. L. Neugarten (ed.). *Middle age and aging*. Chicago: University of Chicago Press, 1968, 173–177.

Neugarten, B. L., & Weinstein, K. K. The changing American grandparent. *Journal of Marriage and the Family*, 1964, *26*, 199–204.

Neulinger, J., & Raps, C. S. Leisure attitudes of an intellectual elite. *Journal of Leisure Research*, 1972, *4*(3), 196–207.

Newman, G., & Nichols, C. R. Sexual activities and attitudes in older persons. *Journal of the American Medical Association*, 1960, *173*, 33–35.

Nisbet, J. D. Intelligence and age: Retesting after twenty-four years' interval. *British Journal of Educational Psychology*, 1957, *27*, 190–198.

Nowak, C. *Concern with youthfulness and attractiveness in adult women*. Unpublished master's thesis, Wayne State University, 1974.

Odell, C. Counseling for a third of a lifetime. *Personnel and Guidance Journal*, 1976, *55*, 145–147.

Offir, C. Old people's revolt—"At 65, work becomes a four-letter word." *Psychology Today*, 1974, *7*(10), 40.

Overall, J. E., & Gorham, D. Organicity versus old age in objective and projective test performance. *Journal of Consulting and Clinical Psychology*, 1972, *39*, 98–105.

Owens, W. A., Jr. Age and mental abilities: A longitudinal study. *Genetic Psychology Monographs*, 1953, *48*, 3–54.

Owens, W. A., Jr. Age and mental abilities: A second adult followup. *Journal of Educational Psychology*, 1966, *57*, 311–325.

Packer, L., & Smith, J. R. Extension of the lifespan of cultured human diploid cells by vitamin E. *Proceedings of the National Academy of Sciences*, 1974, *71*, 4763–4767.

Packer, L., & Smith, J. R. Extension of the lifespan of cultured normal human diploid cells by vitamin E: A reevaluation. *Proceedings of the National Academy of Sciences*, 1977, *74*, 1640–1641.

Paillat, P. M., & Bunch, M. E. (eds.). *Age, work and automation* (vol. 6). White Plains, N.Y.: S. Karger, 1970.

Palmore, E. Physical, mental and social factors in predicting longevity. *Gerontologist*, 1969, *9*, 103–108.

Palmore, E. (ed.). *Normal aging*. Durham, N.C.: Duke University Press, 1970.

Parkes, M. C., Benjamin, B., & Fitzgerald, R. G. Broken heart: A statistical study of increased mortality among widowers. *British Medical Journal*, 1969, *1*, 740–743.

Pastalan, L. A. The simulation of age-related sensory losses. A new approach to the study of environmental barriers. *The New Outlook for the Blind*, Oct. 1974, pp. 356–362.

Pensions: A $38-billion "mortgage." *Greensboro Daily News*, July 13, 1977, p. A2.

Perlman, H. H. *Persona: Social role and personality*. Chicago: University of Chicago Press, 1968.

Perry, P. W. The night of ageism. *MH*, 1974, *58*(3), 13–20.

Peterson, L. R., & Peterson, M. J. Short-term retention of individual verbal items. *Journal of Experimental Psychology*, 1959, *58*, 193–198.

Pfeiffer, E., Verwoerdt, A., & Wang, H. S. Sexual behavior in aged men and women. *Archives of General Psychiatry*, 1968, *19*, 755–758.

Pfeiffer, E., Verwoerdt, A., & Wang, H. S. The natural history of sexual behavior in a biologically advantaged group of aged individuals. *Journal of Gerontology*, 1969, *24*, 193–198.

Phillips, B. S. *The aged in a central Illinois community*. Urbana: University of Illinois Press, 1962.

Pines, M. Age-ism . . . slashing our own tires. *APA Monitor*, 1976, *7*(12), 7.

Porter, S. Retirees' cost of living jumps. *Greensboro Daily News*, August 17, 1977, p. A8.

Puner, M. *To the good long life: What we know about growing old*. New York: Universe Books, 1974.

Pye, E. K. Can we live forever? *The Saturday Evening Post*, 1977, *249*(2), 35, 88.

Quirk, D. A. Life span opportunities for the older adult. *Personnel and Guidance Journal*, 1976, *55*, 140–142.

Rappoport, L. Adult development: "Faster horses . . . and more money." *Personnel and Guidance Journal,* 1976, *55,* 106–108.

Reichard, S., Livson, F., & Petersen, P. G. *Aging and personality.* New York: Wiley, 1962.

Reichard, S., Livson, F., & Petersen, P. G. Adjustment to retirement. In B. L. Neugarten (ed.). *Middle age and aging.* Chicago: University of Chicago Press, 1968.

Reimanis, G., & Green, R. F. Imminence of death and intellectual decrement in the aging. *Developmental Psychology,* 1971, *5,* 270–272.

Retirees may overburden the labor force. *The Futurist,* 1976, *10*(3), 157.

Richter, C. P. On the phenomenon of sudden death in animals and man. *Psychosomatic Medicine,* 1957, *19,* 191–198.

Riley, J. W., Jr. Attitudes toward death. Unpublished. Cited in M. W. Riley, A. Foner, et al. (eds.). *Aging and society.* Vol. 1. *An inventory of research findings.* New York: Russell Sage Foundation, 1968.

Riley, M. W., & Foner, A. (eds.). *Aging and society.* New York: Russell Sage Foundation, 1968.

Roffwarg, H. P., Muzio, J. N., & Dement, W. C. Ontogenetic development of the human sleep-dream cycle. *Science,* 1966, *152,* 604–619.

Romo, M., Siltanen, P., Theorell, T., & Rahe, R. H. World behavior, time urgency, and life-dissatisfactions in subjects with myocardial infarction: A cross-cultural study. *Journal of Psychosomatic Research,* 1974, *18*(1), 1–8.

Rose, C. L. Social factors in longevity. *Gerontologist,* 1964, *4,* 27–37.

Rosenfeld, A. *Prolongevity.* New York: Knopf, 1976. (a)

Rosenfeld, A. The Willy Loman complex. *Saturday Review,* 1976, *3*(22), 24–26. (b)

Rosow, I. Housing and local ties of the aged. In B. L. Neugarten (ed.). *Middle age and aging: A reader in social psychology.* Chicago: University of Chicago Press, 1968.

Sartre, J. P. *Existentialism and human emotions.* New York: Philosophical Library, 1957.

Saul, S. *Aging: An album of people growing old.* New York: Wiley, 1974.

Savitz, H. A. Mental health and aging. *MH,* 1974, *58*(3), 21–22.

Schaie, K. W. Age changes and age differences. *Gerontologist,* 1967, *7,* 128–132.

Schaie, K. W., & Labouvie-Vief, G. Generational versus ontogenetic components of change in cognitive behavior: A fourteen-year cross-sequential study. *Developmental Psychology,* 1974, *10,* 305–320.

Schaie, K. W., & Strother, C. R. A cross-sequential study of age changes in cognitive behavior. *Psychological Bulletin,* 1968, *70,* 671–680.

Schonfield, D. Memory changes with age. *Nature,* 1965, *208,* 918.

Schultz, J. H. *The economics of aging.* Belmont, Calif.: Wadsworth, 1976.

Seligman, M. E. P. *Helplessness: On depression, development, and death.* San Francisco: W. H. Freeman, 1975. Chap. 8.

Selkurt, E. E. Death. *The world book encyclopedia* (vol. 5). Chicago: Field Enterprises Educational Corp., 1975.

Selye, H. *The stress of life* (rev. ed.). New York: McGraw-Hill, 1976.

Serock, K., Seefeldt, C., Jantz, R. K., & Galper, A. As children see old folks. *Today's Education,* 1977, *66*(2), 70–73.

Shanas, E., Townsend, P., Wederburn, D., Friis, H., Milhoj, P., & Stehouwer, J. The psychology of health. In B. L. Neugarten (ed.). *Middle age and aging.* Chicago: University of Chicago Press, 1968.

Sheldon, A., McEwan, P. J. M., & Ryser, C. P. *Retirement patterns and predictions.* National Institute of Mental Health, DHEW. Publication No. (ADM) 74–79, 1975.

Shock, N. W. Aging and psychological adjustment. *Review of Educational Research,* 1952, *22,* 439–458. (a)

Shock, N. W. Aging of homeostatic mechanisms. In A. I. Lansing (ed.). *Cowdry's problems of aging* (3rd ed.). Baltimore: Williams & Wilkins, 1952. (b)

Sinaki, M., Opitz, J. L., & Wahner, H. W. Bone mineral content: Relationship to muscle strength in normal subjects. *Archives of Physical Medicine and Rehabilitation,* 1974, *55,* 508–512.

Sinick, D. W. Aging. *Personnel and Guidance Journal,* 1976, *55,* 100.

Smith, M. E. Delayed recall of previously memorized material after forty years. *Journal of Genetic Psychology,* 1963, *102,* 3–4.

Social security checks rise with living costs. *Greensboro Daily News,* June 30, 1977, p. A2.

Soviets say work spurs longevity. *Greensboro Daily News,* August 22, 1977, p. A11.

Spence, D. L. Patterns of retirement in San Francisco. In F. M. Carp (ed.). *The retirement process.* U.S. Dept. of Health, Education and Welfare, PHS Publication No. 1778. Washington, D.C.: U.S. Government Printing Office, 1966.

Spence, D. L., Feigenbaum, E. M., Fitzgerald, F., & Roth, J. Medical student attitudes toward the geriatric patient. *Journal of American Geriatrics Society,* 1968, *16,* 976–983.

Spoor, A. Presbycusis values in relation to noise induced hearing loss. *International Audiology,* 1967, *6,* 48–57.

Steinbaum, B. *Attitudes toward the aged in nursing students before and after a course in gerontology.* Unpublished doctoral dissertation, Columbia University, 1973.

Step-up in fight on crimes against elderly. *U.S. News & World Report,* 1977, *82*(23), 62.

Streib, G. F., & Schneider, C. J. *Retirement in American society.* Ithaca, N.Y.: Cornell University Press, 1971.

Sussman, M. B. *Incentives and family environments for the elderly.* (Final Report AOA Grant No. 90-A-316). Washington, D.C.: Administration on Aging, Feb. 12, 1977.

Taves, M. J., & Hansen, G. O. 1700 elderly citizens. In A. M. Rose (ed.). *Aging in Minnesota.* Minneapolis: University of Minnesota Press, 1963, pp. 73–181.

Terry, R., & Wisniewski, H. Sans teeth, sans eyes, sans taste, sans everything. *Behavior Today,* 1974, *5,* 84.

The graying of America. *Newsweek,* 1977, *89*(9), 50–52; 55–58; 63–65.

Thomas, D. *Collected poems.* New York: New Directions, 1957.

Tiede, T. Brandeis prof says citizens get too old to vote. *Champaign-Urbana Courier,* Nov. 3, 1970, p. 19.

Timiras, P. S. *Developmental physiology and aging.* New York: Macmillan, 1972.

Tobin, S. S., & Lieberman, M. A. *Last home for the aged: Critical implications of institutionalization.* San Francisco: Jossey-Bass, 1976.

Tolstoy, L. The death of Ivan Ilych. In L. Tolstoy. *Death of Ivan Ilych and other stories.* New York: New American Library, 1960. (Originally published in 1886.)

Tuckman, J., & Lorge, I. Attitudes toward old people. *Journal of Social Psychology,* 1953, *37,* 249–260.

Tuddenham, R. D., Blumenkrantz, J., & Wilkin, W. R. Age changes in AGCT: A longitudinal study of average adults. *Journal of Counseling and Clinical Psychology,* 1968, *32,* 659–663.

Ullmann, C. A. Preretirement planning: Does it prevent postretirement shock? *Personnel and Guidance Journal,* 1976, *55,* 115–118.

U.S. Bureau of the Census. Some demographic aspects of aging in the United States. *Current Population Reports,* Series P-23, No. 43. Washington, D.C.: U.S. Government Printing Office, 1973.

U.S. Bureau of the Census. Projections of the population of the United States: 1977 to 2050. *Current Population Reports,* Series P-25, No. 704. Washington, D.C.: U.S. Government Printing Office, 1977.

U.S. Department of Housing and Urban Development. *Older Americans: Facts about incomes and housing.* Washington, D.C.: U.S. Government Printing Office, 1973.

Van Wey, L. Dramatic rise in elderly reversing "youth society." *Stockton Record,* August 31, 1977. (a)

Van Wey, L. Problems of getting older. *Stockton Record,* Sept. 1, 1977. (b)

Verwoerdt, A. Biological characteristics of the elderly. In R. R. Boyd and C. G. Oakes (eds.). *Foundations of practical gerontology.* Columbia, S. C.: University of South Carolina Press, 1969. (a)

Verwoerdt, A. Psychiatric aspects of aging. In R. R. Boyd and C. G. Oakes (eds.). *Foundations of practical gerontology.* Columbia, S. C.: University of South Carolina Press, 1969. (b)

Vinick, B. *Remarriage in old age.* Paper presented at the annual meeting of the American Sociological Association, Chicago, Sept. 1977.

Volpe, A., and Kastenbaum, R. Beer and TLC. *American Journal of Nursing,* 1967, *67,* 100–103.

Vontress, C. E. Counseling middle-age and aging cultural minorities. *Personnel and Guidance Journal,* 1976, *55,* 132–135.

Wechsler, D. *The measurement and appraisal of adult intelligence* (4th ed.). Baltimore: Williams & Wilkins, 1958.

Weisman, A. D. *On dying and denying: A psychiatric study of terminality.* New York: Behavioral Publications, 1972.

Weisman, A. D., & Kastenbaum, R. The psychological autopsy: A study of the terminal phase of life. *Community Mental Health Journal,* Monograph No. 4. New York: Behavioral Publications, 1968.

Welford, A. T. *Aging and human skill.* New York: Oxford University Press, 1958.

Wesman, A. G. Intelligent testing. *American Psychologist,* 1968, 23, 267–274.

Whaley, W. G. Life. *World book encyclopedia* (vol. 12). Chicago: Field Educational Enterprises Corp., 1974.

Wilkie, F., and Eisdorfer, C. Intelligence and blood pressure in the aged. *Science,* 1971, *172*, 959–962.

Winokur, G. The types of affective disorders. *Journal of Nervous and Mental Diseases,* 1973, *156*, 82–96.

Witkin, H. The perception of the upright. *Scientific American,* 1959, *200*(2), 50–56.

Yerkes, R. M. Psychological examining in the U.S. Army. *Memoirs: National Academy of Science,* 1921, *15*, 1–890.

Young, M. L. Age and sex differences in problem solving. *Journal of Gerontology,* 1971, *26*, 330–336.

Index of
Authors and Names

Numbers in *italics* refer to pages in the References.

217

Index of Terms and Organizations

Numbers in *italics* refer to pages in the Glossary.